The Bontoc Igorot

The Bontoc Igorot

Albert Ernest Jenks

THE BONTOC IGOROT

Published in the United States by IndyPublish.com
Boston, Massachusetts

ISBN 1-58827-877-8 (paperback)

Letter of Transmittal

Department of the Interior, The Ethnological Survey,

MANILA, FEBRUARY 3, 1904.

Sir: I have the honor to submit a study of the Bontoc Igorot made for this Survey during the year 1903. It is transmitted with the recommendation that it be published as Volume I of a series of scientific studies to be issued by The Ethnological Survey for the Philippine Islands.

Respectfully,

Albert Ernst Jenks,

CHIEF OF THE ETHNOLOGICAL SURVEY.

Hon. Dean C. Worcester,
SECRETARY OF THE INTERIOR, MANILA, P. I.

Preface

After an expedition of two months in September, October, and November, 1902, among the people of northern Luzon it was decided that the Igorot of Bontoc pueblo, in the Province of Lepanto-Bontoc, are as typical of the primitive mountain agriculturist of Luzon as any group visited, and that ethnologic investigations directed from Bontoc pueblo would enable the investigator to show the culture of the primitive mountaineer of Luzon as well as or better than investigations centered elsewhere.

Accompanied by Mrs. Jenks, the writer took up residence in Bontoc pueblo the 1st of January, 1903, and remained five months. The following data were gathered during that Bontoc residence, the previous expedition of two months, and a residence of about six weeks among the Benguet Igorot.

The accompanying illustrations are mainly from photographs. Some of them were taken in April, 1903, by Hon. Dean C. Worcester, Secretary of the Interior; others are the work of Mr. Charles Martin, Government photographer, and were taken in January, 1903; the others were made by the writer to supplement those taken by Mr. Martin, whose time was limited in the area. Credit for each photograph is given with the halftone as it appears.

I wish to express my gratitude for the many favors of the only other Americans living in Bontoc Province during my stay there, namely, Lieutenant-Governor Truman K. Hunt, M.D.; Constabulary Lieutenant (now Captain) Elmer A. Eckman; and Mr. William F. Smith, American teacher.

In the following pages native words have their syllabic divisions shown by hyphens and their accented syllables and vowels marked in the various sections wherein the words are considered technically for the first time, and also in the vocabulary in the last chapter. In all other places they are unmarked. A later study of the language may show that errors have been made in writing sentences, since it was not always possible to get a consistent answer to the question as to what part of a sentence constitutes a single word, and time was too limited for any extensive language study. The following alphabet has been used in writing native words.

A as in FAR; Spanish RAMO
A as in LAW; as O in French OR
AY as AI in AISLE; Spanish HAY
AO as OU in OUT; as AU in Spanish AUTO
B as in BAD; Spanish BAJAR
CH as in CHECK; Spanish CHICO
D as in DOG; Spanish DAR
E as in THEY; Spanish HALLE
E as in THEN; Spanish COMEN
F as in FIGHT; Spanish FIRMAR
G as in GO; Spanish GOZAR
H as in HE; Tagalog BAHAY
I as in PIQUE; Spanish HIJO
I as in PICK
K as in KEEN
L as in LAMB; Spanish LENTE
M as in MAN; Spanish MENOS
N as in NOW; Spanish JABON
NG as in FINGER; Spanish LENGUA
O as in NOTE; Spanish NOSOTROS
OI as in BOIL
P as in POOR; Spanish PERO
Q as CH in German ICH
S as in SAUCE; Spanish SORDO
SH as in SHALL; as CH in French CHARMER
T as in TOUCH; Spanish TOMAR
U as in RULE; Spanish UNO
U as in BUT
U as in German KUHL
V as in VALVE; Spanish VOLVER
W as in WILL; nearly as OU in French OUI
Y as in YOU; Spanish YA

It seems not improper to say a word here regarding some of my commonest impressions of the Bontoc Igorot.

Physically he is a clean-limbed, well-built, dark-brown man of medium stature, with no evidence of degeneracy. He belongs to that extensive stock of primitive people of which the Malay is the most commonly named. I do not believe he has received any of his characteristics, as a group, from either the Chinese or Japanese, though this theory has frequently been presented. The Bontoc man would be a savage if it were not that his geographic location compelled him to become an agriculturist; necessity drove him to this art of peace. In everyday life his actions are deliberate, but he is not lazy. He is remarkably industrious for a primitive man. In his agricultural labors he has strength, determination, and endurance. On the trail, as a cargador or burden bearer for Americans, he is patient and uncomplaining, and earns his wage in the sweat of his brow. His social life is lowly, and before marriage is most primitive; but a man has only one wife, to whom he is usually faithful. The social group is decidedly democratic; there are no slaves. The people are neither drunkards, gamblers, nor "sportsmen." There is little "color" in the life of the Igorot; he is not very inventive and seems to have little imagination. His chief recreation -- certainly his most-enjoyed and highly prized recreation -- is head-hunting. But head-hunting is not the passion with him that it is with many Malay peoples.

His religion is at base the most primitive religion known -- animism, or spirit belief -- but he has somewhere grasped the idea of one god, and has made this belief in a crude way a part of his life.

He is a very likable man, and there is little about his primitiveness that is repulsive. He is of a kindly disposition, is not servile, and is generally trustworthy. He has a strong sense of humor. He is decidedly friendly to the American, whose superiority he recognizes and whose methods he desires to learn. The boys in school are quick and bright, and their teacher pronounces them superior to Indian and Mexican children he has taught in Mexico, Texas, and New Mexico.[1]

Briefly, I believe in the future development of the Bontoc Igorot for the following reasons: He has an exceptionally fine physique for his stature and has no vices to destroy his body. He has courage which no one who knows him seems ever to think of questioning; he is industrious, has a bright mind, and is willing to learn. His institutions -- governmental, religious, and social -- are not radically opposed to those of modern civilization -- as, for instance, are many institutions of the Mohammedanized people of Mindanao and the Sulu Archipelago -- but are such, it seems to me, as will quite readily yield to or associate themselves with modern institutions.

I recall with great pleasure the months spent in Bontoc pueblo, and I have a most sincere interest in and respect for the Bontoc Igorot as a man.

Introduction

The readers of this monograph are familiar with the geographic location of the Philippine Archipelago. However, to have the facts clearly in mind, it will be stated that the group lies entirely within the north torrid zone, extending from 4[degree] 40' northward to 21[degree] 3' and from 116[degree] 40' to 126[degree] 34' east longitude. It is thus about 1,000 miles from north to south and 550 miles from east to west. The Pacific Ocean washes its eastern shores, the Sea of Celebes its southern, and the China Sea its western and northern shores. It is about 630 kilometers, or 400 miles, from the China coast, and lies due east from French Indo-China. The Batanes group of islands, stretching north of Luzon, has members nearer Formosa than Luzon. On the southwest Borneo is sighted from Philippine territory.

Briefly, it may be said the Archipelago belongs to Asia -- geologically, zoologically, and botanically -- rather than to Oceania, and that, apparently, the entire Archipelago has shared a common origin and existence. There is evidence that it was connected with the mainland by solid earth in the early or Middle Tertiary. For a long geologic time the land was low and swampy. At the end of the Eocene a great upheaval occurred; there were foldings and crumplings, igneous rock was thrust into the distorted mass, and the islands were considerably elevated above the sea. During the latter part of the Tertiary period the lands seem to have subsided and to have been separated from the mainland.

About the close of the subsidence eruptions began which are continued to the present by such volcanoes as Taal and Mayon in Luzon and Apo in Mindanao. No further subsidence appears to have occurred after the close of the Tertiary, though the gradual elevation beginning then had many lapses, as is evidenced by the numerous sea beaches often seen one above the other in horizontal tiers. The elevation continues to-day in an almost invisible way. The Islands have been greatly enlarged during the elevation by the constant building of coral around the sub-merged shores.

It is believed that man had appeared in the great Malay Archipelago before this elevation began. It is thought by some that he was in the Philippines in the later Tertiary, but there are no data as yet throwing light on this question.

To-day the Archipelago lies like a large net in the natural pathway of people flee-ing themselves from the supposed birthplace of the primitive Malayan stock, namely, from Java, Sumatra, and the adjacent Malay Peninsula, or, more likely, the larger mainland. It spreads over a large area, and is well fitted by its numer-ous islands -- some 3,100 -- and its innumerable bays and coastal pockets to catch up and hold a primitive, seafaring people.

There are and long have been daring Malayan pirates, and there is to-day among the southern islands a numerous class -- the Samal -- living most of the time on the sea, yet they all keep close to land, except in time of calm, and when a storm is brewing they strike out straight for the nearest shore like scared children. The ocean currents and the monsoons have been greatly instrumental in driving dif-ferent people through the seas into the Philippine net.[2] The Tagakola on the west coast of the Gulf of Davao, Mindanao, have a tradition that they are descen-dants of men cast on their present shores from a distant land and of the Manobo women of the territory. The Bagobo, also in the Gulf of Davao, claim they came to their present home in a few boats generations ago. They purposely left their former land to flee from head-hunting, a practice in their earlier home, but one they do not follow in Mindanao. What per cent of the people coming originally to the Archipelago was castaway, nomadic, or immigrant it is impossible to judge, but there have doubtless also been many systematic and prolonged migrations from nearby lands, as from Borneo, Celebes, Sangir, etc.

Primitive man is represented in the Philippines to-day not alone by one of the lowest natural types of savage man the historic world has looked upon -- the small, dark-brown, bearded, "crisp-woolly"-haired Negritos -- but by some thirty distinct primitive Malayan tribes or dialect groups, among which are believed to be some of the lowest of the stock in existence.

In northern Luzon is the Igorot, a typical primitive Malayan. He is a muscular, smooth-faced, brown man of a type between the delicate and the coarse. In Mindoro the Mangiyan is found, an especially lowly Malayan, who may prove to be a true savage in culture. In Mindanao is the slender, delicate, smooth-faced brown man of which the Subano, in the western part, is typical. There are the

Bagobo and the extensive Manobo of eastern Mindanao in the neighborhood of the Gulf of Davao, the latter people following the Agusan River practically to the north coast of Mindanao. In southeastern Mindanao, in the vicinity of Mount Apo and also north of the Gulf of Davao, are the Ata. They are a scattered people and evidently a Negrito and primitive Malayan mixture. In Nueva Vizcaya, Nueva Ecija, Isabela, and perhaps Principe, of Luzon, are the Ibilao. They are a slender, delicate, bearded people, with an artistic nature quite different from any other now known in the island, but somewhat like that of the Ata of Mindanao. Their artistic wood productions suggest the incised work of distant dwellers of the Pacific, as that of the people of New Guinea, Fiji Islands, or Hervey Islands. The seven so-called Christian tribes,[3] occupying considerable areas in the coastwise lands and low plains of most of the larger islands of the Archipelago, represent migrations to the Archipelago subsequent to those of the Igorot and comparable tribes.

The last migrations of brown men into the Archipelago are historic. The Spaniard discovered the inward flow of the large Samal Moro group -- after his arrival in the sixteenth century. The movement of this nomadic "Sea Gipsy" Samal has not ceased to-day, but continues to flow in and out among the small southern islands.

Besides the peoples here cited there are a score of others scattered about the Archipelago, representing many grades of primitive culture, but those mentioned are sufficient to suggest that the Islands have been very effective in gathering up and holding divers groups of primitive men.[4]

PART 1

The Igorot Culture Group

Igorot land

Northern Luzon, or Igorot land, is by far the largest area in the Philippine Archipelago having any semblance of regularity. It is roughly rectangular in form, extending two and one-half degrees north and south and two degrees east and west.

There are two prominent geographic features in northern Luzon. One is the beautifully picturesque mountain system, the Caraballos, the most important range of which is the Caraballos Occidentales, extending north and south throughout the western part of the territory. This range is the famous "Cordillera Central" for about three-quarters of its extent northward, beyond which it is known as "Cordillera del Norte." The other prominent feature is the extensive drainage system of the eastern part, the Rio Grande de Cagayan draining northward into the China Sea about two-thirds of the territory of northern Luzon. It is the largest drainage system and the largest river in the Archipelago.

The surface of northern Luzon is made up of four distinct types. First is the coastal plain -- a consistently narrow strip of land, generally not over 3 or 4 miles wide. The soil is sandy silt with a considerable admixture of vegetable matter. In some places it is loose, and shifts readily before the winds; here and there are stretches of alluvial clay loam. The sandy areas are often covered with coconut trees, and the alluvial deposits along the rivers frequently become beds of nipa palm as far back as tide water. The plain areas are generally poorly watered except during the rainy season, having only the streams of the steep mountains passing through them. These river beds are broad, "quicky," impassable torrents in the rainy season, and are shallow or practically dry during half the year, with only a narrow, lazy thread flowing among the bowlders.

This plain area on the west coast is the undisputed dwelling place of the Christian Ilokano, occupying pueblos in Union, Ilokos Sur, and Ilokos Norte Provinces. Almost nothing is known of the eastern coastal plain area. It is believed to be extremely narrow, and has at least one pueblo, of Christianized Tagalog -- the famous Palanan, the scene of Aguinaldo's capture.

The second type of surface is the coastal hill area. It extends from the coastal plain irregularly back to the mountains, and is thought to be much narrower on the eastern coast than on the western -- in fact, it may be quite absent on the eastern. It is the remains of a tilted plain sloping seaward from an altitude of about 1,000 feet to one of, say, 100 feet, and its hilly nature is due to erosion. These hills are generally covered only with grasses; the sheltered moister places often produce rank growths of tall, coarse cogon grass.[5] The soil varies from dark clay loam through the sandy loams to quite extensive deposits of coarse gravel. The level stretches in the hills on the west coast are generally in the possession of the Christian peoples, though here and there are small pueblos of the large Igorot group. The Igorot in these pueblos are undergoing transformation, and quite generally wear clothing similar to that of the Ilokano.

The third type of surface is the mountain country -- the "temperate zone of the Tropics"; it is the habitat of the Igorot. From the western coastal hill area the mountains rise abruptly in parallel ranges lying in a general north and south direction, and they subside only in the foothills west of the great level bottom land bordering the Rio Grande de Cagayan. The Cordillera Central is as fair and about as varied a mountain country as the tropic sun shines on. It has mountains up which one may climb from tropic forest jungles into open, pine-forested parks, and up again into the dense tropic forest, with its drapery of vines, its varied hanging orchids, and its graceful, lilting fern trees. It has mountains forested to the upper rim on one side with tropic jungle and on the other with sturdy pine trees; at the crest line the children of the Tropics meet and intermingle with those of the temperate zone. There are gigantic, rolling, bare backs whose only covering is the carpet of grass periodically green and brown. There are long, rambling, skeleton ranges with here and there pine forests gradually creeping up the sides to the crests. There are solitary volcanoes, now extinct, standing like things purposely let alone when nature humbled the surrounding earth. There are sculptured lime rocks, cities of them, with gray hovels and mansions and cathedrals.

The mountains present one interesting geologic feature. The "hiker" is repeatedly delighted to find his trail passing quite easily from one peak or ascent to another over a natural connecting embankment. On either side of this connecting ridge is the head of a deep, steep-walled canyon; the ridge is only a few hundred feet broad at base, and only half a dozen to twenty feet wide at the top. These ridges invariably have the appearance of being composed of soft earth, and not of rock. They are appreciated by the primitive man, who takes advantage of them as of bridges.

The mountains are well watered; the summits of most of the mountains have perpetual springs of pure, cool waters. On the very tops of some there are occasional perpetual water holes ranging from 10 to 100 feet across. These holes have neither surface outlet nor inlet; there are two such within two hours of Bontoc pueblo. They are the favorite wallowing places of the carabao, the so-called "water buffalo,"[6] both the wild and the half-domesticated animals.

The mountain streams are generally in deep gorges winding in and out between the sharp folds of the mountains. Their beds are strewn with bowlders, often of immense size, which have withstood the wearing of waters and storms. During the rainy season the streams racing between the bases of two mountain ridges are maddened torrents. Some streams, born and fed on the very peaks, tumble 100, 500, even 1,500 feet over precipices, landing white as snow in the merciless torrent at the mountain base. During the dry season the rivers are fordable at frequent intervals, but during the rainy season, beginning in the Cordillera Central in June and lasting well through October, even the natives hesitate often for a week at a time to cross them.

The absence of lakes is noteworthy in the mountain country of northern Luzon -- in fact, in all of northern Luzon. The two large lakes frequently shown on maps of Cagayan Province, one east and one west of the Rio Grande de Cagayan near the eighteenth parallel, are not known to exist, though it is probable there is some foundation for the Spaniards' belief in the existence of at least the eastern one. In the bottom land of the Rio Grande de Cagayan, about six hours west of Cabagan Nuevo, near the provincial border of Cagayan and Isabela, there were a hundred acres of land covered with shallow water the last of October, 1902, just at the end of the dry season of the Cagayan Valley. The surface was well covered with rank, coarse grasses and filled with aquatic plants, especially with lilies. Apparently the waters were slowly receding, since the earth about the margins was supporting the short, coarse grasses that tell of the gradual drying out of soils once covered with water. In the mountains near Sagada, Bontoc Province, there is a very small lake, and one or two others have been reported at Bontoc; but the mountains must be said to be practically lakeless.

Another mountain range of northern Luzon, of which practically no details are known, is the Sierra Madre, extending nearly the full length of the country close to the eastern coast. It seems to be an unbroken, continuous range, and, as such, is the longest mountain range in the Archipelago.

The fourth type of surface is the level areas. These areas lie mainly along the river courses, and vary from a few rods in width to the valley of the Rio Grande de Cagayan, which is often 50 miles in width, and probably more. There are, besides these river valleys, varying tracts of level plains which may most correctly be termed mountain table-lands. The limited mountain valleys and table-lands are the immediate home of the Igorot. The valleys are worn by the streams, and, in turn, are built up, leveled, and enriched by the sand and alluvium deposited annually by the floods. They are generally open, grass-covered areas, though some have become densely forested since being left above the high water of the streams.

The broad valley of the Rio Grande de Cagayan is not occupied by the Igorot. It is too poorly watered and forested to meet his requirements. It is mainly a vast pasture, supporting countless deer; along the foothills and the forest-grown creek and river bottoms there are many wild hogs; and in some areas herds of wild carabaos and horses are found. Near the main river is a numerous population of Christians. Many are Ilokano imported originally by the tobacco companies to carry on the large tobacco plantations of the valley, and the others are the native Cagayan.

The table-lands were once generally forested, but to-day many are deforested, undulating, beautiful pastures. Some were cleared by the Igorot for agriculture, and doubtless others by forest fires, such as one constantly sees during the dry season destroying the mountain forests of northern Luzon.

General observations have not been made on the temperature and humidity of much of the mountain country of northern Luzon. However, scientific observations have been made and recorded for a series of about ten years at Baguio, Benguet Province, at an altitude of 4,777 feet, and it is from the published data there gathered that the following facts are gained.[7] The temperature and rainfall are the average means deduced from many years' observations:

Month	Mean temperature [DEGREE]F	Number of rainy days	Rainfall INCHES
January	63.5	1	0.06
February	62.1	2	0.57
March	66.9	3	1.46
April	70.5	1	0.32
May	68.3	16	4.02
June	67.2	26	12.55
July	66.5	26	14.43
August	64.6	31	37.03
September	67.0	23	11.90
October	67.0	13	4.95
November	68.2	13	2.52
December	66.0	16	5.47

It is seen that April is the hottest month of the year and February is the coldest. The absolute lowest temperature recorded is 42.10[degree] Fahrenheit, noted February 18, 1902. Of course the temperature varies considerably -- a fact due largely to altitude and prevailing winds. The height of the rainy season is in August, during which it rains every day, with an average precipitation of 37.03 inches. Baguio is known as much rainier than many other places in the Cordillera Central, yet it must be taken as more or less typical of the entire mountain area of northern Luzon, throughout which the rainy season is very uniform. Usually the days of the rainy season are beautiful and clear during the forenoon, but all-day rains are not rare, and each season has two or three storms of pelting, driving rain which continues without a break for four or five days.

Igorot peoples

In several languages of northern Luzon the word "Ig-o-rot'" means "mountain people." Dr. Pardo de Tavera says the word "Igorrote" is composed of the root word "golot," meaning, in Tagalog, "mountain chain," and the prefix "i," meaning "dweller in" or "people of." Morga in 1609 used the word as "Igolot;" early Spaniards also used the word frequently as "Ygolotes" -- and to-day some groups of the Igorot, as the Bontoc group, do not pronounce the "r" sound, which common usage now puts in the word. The Spaniards applied the term to the wild peoples of present Benguet and Lepanto Provinces, now a short-haired, peaceful people. In after years its common application spread eastward to the natives of the comandancia of Quiangan, in the present Province of Nueva Vizcaya, and northward to those of Bontoc.

The word "Ig-o-rot'" is now adopted tentatively as the name of the extensive primitive Malayan people of northern Luzon, because it is applied to a very large number of the mountain people by themselves and also has a recognized usage in ethnologic and other writings. Its form as "Ig-o-rot'" is adopted for both singular and plural, because it is both natural and phonetic, and, because, so far as it is possible to do so, it is thought wise to retain the simple native forms of such words as it seems necessary or best to incorporate in our language, especially in scientific language.

The sixteenth degree of north latitude cuts across Luzon probably as far south as any people of the Igorot group are now located. It is believed they occupy all the mountain country northward in the island except the territory of the Ibilao in the southeastern part of the area and some of the most inaccessible mountains in eastern Luzon, which are occupied by Negritos.

There are from 150,000 to 225,000 Igorot in Igorot land. The census of the Archipelago taken in 1903 will give the number as about 185,000. In the northern part of Pangasinan Province, the southwestern part of the territory, there are reported about 3,150 pagan people under various local names, as "Igorrotes," "Infieles" [pagans], and "Nuevos Christianos." In Benguet Province there are some 23,000, commonly known as "Benguet Igorrotes." In Union Province there are about 4,400 primitive people, generally called "Igorrotes." Ilokos Sur has nearly 8,000, half of whom are known to history as "Tinguianes" and half as "Igorrotes." The Province of Ilokos Norte has nearly 9,000, which number is divided quite evenly between "Igorrotes," "Tinguianes," and "Infieles." Abra Province has in round numbers 13,500 pagan Malayans, most of whom are historically known as "Alzados" and "Tinguianes." These Tinguian ethnically belong to the great Igorot group, and in northern Bontoc Province, where they are known as Itneg, flow into and are not distinguishable from the Igorot; but no effort is made in this monograph to cut the Tinguian asunder from the position they have gained in historic and ethnologic writings as a separate people. The Province of Lepanto-Bontoc has, according to records, about 70,500 "Igorrotes," "Tinguianes," and "Caylingas," but I believe a more careful census will show it has nearer 100,000. Nueva Ecija is reported to have half a hundred "Tinguianes." The Province of Nueva Vizcaya has some 46,000 people locally and historically known as "Bunnayans," a large group in the Spanish comandancia of Quiangan; the "Silapanes," also a large group of people closely associated with the Bunayan; the Isinay, a small group in the southern part of the province; the Alamit, a considerable group of Silipan people dwelling along the Alamit River in the comandancia of Quiangan; and the small Ayangan group of the Bunayan people of Quiangan. Cagayan Province has about 11,000 "Caylingas" and "Ipuyaos." Isabela Province is reported as having about 2,700 primitive Malayans of the Igorot group; they are historically known as "Igorrotes," "Gaddanes," "Calingas," and "Ifugaos."

The following forms of the above names of different dialect groups of Ig-o-rot' have been adopted by The Ethnological Survey: Tin-gui-an', Ka-lin'-ga, Bun-a-yan', I-sa-nay', A-la'-mit, Sil-i-pan', Ay-an'-gan, I-pu-kao', and Gad-an'.

It is believed that all the mountain people of the northern half of Luzon, except the Negritos, came to the island in some of the earliest of the movements that swept the coasts of the Archipelago from the south and spread over the inland areas -- succeeding waves of people, having more culture, driving their cruder blood fellows farther inland. Though originally of one blood, and though they are all to-day in a similar broad culture-grade -- that is, all are mountain agriculturists, and all are, or until recently have been, head-hunters -- yet it does not follow that the Igorot groups have to-day identical culture; quite the contrary is true. There are many and wide differences even in important cultural expressions which are due to environment, long isolation, and in some cases to ideas and processes borrowed from different neighboring peoples. Very misleading statements have sometimes been made in regard to the Igorot -- customs from different groups have been jumbled together in one description until a man has been pictured who can not be found anywhere. All except the most general statements are worse than wasted unless a particular group is designated.

An illustration of some of the differences between groups of typical Igorot will make this clearer. I select as examples the people of Bontoc and the adjoining Quiangan district in northern Nueva Vizcaya Province, both of whom are com-

monly known as Igorot. It must be noted that the people of both areas are practically unmodified by modern culture and both are constant head-hunters. With
scarcely one exception Bontoc pueblos are single clusters of buildings; in Banawi
pueblo of the Quiangan area there are eleven separate groups of dwellings, each
group situated on a prominence which may be easily protected by the inhabitants
against an enemy below them; and other Quiangan pueblos are similarly built. As
will be brought out in succeeding chapters, the social and political institutions of
the two peoples differ widely. In Bontoc the head weapon is a battle-ax, in
Quiangan it is a long knife. Most of the head-hunting practices of the two peoples are different, especially as to the disposition of the skulls of the victims.
Bontoc men wear their hair long, and have developed a small pocket-hat to con-
fine the hair and contain small objects carried about; the men of Quiangan wear
their hair short, have nothing whatever of the nature of the pocket-hat, but have
developed a unique hand bag which is used as a pocket. In the Quiangan area a
highly conventionalized wood-carving art has developed -- beautiful eating
spoons with figures of men and women carved on the handles and food bowls cut
in animal figures are everywhere found; while in Bontoc only the most crude and
artless wood carving is made. In language there is such a difference that Bontoc
men who accompanied me into the northern part of the large Quiangan area,
only a long day from Bontoc pueblo, could not converse with Quiangan men,
even about such common things as travelers in a strange territory need to learn.

It is because of the many differences in cultural expressions between even small
and neighboring communities of the primitive people of the Philippine
Archipelago that I wish to be understood in this paper as speaking of the one
group -- the Bontoc Igorot culture group; a group however, in every essential typical of the numerous Igorot peoples of the mountains of northern Luzon.

PART 2

The Bontoc Culture Group

Bontoc culture area

The Bontoc culture area nearly equals the old Spanish Distrito Politico-Militar of Bontoc, presented to the American public in a Government publication in 1900.[8]

The Spanish Bontoc area was estimated about 4,500 square kilometers. This was probably too large an estimate, and it is undoubtedly an overestimate for the Bontoc culture area, the northern border of which is farther south than the border of the Spanish Bontoc area.

The area is well in the center of northern Luzon and is cut off by watersheds from other territory, except on the northeast. The most prominent of these watersheds is Polis Mountain, extending along the eastern and southern sides of the area; it is supposed to reach a height of over 7,000 feet. The western watershed is an undifferentiated range of the Cordillera Central. To the north stretches a large area of the present Province of Bontoc, though until 1903 most of that northern territory was embraced in the Province of Abra. The Province of Isabela lies to the east; Nueva Vizcaya and Lepanto border the area on the south, and Lepanto and Abra border it on the west.

The Bontoc culture area lies entirely in the mountains, and, with the exception of two pueblos, it is all drained northeastward into the Rio Grande de Cagayan by one river, the Rio Chico de Cagayan; but the Rio Sibbu, coursing more directly eastward, is a considerable stream.

To-day one main trail enters Bontoc Province. It was originally built by the Spaniards, and enters Bontoc pueblo from the southwest, leading up from Cervantes in Lepanto Province. From Cervantes there are two trails to the coast. One passes southward through Baguio in Benguet Province and then stretches westward, terminating on the coast at San Fernando, in Union Province. The other, the one most commonly traveled to Bontoc, passes to the northwest, terminating on the coast at Candon, in the Province of Ilokos Sur. The main trail, entering Bontoc from Cervantes, passes through the pueblo and extends to the northeast, quite closely following the trend of the Chico River. In Spanish times it was seldom traveled farther than Bassao, but several parties of Americans have been over it as far as the Rio Grande de Cagayan since November, 1902. A second trail, also of Spanish origin, but now practically unused, enters the area from the south and connects Bontoc pueblo, its northern terminus, with the valley of the Magat River far south. It passes through the pueblos of Bayambang, Quiangan, and Banawi, in the Province of Nueva Vizcaya.

The main trail is to-day passable for a horseman from the coast terminus to Tinglayan, three days beyond Bontoc pueblo. Practically all other trails in the area are simply wild footpaths of the Igorot. Candon, the coast terminus of the main trail, lies in the coastal plain area about 4 1/4 miles from the sea. From the coast to the small pueblo of Concepcion at the western base of the Cordillera Central is a half-day's journey. The first half of the trail passes over flat land, with here and there small pueblos surrounded by rice sementeras. There are almost no forests. The latter half is through the coastal hill area, and the trail frequently passes through small forests; it crosses several rivers, dangerous to ford in the rainy season, and winds in and out among attractive hills bearing clumps of graceful, plume-like bamboo.

From Concepcion the trail leads up the mountain to Tilud Pass, historic since the insurrection because of the brave stand made there by the young, ill-fated General del Pilar. The climb to Tilud Pass, from either side of the mountain, is one of the longest and most tedious in northern Luzon. The trail frequently turns short on itself, so that the front and rear parts of a pack train are traveling face to face, and one end is not more than eight or ten rods above the other on the side of the mountain. The last view of the sea from the Candon-Bontoc trail is obtained at Tilud Pass. From Concepcion to Angaki, at the base of the mountain on the eastern side of the pass, the trail is about half a day long. From the pass it is a ceaseless drop down the steep mountain, but affords the most charming views of mountain scenery in northern Luzon. The shifting direction of the turning trail and the various altitudes of the traveler present constantly changing scenes -- mountains and mountains ramble on before one. From Angaki to Cervantes the trail passes over deforested rolling mountain land, with safe drinking water in only one small spring. Many travelers who pass that part of the journey in the middle of the day complain loudly of the heat and thirst experienced there.

Cervantes, said to be 70 miles from Candon, is the capital of the dual Province of Lepanto-Bontoc. Bontoc pueblo lies inland only about 35 miles farther, but the greater part of two days is usually required to reach it. Twenty minutes will carry a horseman down the bluff from Cervantes, across the swift Abra -- if the stream is fordable -- and start him on the eastward mountain climb.

The first pueblo beyond Cervantes is Cayan, the old Spanish capital of the district. About twenty-five years ago the site was changed from Cayan to Cervantes because there was not sufficient suitable land at Cayan. Cayan is about four hours from Cervantes, and every foot of the trail is up the mountain. A short distance beyond Cayan the trail divides to rejoin only at the outskirts of Bontoc pueblo; but the right-hand or "lower" trail is not often traveled by horsemen. Up and up the mountain one climbs from about 1,800 feet at Cervantes to about 6,000 feet among the pines, and then slowly descends, having crossed the boundary line between Lepanto and Bontoc subprovinces to the pueblo of Bagnen -- the last one before the Bontoc culture area is entered. It is customary to spend the night on the trail, as one goes into Bontoc, either at Bagnen or at Sagada, a pueblo about two hours farther on.

Only along the top of the high mountain, before Bagnen is reached, does the trail pass through a forest -- otherwise it is always climbing up or winding about the mountains deforested probably by fires. Practically all the immediate territory on the right hand of the trail between Bagnen and Sagada is occupied by the beautifully terraced rice sementeras of Balugan; the valley contains more than a thousand acres so cultivated. At Sagada lime rocks -- some eroded into gigantic, massive forms, others into fantastic spires and domes -- everywhere crop out from the grassy hills. Up and down the mountains the trail leads, passing another small pine forest near Ankiling and Titipan, about four hours from Bontoc, and then creeps on and at last through the terraced entrance way into the mountain pocket where Bontoc pueblo lies, about 100 miles from the western coast, and, by Government aneroid barometer, about 2,800 feet above the sea.

<u>Marks of Bontoc culture</u>

It is difficult and often impossible to state the essential difference in culture which distinguishes one group of people from another. It is more difficult to draw lines of distinction, for the culture of one group almost imperceptibly flows into that of another adjoining it.

However, two fundamental institutions of the people of Bontoc seem to differ from those of most adjoining people. One of these institutions has to do with the control of the pueblo. Bontoc has not developed the headman -- the "principal" of the Spaniard, the "Bak-nan'" of the Benguet Igorot -- the one rich man who becomes the pueblo, leader. In Benguet Province the headman is found in every pueblo, and he is so powerful that he often dominates half a dozen outlying barrios to the extent that he receives a large share, often one-half, of the output of all the productive labors of the barrio. Immediately north of the Bontoc area, in Tinglayan, the headman is again found. He has no place whatever in Bontoc. The control of the pueblos of the Bontoc area is in the hands of groups of old men; however, each group, called "intugtukan," operates only within a single political and geographic portion of the pueblo, so that no one group has in charge the control of the pueblo. The pueblo is a loose federation of smaller political groups.

The other institution is a social development. It is the olag, an institution of trial marriage. It is not known to exist among adjoining people, but is found throughout the area in which the intugtukan exists; they are apparently coextensive. I was repeatedly informed that the olag is not found in the Banawi area south of Bontoc, or in the Tinglayan area east, or among the Tinguian to the north, or in Benguet far southwest, or in Lepanto immediately southwest -- though I have some reason to believe that both the intugtukan and olag exist in a crumbling way among certain Lepanto Igorot.

Besides these two institutions there are other differing marks of culture between the Bontoc area and adjoining people. Some of these were suggested a few pages back, others will appear in following pages.

Without doubt the limits of the spread of the common culture have been determined mainly by the physiography of the country. One of the two pueblos in the area not on the common drainage system is Lias, but Lias was largely built by a migration from Bontoc pueblo -- the hotbed of Bontoc culture. Barlig, the other pueblo not on the common drainage system (both Barlig and Lias are on the Sibbu River), lies between Lias and the other pueblos of the Bontoc culture area, and so naturally has been drawn in line and held in line with the culture of the geographic area in which it is located -- its institutions are those of its environment.

The Bontoc man

Introduction

The Bontoc Igorot has been in Bontoc longer than the endurance of tradition, for he says he never lived elsewhere, that he never drove any people out before him, and that he was never driven; and has always called himself the "I-pu-kao'" or "I-fu-gao'" -- the "people."

This word for people survives not only throughout the Province of Bontoc but also far toward the northern end of Luzon, where it appears as "Apayao" or "Yaos." Bontoc designates the people of the Quiangan region as "I-fu-gao'," though a part of them at least have a different name for themselves.

The Bontoc Igorot have their center in the pueblo of Bontoc, pronounced "Ban-tak'," a Spanish corruption of the Igorot name "Fun-tak'," a common native word for mountain, the original name of the pueblo. To the northwest their culture extends to that of the historic Tinguian, a long-haired folk physiographically cut off by a watershed. To the east of the Cordillera Central the Tinguian call themselves "It-neg'." To the northeast the Bontoc culture area embraces the pueblo of Basao, stopping short of Tinglayan. The eastern limit of Bontoc culture is fixed by the pueblos of Lias and Barlig, and is thus about coextensive with the province. Southward the area includes all to the top of the watershed of Polis Mountain, which turns southward the numerous streams feeding the Rio Magat. The pueblos south of this watershed -- Lubong, Gisang, Banawi, etc. -- belong to the short-haired people of Quiangan culture. To the west Bontoc culture extends to the watershed of the Cordillera Central, which turns westward the various affluents of the Rio del Abra. On the southwest this cuts off the short-haired Lepanto Igorot, whose culture seems to be more allied to that of Benguet than Bontoc.

The men of the Bontoc area know none of the peoples by whom they are surrounded by the names history gives or the peoples designate themselves, with the exception of the Lepanto Igorot, the It-neg', and the Ilokano of the west coast. They do not know the "Tinguian" of Abra on their north and northwest by that name; they call them "It-neg'." Farther north are the people called by the Spaniards "Nabayuganes," "Aripas," and "Ipugaos;" to the northeast and east are the "Caylingas," "Comunanges," "Bayabonanes," "Dayags," and "Gaddannes" -- but Bontoc knows none of these names. Bontoc culture and Kalinga culture lie close together on the east, and the people of Bontoc pueblo name all their eastern neighbors It-neg' -- the same term they apply to the Tinguian to the west and northwest, because, they say, they all wear great quantities of brass on the arms and legs. To the south of Bontoc are the Quiangan Igorot, the Banawi division of which, at least, names itself May'-yo-yet, but whom Bontoc calls "I-fu-gao'." They designate the people of Benguet the "Igorot of Benguet," but these peoples designate themselves "Ib-a-loi'" in the northern part, and "Kan-ka-nay'" in the southern part, neither of which names Bontoc knows.

She has still another set of names for the people surrounding her -- people whom she vaguely knows are there but of whom or of whose lands she has no first-hand knowledge. The people to the north are "Am-yan'-an," and the northern country is "La'-god." The "Day'-ya" are the eastern people, while "Bar'-lig" is the name of the eastern and southeastern land. "Ab-a-ga'-tan" are the people of the south, and "Fi'-lig ab-a-ga'-tan," is the south land. The people of the west are "Loa'-od," and "Fi'-lig lao'-od," or "Lo'-ko" (the Provinces of Ilokos Norte and Ilokos Sur) is the country lying to the west and southwest.

Some of the old men of Bontoc say that in the past the Igorot people once extended to the seacoast in the Provinces of Ilokos Norte and Ilokos Sur. This, of course, is a tradition of the prehistoric time before the Ilokano invaded northern Luzon; but, as has been stated, the Bontoc people claim never to have been driven by that invasion, neither have they any knowledge of such a movement. It is not improbable, however, that traditions of the invasion may linger with the people nearer the coast and farther north.

<u>Historical sketch</u>

It is regretted that the once voluminous historical records and data which the Spaniards prepared and kept at Bontoc were burned -- tons of paper, they say -- probably late in 1898 or early in 1899 by Captain Angels, an insurrecto. However, from scanty printed historical data, but mostly from information gathered in Bontoc from Igorot and resident Ilokano, the following brief sketch is presented, with the hope that it will show the nature of the outside influences which have been about Bontoc for the past half century prior to American occupation. It is believed that the data are sufficiently truthful for this purpose, but no claim is made for historical accuracy.

It seems that in 1665 the Spanish governor of the Philippines, Governor-General D. Diego de Salcedo, sent an expedition from Manila into northern Luzon. Some time during the three years the expedition was out its influence was felt in Fidelisan and Tanolang, two pueblos in the western part of the Bontoc culture area, for history says they paid tribute.[9] It is not probable that any considerable party from the expedition penetrated the Igorot mountain country as far as the above pueblos.

After the year 1700 expeditions occasionally reached Cayan, which, until about twenty-five years ago, as has been stated, was a Spanish capital. In 1852 the entire territory of present Lepanto-Bontoc and a large part of northern Nueva Vizcaya were organized as an independent "distrito," under the name of "Valle de Cayan;"[10] and a few years later, though the author does not give the date, Bontoc was established as an independent "distrito."

The Spaniards and Ilokano in and about Bontoc Province say that it was about fifty years ago that the Spaniards first came to Bontoc. The time agrees very accurately with the time of the establishment of the district. From then until 1899 there was a Spanish garrison of 200 or 300 men stationed in Bontoc pueblo. Christian Ilokano from the west coast of northern Luzon and the Christian Tagalog from Manila and vicinity were the soldiers.

The Spanish comandante of the "distrito," the head of the political-military government, resided there, and there were also a few Spanish army officers and an army chaplain. A large garrison was quartered in Cervantes; there was a church in both Bontoc and Cervantes. In the district of Bontoc there was a Spanish post at Sagada, between the two capitals, Bontoc and Cervantes. Farther to the east was a post at Tukukan and Sakasakan, and farther east, at Basao, there was a post, a church, and a priest.

Most of the pueblos had Ilokano presidentes. The Igorot say that the Spaniards did little for them except to shoot them. There is yet a long, heavy wooden stock in Bontoc pueblo in which the Igorot were imprisoned. Igorot women were made the mistresses of both officers and soldiers. Work, food, fuel, and lumber were not always paid for. All persons 18 or more years old were required to pay an annual tax of 50 cents or an equivalent value in rice. A day's wage was only 5 cents, so each family was required to pay an equivalent of twenty days' labor annually. In wild towns the principal men were told to bring in so many thousand bunches of palay -- the unthreshed rice. If it was not all brought in, the soldiers frequently went for it, accompanied by Igorot warriors; they gathered up the rice, and sometimes burned the entire pueblo. Apad, the principal man of Tinglayan, was confined six years in Spanish jails at Bontoc and Vigan because he repeatedly failed to compel his people to bring in the amount of palay assessed them.

They say there were three small guardhouses on the outskirts of Bontoc pueblo, and armed Igorot from an outside town were not allowed to enter. They were disarmed, and came and went under guard.

The Spanish comandantes in charge of the province seem to have remained only about two years each. Saldero was the last one. Early in the eighties of the nineteenth century the comandante took his command to Barlig, a day east of Bontoc, to punish that town because it had killed people in Tulubin and Samoki; Barlig all but exterminated the command -- only three men escaped to tell the tale. Mandicota, a Spanish officer, went from Manila with a battalion of 1,000 soldiers to erase Barlig from the map; he was also accompanied from Bontoc by 800 warriors from that vicinity. The Barlig people fled to the mountains, losing only seven men, whose heads the Bontoc Igorot cut off and brought home.

Comandante Villameres is reported to have taken twenty soldiers and about 520 warriors of Bontoc and Samoki to punish Tukukan for killing a Samoki woman; the warriors returned with three heads.

They say that in 1891 Comandante Alfaro took 40 soldiers and 1,000 warriors from the vicinity of Bontoc to Ankiling; sixty heads adorned the triumphant return of the warriors.

In 1893 Nevas is said to have taken 100 soldiers and 500 warriors to Sadanga; they brought back one head.

A few years later Saldero went to "clear up" rebellious Sagada with soldiers and Igorot warriors; Bontoc reports that the warriors returned with 100 heads.

The insurrectos appeared before Cervantes two or three months after Saldero's bloody work in Sagada. The Spanish garrison fled before the insurrectos; the Spanish civilians went with them, taking their flocks and herds to Bontoc. A thousand pesos was the price offered by the Igorot of Sagada to the insurrectos for Saldero's head when the Philippine soldiers passed through the pueblo; but Saldero made good his escape from Bontoc, and left the country by boat from Vigan.

The Bontoc Igorot assisted the insurrectos in many ways when they first came. About 2 miles west of Bontoc is a Spanish rifle pit, and there the Spanish soldiers, now swelled to about 600 men, lay in wait for the insurrectos. There on two hilltops an historic sham battle occurred. The two forces were nearly a mile apart, and at that distance they exchanged rifle bullets three days. The Spaniards finally surrendered, on condition of safe escort to the coast. For fifty years they had conquered their enemy who were armed only with spear and ax; but the insurrectos were armed with guns. However, the really hard pressing came from the rear -- there were still the ax and spear -- and few soldiers from cuartel or trench who tried to bring food or water for the fighting men ever reported why they were delayed.

The feeling of friendship between the Igorot and insurrectos was so strong that when the insurrectos asked the Igorot to go to Manila to fight the new enemy (the Americans), 400 warriors, armed only with spear, battle-ax, and shield, went a three weeks' journey to get American heads. At Caloocan, just outside Manila, they met the American Army early in February, 1899. They threw their spears, the Americans fired their guns -- "which must be brothers to the thunder," the Igorot said -- and they let fall their remaining weapons, and, panic stricken, started home. All but thirteen arrived in safety. They are not ashamed of their defeat and retreat; they made a mistake when they went to fight the Americans, and they were quick to see it. They are largely blessed with the saving sense of humor, and some of the warriors who were at Caloocan have been known to say that they never stopped running until they arrived home.

When these men told their people in Bontoc what part they and the insurrectos played in the fight against the Americans, the tension between the Igorot and insurrectos was at its greatest. The insurrectos were evidently worse than the Spaniards. They did all the things the Spaniards had done, and more -- they robbed through falsehood. Consequently, insurrectos frequently lost their heads.

Major Marsh went through Bontoc close after Aguinaldo in December, 1899. The Igorot befriended the Americans; they brought them food and guided them faithfully along the bewildering mountain trails when the insurrectos split and scattered -- anywhere, everywhere, fleeing eastward, northward, southward, in the mountains.

When Major Marsh returned through Bontoc, after following Aguinaldo into the heart of the Quiangan area, he left in the pueblo some sixty shoeless men under a volunteer lieutenant. The lieutenant promptly appointed an Ilokano presidente, vice-presidente, secretary, and police force in Bontoc and also in Sagada, and when the soldiers left in a few weeks he gave seven guns to the "officials" in Bontoc and two to those in Sagada. A short time proved that those "officials" were untrustworthy men; many were insurrectos who had dropped behind Aguinaldo. They persecuted the Igorot even worse than had the insurrectos. They seemed to have the American Army behind them -- and the Igorot stood in awe of American arms.

The crisis came. An Igorot obtained possession of one of the guns, and the Ilokano chief of police was killed and his corporal wounded.

This shooting, at the time apparently unpremeditated, but, in reality, carefully planned and successfully executed, was the cause of the arrival in Bontoc pueblo of the first American civilians. At that time a party of twenty Americans was at Fidelisan, a long day northwest of Bontoc; they were prospecting and sightseeing. The Ilokano sent these men a letter, and the Igorot sent a messenger, begging them to come to the help of the pueblo. Three men went on August 27, 1900; they were Truman K. Hunt, M.D., Mr. Frank Finley, and Mr. Riley. The disagreement was settled, and several Ilokano families left Bontoc under the protection of Mr. Riley.

August 9, 1901, when the Board of Health for the Philippine Islands was organized, Dr. Hunt, who had remained in Bontoc most of the preceding year, was appointed "superintendent of public vaccination and inspection of infectious diseases for the Provinces of Bontoc and Lepanto." He was stationed at Bontoc. About that time another American civilian came to the province -- Mr. Reuben H. Morley, now secretary-treasurer of the Province of Nueva Vizcaya, who lived nearly a year in Tulubin, two hours from Bontoc. December 14 Mr. William F. Smith, an American teacher, was sent to Bontoc to open a school.

Early in 1902 Constabulary inspectors, Lieutenants Louis A. Powless and Ernest A. Eckman, also came. May 28, 1902, the Philippine Commission organized the Province of Lepanto-Bontoc; on June 9 Dr. Hunt was appointed lieutenant-governor of the province. May 1, 1903, Dr. Hunt resigned and E. A. Wagar, M.D., became his successor.

The Spaniard was in Bontoc about fifty years. To summarize the Spanish influence on the Igorot -- and this includes any influence which the Ilokano or Tagalog may have had since they came among the people under Spanish protection -- it is believed that no essential institution of the Igorot has been weakened or vitiated to any appreciable degree. No Igorot attended the school which the Spaniards had in Bontoc; to-day not ten Igorot of the pueblo can make themselves understood in Spanish about the commonest things around them. I fail to detect any occupation, method, or device of the Igorot which the Spaniards' influence improved; and the Igorot flatly deny any such influence.

The Spaniard put the institution of pueblo presidente pretty well throughout the area now in province, but the presidente in no way interferes with the routine life of the people -- he is the mouthpiece of the Government asking for labor and the daily necessities of a nonproductive, resident foreign population.

The "tax" levied was scarcely in the nature of a modern tax; it was more the means taken by the Spaniard to secure his necessary food. In no other way was the political life and organization of the pueblo affected. In the realm of religion and spirit belief the surface has scarcely been scratched. The only Igorot who became Christians were the wives of some of the Christian natives who came in with the Spaniard, mainly as soldiers. There are now eight or ten such women, wives of the resident Ilokanos of Bontoc pueblo, but those whose husbands left the pueblo have reverted to Igorot faith.

In the matter of war and head-hunting the effect of the Spaniard was to intensify the natural instinct of the Igorot in and about Bontoc pueblo. Nineteen men in twenty of Bontoc and Samoki have taken a human head, and it has been seen under what conditions and influences some of those heads were taken. An Igorot, whose confidence I believe I have, an old man who represents the knowledge and wisdom of the people, told me recently that if the Americans wanted the people of Bontoc to go out against a pueblo they would gladly go; and he added, suggestively, that when the Spaniards were there the old men had much better food than now, for many hogs were killed in the celebration of war expeditions -- and the old men got the greater part of the meat. The Igorot is a natural head-hunter, and his training for the last sixty years seems to have done little more for him than whet this appetite.

Somatology

Man

The Bontoc men average about 5 feet 4 1/8 inches in height, and have the appearance of being taller than they are. Again and again one is deceived by their height, and he repeatedly backs a 5-foot-7-inch Igorot up against a 6-foot American, vainly expecting the stature of the brown man to equal that of the white. Almost never does the Bontoc man appear heavy or thickset, as does his brother, the Benguet Igorot -- the human pack horse seen so constantly on the San Fernando-Baguio trail -- muscularly one of the most highly developed primitive people in the world to-day

Of thirty-two men measured from Bontoc and vicinity the shortest was 4 feet 9 1/8 inches and the tallest was slightly more than 5 feet 9 inches. The following table presents the average measurements of the thirty-two men:

Average measurements of Bontoc men

Measurements

CM.

Stature
160.287

Spread of arms
165.684

Head length
19.212

Head breadth
15.203

Cephalic index (per cent)
79.1328

Nasal length
5.25625

Nasal breadth
4.1625

Nasal index (per cent)
79.191

From these measurements it appears that the composite man -- the average of the combined measurements of thirty-two men -- is mesaticephalic. Among the thirty-two men the extremes of cephalic index are 91.48 and 67.48. This first measurement is of a young man between 20 and 25 years of age. It stands far removed from other measurements, the one nearest it being 86.78, that of a man about 60 years old. The other extreme is 67.48, the measure of a young man between 25 and 30 years of age. Among the thirty-two men, nine are brachycephalic -- that is, their cephalic index is greater than 80; twenty of the thirty-two are mesati-

cephalic, with cephalic index between 75 and 80; and only three are dolichocephalic -- that is, the cephalic index is below 75.

The nasal indexes of the thirty-two men show that the Bontoc man has the
"medium" or mesorhine nose. They also show that one is very extremely
platyrhine, the index being 104.54, and one is very leptorhine, being 58.18. Of
the total, five are leptorhine -- that is, have the "narrow" nose with nasal index
below 70. Seventeen men are mesorhine, with the "medium" nose with nasal
index between 70 and 85; and ten are platyrhine -- that is, the noses are "broad,"
with an index greater than 85.

The Bontoc men are never corpulent, and, with the exception of the very old,
they are seldom poor. During the period of a man's prime he is usually muscled
to an excellent symmetry. His neck, never long, is well formed and strong and
supports the head in erect position. His shoulders are broad, even, and full muscled, and with seeming ease carry transportation baskets laden with 75 to 100
pounds. His arms are smoothly developed and are about the same relative length
as the American's. The hands are strong and short. The waist line is firm and
smaller than the shoulders or hips. The buttocks usually appear heavy. His legs are
generally straight; the thighs and calves are those of a prime pedestrian accustomed to long and frequent walks. The ankles are seldom thick; and the feet are
broad and relatively short, and, almost without exception, are placed on the
ground straight ahead. He has the feet of a pedestrian -- not the inturned feet of
the constant bearer of heavy burdens on the back or the outturned feet of the man
who sits or stands. The perfection of muscular development of two-thirds of the
men of Bontoc between the ages of 25 and 30 would be the envy of the average
college athlete in the States.

In color the men are brown, though there is a wide range of tone from a light
brown with a strong saffron undertone to a very dark brown -- as near a bronze
as can well be imagined. The sun has more to do with the different color tones
than has anything else, after which habits of personal cleanliness play a very large
role. There are men in the Bontoc Igorot Constabulary of an extremely light-
brown color, more saffron than brown, who have been wearing clothing for only
one year. During the year the diet of the men in the Constabulary has been practically the same as that of their darker brothers among whom they were enlisted
only twelve months ago. All the members of the Constabulary differ much more
in color from the unclothed men than the unclothed differ among themselves.
Man after man of these latter may pass under the eye without revealing a tint of
saffron, yet there are many who show it faintly. The natural Igorot never washes
himself clean. He washes frequently, but lacks the means of cleansing the skin,

and the dirtier he is the more bronze-like he appears. At all times his face looks lighter and more saffron-tinted than the remainder of his body. There are two reasons for this -- because the face is more often washed and because of its contrast with the black hair of the head.

The hair of the head is black, straight, coarse, and relatively abundant. It is worn long, frequently more than half way to the hips from the shoulders. The front is "banged" low and square across the forehead, cut with the battle-ax; this line of cut runs to above and somewhat back of the ear, the hair of the scalp below it being cut close to the head. When the men age, a few gray hairs appear, and some old men have heads of uniform iron-gray color. I have never seen a white-haired Igorot. A few of the old men have their hair thinning on the crown, but a tendency to baldness is by no means the rule.

Bontoc pueblo is no exception to the rule that every pueblo in the Philippines has a few people with curly or wavy hair. I doubt whether to-day an entire tribe of perfectly straight-haired primitive Malayan people exists in the Archipelago. Funit is a curly-haired Bontoc man of about 45 years of age. Many people told me that his father and also his grandfather were members of the pueblo and had curly hair. I have never been able to find any hint at foreign or Negrito blood in any of the several curly haired people in the Bontoc culture area whose ancestors I have tried to discover.

The scanty growth of hair on the face of the Bontoc man is pulled out. A small pebble and the thumb nail or the blade of the battle-ax and the bulb of the thumb are frequently used as forceps; they never cut the hair of the face. It is common to see men of all ages with a very sparse growth of hair on the upper lip or chin, and one of 50 years in Bontoc has a fairly heavy 4-inch growth of gray hair on his chin and throat; he is shown in Pl. XIII. Their bodies are quite free from hair. There is none on the breast, and seldom any on the legs. The pelvic growth is always pulled out by the unmarried. The growth in the armpits is scant, but is not removed.

The iris of the eye is brown -- often rimmed with a lighter or darker ring. The brown of the iris ranges from nearly black to a soft hazel brown. The cornea is frequently blotched with red or yellow. The Malayan fold of the upper eyelid is seen in a large majority of the men, the fold being so low that it hangs over and hides the roots of the lashes. The lashes appear to grow from behind the lid rather than from its rim.

The teeth are large and strong, and, whereas in old age they frequently become few and discolored, during prime they are often white and clean. The people never artificially stain the teeth, and, though surrounded by betel-nut chewers with dark teeth or red-stained lips, they do not use the betel.

Since the Igorot keeps no record of years, it is impossible to know his age, but it is believed that sufficient comparative data have been collected in Bontoc to make the following estimates reliable:

At the age of 20 a man seems hardly to have reached his physical best; this he attains, however, before he is 25. By 35 he begins to show the marks of age. By 45 most of the men are fast getting "old"; their faces are seamed, their muscles losing form, their carriage less erect, and the step slower. By 55 all are old -- most are bent and thin. Probably not over one or two in a hundred mature men live to be 70 years old.

The following census taken from a Spanish manuscript found in Quiangan, and written in 1894, may be taken as representative of an average Igorot pueblo:

Census of Magulang, district of Quiangan

Years	Females	Males
0 to 1	191	200
1 to 5	209	210
5 to 10	144	123
10 to 15	132	159
15 to 20	129	114
20 to 30	121	134
30 to 40	212	239
40 to 50	118	126
50 and over	79	62
Total	1,335	1,367

From this census it seems that the Magulang Igorot man is at his prime between the ages of 30 and 40 years, and that the death rate for men between the ages of 40 and 50 is nearly as great as the death rate among children between 5 to 10 years of age, being 52.7 per cent. Beyond the age of 50 collapse is sudden, since all the men more than 50 years old are less than half the number of those between the ages of 40 and 50 years.

Woman

The women average 4 feet 9 3/8 inches in height. In appearance they are short and stocky. Twenty-nine women from Bontoc and vicinity were measured; the tallest was 5 feet 4 3/4 inches, and the shortest 4 feet 4 3/4 inches. The following table presents the average measurements of twenty-nine women:

Average measurements of Bontoc women

Measurements

CM.

Stature 145.800

Spread of arms 149.603

Head length 18.593

Head breadth 14.706

Cephalic index (per cent) 79.094

Nasal length 4.582

Nasal breadth 3.608

Nasal index (per cent) 78.744

These measurements show that the composite woman -- the average of the measurements of twenty-nine women -- is mesaticephalic. The extremes of cephalic index are 87.64 and 64.89; both are measurements of women about 35 years of age. Of the twenty-nine women twelve are brachycephalic; twelve are mesaticephalic; and five are dolichocephalic.

The Bontoc woman has a "medium," or mesorhine, nose, as is shown by the above figures. Four of the twenty-nine women have the "narrow" leptorhine nose with nasal index below 70; seven have platyrhine or the "broad" nose with index greater than 85; while seventeen have the "medium" or mesorhine nose with nasal index between 70 and 85. The broadest nose has an index of 97.56, and the narrowest an index of 58.53.

The women reach the age of maturity well prepared for its responsibilities. They have more adipose tissue than the men, yet are never fat. The head is carried erect, but with a certain stiffness -- often due, in part, no doubt, to shyness, and in part to the fact that they carry all their burdens on their heads. I believe the neck more often appears short than does the neck of the man. The shoulders are broad, and flat across the back. The breasts are large, full, and well supported. The hips are broad and well set, and the waist (there is no natural waist line) is frequently no smaller than the hips, though smaller than the shoulders. Their arms are smooth and strong, and they throw stones as men do, with the full-arm throw from the shoulder. Their hands are short and strong. Their legs are almost invariably straight, but are probably more frequently bowed at the knees than are the men's. The thighs are sturdy and strong, and the calves not infrequently over-large. This enlargement runs low down, so the ankles, never slender, very often appear coarse and large. In consequence of this heavy lower leg, the feet, short at best, usually look much too short. They are placed on the ground straight ahead, though the tendency to inturned feet is slightly more noticeable than it is among the men.

Their carriage is a healthful one, though it is not always graceful, since their long strides commonly give the prominent buttocks a jerky movement. They prove the naturalness of that style of walking which, in profile, shows the chest thrust forward and the buttocks backward; the abdomen is in, and the shoulders do not swing as the strides are made.

It can not be said that at base the color of the women's skin differs from that of the men, but the saffron undertone is more commonly seen than it is in the unclothed men. It shows on the shaded parts of the body, and where the skin is distended, as on the breast and about certain features of the face.

The hair of the head is like that of the man's; it is worn long, and is twisted and wound about the head. It has a tendency to fall out as age comes on, but does not seem thin on the head. The tendency to gray hairs is apparently somewhat less than it is with the men. The remainder of the body is exceptionally free from hair. The growth in the armpits and the pelvic hair are always pulled out by the unmarried, and a large per cent of the women do not allow it to grow even in old age.

Their eyes are brown, varied as are those of the men, and with the Malayan fold of the upper eyelid.

Their teeth are generally whiter and cleaner than are those of their male companions, a condition due largely, probably, to the fact that few of the women smoke.

They seem to reach maturity at about 17 or 18 years of age. The first child is commonly born between the ages of 16 and 22. At 23 the woman has certainly reached her prime. By 30 she is getting "old"; before 45 the women are old, with flat, pendent folds of skin where the breasts were. The entire front of the body -- in prime full, rounded, and smooth -- has become flabby, wrinkled, and folded. It is only a short time before collapse of the tissue takes place in all parts of the body. An old woman, say, at 50, is a mass of wrinkles from foot to forehead; the arms and legs lose their plumpness, the skin is "bagged" at the knees into half a dozen large folds; and the disappearance of adipose tissue from the trunk-front, sides, and back -- has left the skin not only wrinkled but loose and flabby, folding over the girdle at the waist.

The census of Magulang, page 42, should be again referred to, from which it appears that the death rate among women is greater between the ages of 40 and 50 years than it is with men, being 55.66 per cent. The census shows also that there are relatively a larger number of old women -- that is, over 50 years old -- than there are old men.

Child

The death rate among children is large. Of fifteen families in Bontoc, each having had three or more children, the death rate up to the age of puberty was over 60 per cent. According to the Magulang census the death rate of children from 5 to 10 years of age is 63.73 per cent.

The new-born babe is as light in color as the average American babe, and is much less red, instead of which color there is the slightest tint of saffron. As the babe lies naked on its mother's naked breast the light color is most strikingly apparent by contrast. The darker color, the brown, gradually comes, however, as the babe is exposed to the sun and wind, until the child of a year or two carried on its mother's back is practically one with the mother in color.

Some of the babes, perhaps all, are born with an abundance of dark hair on the head. A child's hair is never cut, except that from about the age of 3 years the boy's hair is "banged" across the forehead. Fully 30 per cent of children up to 5 or 6 years of age have brown hair -- due largely to fading, as the outer is much lighter than the under hair. In rare cases the lighter brown hair assumes a distinctly red cast, though a faded lifeless red. Before puberty is reached, however, all children have glossy black hair.

The iris of a new-born babe is sometimes a blue brown; it is decidedly a different brown from that of the adult or of the child of five years. Most children have the Malayan fold of the eyelid; the lower lid is often much straighter than it is on the average American. When, in addition to these conditions, the outer corner of the eye is higher than the inner, the eye is somewhat Mongolian in appearance. About one-fifth of the children in Bontoc have this Mongolian-like eye, though it is rarer among adults -- a fact due, in part, apparently, to the down curving and sagging of the lower lid as one's prime is reached and passed.

Children's teeth are clean and white, and very generally remain so until maturity.

The child from 1 to 3 years of age is plump and chubby; his front is full and rounded, but lacks the extra abdominal development so common with the children of the lowlands, and which has received from the American the popular name of "banana belly." By the age of 7 the child has lost its plump, rounded form, which is never again had by the boys but is attained by the girls again early in puberty. During these last half dozen years of childhood all children are slender and agile and wonderfully attractive in their naturalness. Both girls and boys reach puberty at a later time than would be expected, though data can not be gathered to determine accurately the age at puberty. All the Ilokano in Bontoc pueblo consistently maintain that girls do not reach puberty until at least 16 and 17 years of age. Perhaps it is arrived at by 14 or 15, but I feel certain it is not as early as 12 or 13 -- a condition one might expect to find among people in the tropics.

Pathology

The most serious permanent physical affliction the Bontoc Igorot suffers is blindness. Fully 2 per cent of the people both of Bontoc and her sister pueblo, Samoki, are blind; probably 2 per cent more are partially so. Bontoc has one blind boy only 3 years old, but I know of no other blind children; and it is claimed that no babes are born blind. There is one woman in Bontoc approaching 20 years of age who is nearly blind, and whose mother and older sister are blind. Blindness is very common among the old people, and seems to come on with the general breaking down of the body.

A few of the people say their blindness is due to the smoke in their dwellings. This doubtless has much to do with the infirmity, as their private and public buildings are very smoky much of the time, and when the nights are at all chilly a fire is built in their closed, low, and chimneyless sleeping rooms. There are many persons with inflamed and granulated eyelids whose vision is little or not at all impaired -- a forerunner of blindness probably often caused by smoke.

Twenty per cent of the adults have abnormal feet. The most common and most striking abnormality is that known as "fa'-wing"; it is an inturning of the great toe. Fa'-wing occurs in all stages from the slightest spreading to that approximating forty-five degrees. It is found widely scattered among the barefoot mountain tribes of northern Luzon. The people say it is due to mountain climbing, and their explanation is probably correct, as the great toe is used much as is a claw in securing a footing on the slippery, steep trails during the rainy reason. Fa'-wing occurs quite as commonly with women as with men, and in Ambuklao, Benguet Province, I saw a boy of 8 or 9 years whose great toes were spread half as much as those shown in Pl. XXV. This deformity occurs on one or both feet, but generally on both if at all.

An enlargement of the basal joint of the great toe, probably a bunion, is also comparatively common. It is not improbable that it is often caused by stone bruises, as such are of frequent occurrence; they are sometimes very serious, laying a person up ten days at a time.

The feet of adults who work in the water-filled rice paddies are dry, seamed, and cracked on the bottoms. These "rice-paddy feet," called "fung-as'," are often so sore that the person can not go on the trails for any considerable distance.

I believe not 5 per cent of the people are without eruptions of the skin. It is practically impossible to find an adult whose body is not marked with shiny patches showing where large eruptions have been. Babes of one or two months do not appear to have skin diseases, but those of three and four are sometimes half covered with itching, discharging eruptions. Babes under a year old, such as are most carried on their mother's backs, are especially subject to a mass of sores about the ankles; the skin disease is itch, called ku'-lid. I have seen babes of this age with sores an inch across and nearly an inch deep in their backs.

Relatively there are few large sores on the people such as boils and ulcers, but a person may have a dozen or half a hundred itching eruptions the size of a half pea scattered over his arms, legs, and trunk. From these he habitually squeezes the pus onto his thumb nail, and at once ignorantly cleans the nail on some other part of the body. The general prevalence of this itch is largely due to the gregarious life of the people -- to the fact that the males lounge in public quarters, and all, except married men and women, sleep in these same quarters where the naked skin readily takes up virus left on the stone seats and sleeping boards by an infected companion. In Banawi, in the Quiangan culture area, a district having no public buildings, one can scarcely find a trace of skin eruption.

There are two adult people in Samoki pueblo who are insane; one of them at least is supposed to be affected by Lumawig, the Igorot god, and is said, when he hallooes, as he does at times, to be calling to Lumawig. Bontoc pueblo has a young woman and a girl of five or six years of age who are imbecile. Those four people are practically incapacitated from earning a living, and are cared for by their immediate relatives. There are two adult deaf and dumb men in Bontoc pueblo, but both are industrious and self-supporting.

Igorot badly injured in war or elsewhere are usually killed at their own request. In May, 1903, a man from Maligkong was thrown to the earth and rendered unconscious by a heavy timber he and several companions brought to Bontoc for the school building. His companions immediately told Captain Eckman to shoot him as he was "no good." I can not say whether it is customary for the Igorot to weed out those who faint temporarily -- as the fact just cited suggests; however, they do not kill the feeble aged, and the presence of the insane and the imbecile shows that weak members of the group are not always destroyed voluntarily.

PART 3

General Social Life

The pueblo

Bontoc and Samoki pueblos, in all essentials typical of pueblos in the Bontoc area, lie in the mountains in a roughly circular pocket called Pa-pas'-kan. A perfect circle about a mile in diameter might be described within the pocket. It is bisected fairly accurately by the Chico River, coursing from the southwest to the northeast. Its altitude ranges from about 2,750 feet at the river to 2,900 at the upper edge of Bontoc pueblo, which is close to the base of the mountain ridge at the west, while Samoki is backed up against the opposite ridge to the southeast. The river flows between the pueblos, though considerably closer to Samoki than to Bontoc.

The horizon circumscribing this pocket is cut at the northeast, where the river makes its exit, and lifting above this gap are two ranges of mountains beyond. At the south-southeast there is another cut, through which a small affluent pours into the main stream. At the southwest the river enters the pocket, although no cut shows in the horizon, as the stream bends abruptly and the farther range of mountains folds close upon the near one.

Bontoc lies compactly built on a sloping piece of ground, roughly about half a mile square. Through the pueblo are two water-cut ravines, down which pour the waters of the mountain ridge in the rainy season, and in which, during much of the remainder of the year, sufficient water trickles to supply several near-by dwellings.

Adjoining the pueblo on the north and west are two small groves where a religious ceremonial is observed each month. Granaries for rice are scattered all about the outer fringe of dwellings, and in places they follow the ravines in among the buildings of the pueblo. The old, broad Spanish trail runs close to the pueblo on the south and east, as it passes in and out of the pocket through the gaps cut by the river. About the pueblo at the east and northeast are some fifteen houses built in Spanish time, most of them now occupied by Ilokano men with Igorot or half-breed wives. There also were the Spanish Government buildings, reduced to a church, a convent, and another building used now as headquarters for the Government Constabulary.

The pueblo, now 2,000 or 2,500 people, was probably at one time larger. There is a tradition common in both Bontoc and Samoki that in former years the ancestors of this latter pueblo lived northeast of Bontoc toward the northern corner of the pocket. They say they moved to the opposite side of the river because there they would have more room. There they have grown to 1,200 or 1,500 souls. Still later, but yet before the Spanish came, a large section of people from northeastern Bontoc moved bodily to Lias, about two days to the east. They tell that a Bontoc woman named Fank'-a was the wife of a Lias man, and when a drought and famine visited Bontoc the section of the pueblo from which she came moved as a whole to Lias, then a small collection of people. Still later, La'-nao, a detached section of Bontoc on the lowland near the river, was suddenly wiped out by a disease.

The Igorot is given to naming even small areas of the earth within his well-known habitat, and there are four areas in Bontoc pueblo having distinct names. These names in no way refer to political or social divisions -- they are not the "barrio" of the coast pueblos of the Islands, neither are they in any way like a "ward" in an American city, nor are they "additions" to an original part of the pueblo -- they are names of geographic areas over which the pueblo was built or has spread. From south to north these areas are A-fu', Mag-e'-o, Dao'-wi, and Um-feg'.

<u>Ato</u>

Bontoc is composed of seventeen political divisions, called "a'-to." The geographic area of A-fu' contains four a'-to, namely, Fa-tay'-yan, Po-lup-o', Am-ka'-wa, and Bu-yay'-yeng; Mag-e'-o contains three, namely, Fi'-lig, Mag-e'-o, and Cha-kong'; Dao'-wi has six, namely, Lo-wing'-an, Pud-pud-chog', Si-pa'-at, Si-gi-chan', So-mo-wan', and Long-foy'; Um-feg' has four, Po-ki'-san, Lu-wa'-kan, Ung-kan', and Cho'-ko. Each a'-to is a separate political division. It has its public buildings; has a separate governing council which makes peace, challenges to war, and accepts or rejects war challenges, and it formally releases and adopts men who change residence from one a'-to to another.

Border a'-to Fa-tay'-yan seems to be developing an offspring -- a new a'-to; a part of it, the southwestern border part, is now known as "Tang-e-ao'." It is disclaimed as a separate a'-to, yet it has a distinctive name, and possesses some of the marks of an independent a'-to. In due time it will doubtless become such.

In Sagada, Agawa, Takong, and near-by pueblos the a'-to is said to be known as dap'-ay; and in Balili and Alap both names are known.

The pueblo must be studied entirely through the a'-to. It is only an aggregate of which the various a'-to are the units, and all the pueblo life there is is due to the similarity of interests of the several a'-to.

Bontoc does not know when her pueblo was built -- she was always where she now is -- but they say that some of the a'-to are newer than others. In fact, they divide them into the old and new. The newer ones are Bu-yay'-yeng, Am-ka'-wa, Po-lup-o', Cha-kong', and Po-ki'-san; all these are border a'-to of the pueblo.

The generations of descendants of men who did distinct things are kept carefully in memory; and from the list of descendants of the builders of some of the newer a'-to it seems probable that Cha-kong' was the last one built. One of the builders was Sal-lu-yud'; he had a son named Tam-bul', and Tam-bul' was the father of a man in Bontoc now some twenty-five years old. It is probable that Cha-kong' was built about 1830 -- in the neighborhood of seventy-five years ago. The plat of the pueblo seems to strengthen the impression that Cha-kong' is the newest a'-to, since it appears to have been built in territory previously used for rice granaries; it is all but surrounded by such ground now.

One of the builders of Bu-yay'-yeng, an a'-to adjoining Cha-kong', and also one of the newer ones, was Ba-la-ge'. Ba-la-ge' was the great-great-great-grandfather of Mud-do', who is a middle-aged man now in Bontoc. The generations of fathers descending from Ba-la-ge' to Mud-do' are the following: Bang-eg', Cag-i'-yu, Bit-e', and Ag-kus'. It seems from this evidence that the a'-to Bu-yay'-yeng was built about one hundred and fifty years ago. These facts suggest a much greater age for the older a'-to of the pueblo.

An a'-to has three classes of buildings occupied by the people -- the fawi and paba-funan, public structures for boys and men, and the olag for girls and young women before their permanent marriage; and the dwellings occupied by families and by widows, which are called afong. Each of these three classes of buildings plays a distinct role in the life of the people.

Pabafunan and fawi

The pa-ba-fu'-nan is the home of the various a'-to ceremonials. It is sacred to the men of the a'-to, and on no occasion do the women or girls enter it.

All boys from 3 or 4 years of age and all men who have no wives sleep nightly in the pa-ba-fu'-nan or in the fa'-wi.

The pa-ba-fu'-nan building consists of a low, squat, stone-sided structure partly covered with a grass roof laid on a crude frame of poles; the stone walls extend beyond the roof at one end and form an open court. The roofed part is about 8 by 10 feet, and usually is not over 5 feet high in any part, inside measure; the size of the court is approximately the same as that of the roofed section. In some pa-ba-fu'-nan a part of the court is roofed over for shelter in case of rain, but is not walled in. Under this roof skulls of dogs and hogs are generally found tucked away. Carabao horns and chicken feathers are also commonly seen in such places.

In many cases the open court is shaded by a tree. Posts are found reared above most of the courts. Some are old and blackened; others are all but gone -- a short stump being all that projects above the earth. The tops of some posts are rudely carved to represent a human head; on the tops of others, as in a'-to Lowingan and Sipaat, there are stones which strikingly resemble human skulls. It is to the tops of these posts that the enemy's head is attached when a victorious warrior returns to his a'-to. Both the roofed and court sections are paved with stone, and large stones are also arranged around the sides of the court, some more or less elevated as seats; they are worn smooth and shiny by generations of use. In the center of the court is the smoldering remains of a fire. The only opening into the covered part is a small doorway connecting it with the court. This door is barely large enough to permit a man to squeeze in sidewise; it is often not over 2 1/2 feet high and 10 inches wide. The occupants of the pa-ba-fu'-nan usually sleep curled up naked on the smooth, flat stones. A few people have runo slat mats, some of which roll up, while others are inflexible, and they lie on these over the stone pavement. Fires are built in all sleeping rooms when it is cold, and the rooms all close tightly with a door.

In the court of the building the men lounge when not at work in the fields; they sleep, or smoke and chat, tend babies, or make utensils and weapons. The pa-ba-fu'-nan is the man's club by day, and the unmarried man's dormitory by night, and, as such, it is the social center for all men of the a'-to, and it harbors at night all men visiting from other pueblos.

Each a'-to, except Chakong, has a pa-ba-fu'-nan. When the men of Chakong were building theirs they met the pueblo of Sadanga in combat, and one of the builders lost his head to Sadanga. Then the old men of Chakong counciled together; they came to the conclusion that it was bad for the a'-to to have a pa-ba-fu'-nan, and none has ever been built. This absence of the pa-ba-fu'-nan in some way detracts from the importance of the a'-to in the minds of the people. For instance, in the early stages of this study I was told several times that there are sixteen (and not seventeen) a'-to in Bontoc. The first list of a'-to written did not include Chakong; it was discovered only when the pueblo was platted, and at that time my informants sought to pass it over by saying "It is Chakong, but it has no pa-ba-fu'-nan." The explanation of the obscurity of Chakong in the minds of the Igorot seems to be that the a'-to ceremonial is more important than the a'-to council -- that the emotional and not the mental is held uppermost, that the people of Bontoc flow together through feeling better than they drive together through cold force or control.

The a'-to ceremonials of Chakong are held in the pa-ba-fu'-nan of neighboring a'-to, as in Sigichan, Pudpudchog, or Filig, and this seems partially to destroy the ESPRIT DE CORPS of the unfortunate a'-to.

Each a'-to has a fa'-wi building -- a structure greatly resembling to the pa-ba-fu'-nan, and impossible to be distinguished from it by one looking at the structure from the outside. The fa'-wi and pa-ba-fu'-nan are shown in Pls. XXX, XXXI, and XXXII. Pl. XXIX shows a section of Sipaat a'-to with its fa'-wi and pa-ba-fu'-nan. The fa'-wi is the a'-to council house; as such it is more frequented by the old men than by the younger. The fa'-wi also shelters the skulls of human heads taken by the a'-to. Outside the pueblo, along certain trails, there are simple structures also called "fa'-wi," shelters where parties halt for feasts, etc., while on various ceremonial journeys.

The fa'-wi and pa-ba-fu'-nan of each a'-to are near together, and in five they are under the same roof, though there is no doorway for intercommunication. What was said of the pa-ba-fu'-nan as a social center is equally true of the fa'-wi; each is the lounging place of men and boys, and the dormitory of unmarried males.

In Samoki each of the eight a'-to has only one public building, and that is known simply as "a'-to."

One is further convinced of an extensive early movement of the primitive Malayan from its pristine nest by the presence of institutions similar to the pa-ba-fu'-nan and fa'-wi over a vast territory of the Asiatic mainland as well as the Asiatic Islands and Oceania. That these widespread institutions sprang from the same source will be seen clearly in the quotations appearing in the footnote below.[11] The visible exponent of the institutions is a building forbidden to women, the functions of which are several; it is a dormitory for men -- generally unmarried men -- a council house, a guardhouse, a guest house for men, a center for ceremonials of the group, and a resting place for the trophies of the chase and war -- a "head house."

<u>Olag</u>

The o'-lag is the dormitory of the girls in an a'-to from the age of about 2 years until they marry. It is a small stone and mud-walled structure, roofed with grass, in which a grown person can seldom stand erect. It has but a single opening -- a door some 30 inches high and 10 inches wide. Occupying nearly all the floor space are boards about 4 feet long and from 8 to 14 inches wide; each board is a girl's bed. They are placed close together, side by side, laid on a frame about a foot above the earth. One end, where the head rests, is slightly higher that the other, while in most o'-lag a pole for a foot rest runs along the foot of the beds a few inches from them. The building as shown in Pl. XXXIII is typical of the nineteen found in Bontoc pueblo -- though it does not show, what is almost invariably true, that it is built over one or more pigsties. This condition is illustrated in Pl. XXIX, where a widow's house is shown literally resting above the stone walls of several sties. Unlike the fawi and pabafunan, the o'-lag has no adjoining court, and no shady surroundings. It is built to house the occupants only at night.

The o'-lag is not so distinctly an ato institution as the pabafunan and fawi. Ato Ungkan never had an o'-lag. The demand is not so urgent as that of some ato, since there are only thirteen families in Ungkan. The girls occupy o'-lag of neighboring ato.

The o'-lag of Luwakan, of Lowingan, and of Sipaat (the last situated in Lowingan) are broken down and unused at present. There are no marriageable girls in any of these three ato now, and the small girls occupy near-by o'-lag. These three o'-lag will be rebuilt when the girls are large enough to cook food for the men who build. The o'-lag of Amkawa is in Buyayyeng near the o'-lag of the latter; it is there by choice of the occupants.

Mageo, with her twenty families, also has two o'-lag, but both are situated in Pudpudchog.

The o'-lag is the only Igorot building which has received a specific name, all others bear simply the class name.[12]

In Sagada and some nearby pueblos, as Takong and Agawa, the o'-lag is said to he called If-gan'.

Mr. S. H. Damant is quoted from the Calcutta Review (vol. 61, p. 93) as saying that among the Nagas, frontier tribes of northeast India --

Only very young children live entirely with their parents; ... the women have also a house of their own called the "dekhi chang," where the unmarried girls are supposed to live.

Again Mr. Damant wrote:

I saw Dekhi chang here for the first time. All the unmarried girls sleep there at night, but it is deserted in the day. It is not much different from any ordinary house.[13]

Separate sleeping houses for girls similar to the o'-lag, I judge, are also found occasionally in Assam.[14]

Whereas, so far as known, the o'-lag occurs with the Igorot only among the Bontoc culture group, yet the above quotations and references point to a similar institution among distant people -- among some of the same people who have an institution very similar to the pabafunan and fawi.

Afong

A'-fong is the general name for Bontoc dwellings, of which there are two kinds. The first is the fay'-u (Pls. XXXIV and XXXVI), the large, open, board dwelling, some 12 by 15 feet square, with side walls only 3 1/2 feet high, and having a tall, top-heavy grass roof. It is the home of the prosperous. The other is the kat-yu'-fong (Pl. XXXVII), the smaller, closed, frequently mud-walled dwelling of poor families, and commonly of the widows.

The family dwelling primarily serves two purposes -- it is the place where the man, his wife, and small child sleep, and where the entire family takes its food.

The fay'-u is built at considerable expense. Three or four men are required for a period of about two months to get out the pine boards and timbers in the forest.

Each piece of timber for any permanent building is completed at the time it is cut from the tree, and is left to season in the mountains; sometimes it remains several years. (See Pl. XXXV.) When all is ready to construct the dwelling the owner announces his intention. Some 200 men of the pueblo gather to erect the building, and two or three dozen women come to prepare and cook the necessary food, for, whereas no wage is paid the laborers, all are feasted at the cost of much rice and several hogs and a carabao or two. The toiling and feasting continue about ten days.

The following description of a fay'-u is of an ordinary dwelling in Bontoc pueblo: The fay'-u are all constructed on the same plan, though a few are larger than the one here described, and some few are smaller. The front and back walls of the house are 3 feet 6 inches high and 12 feet 6 inches long. The two side walls are the same height as the ends, but are 15 feet 6 inches long. The rear wall is built of stones carefully chinked with mud. The side walls consist each of two boards extending the full length of the structure. The front wall is cut near the middle from top to bottom with a doorway 1 foot 4 inches wide; otherwise the front wall is like the two side walls, except that it has a roughly triangular timber grooved along the lower side and fitted over the top board as a cap. The doorposts are two timbers sunk in the ground; their tops fit into the two "caps," and each has a groove from top to bottom into which the ends of the boards of the front wall are inserted. A few dwellings have a door consisting of a single board set on end and swinging on a projection sunk in a hole in a doorsill buried in the earth; the upper part of the door swings on a string secured to the doorpost and passing through a hole in the door.

At each of the four corners of the building, immediately inside the walls, is a post set in the ground and standing 6 feet 9 inches high. The boards of the walls are tied to these corner posts, and the greater part of the weight of the roof rests on their tops. Four other posts, also planted in the ground and about as high as the corner posts, stand about 4 feet inside the walls of the house equidistant from the corner post and marking the corners of a rectangle about 5 1/2 feet square. They directly support the second story of the building.

There is no floor except the earth in the first story of the Bontoc dwelling, and from the door at the front of the building to the two rear posts of the four central ones there is an unobstructed passage or aisle called "cha-la'-nan." At one's left, as he enters the door, is a small room called "chap-an'" 5 1/2 feet square separated from the aisle by a row of low stones partially sunk in the earth. The earth in this room is excavated so that the floor is about 1 foot lower than that of the remainder of the building, and in its center the peculiar double wooden rice mortar is imbedded in the earth. It is in the chap-an' that the family rice and millet is threshed. At the left of the aisle and immediately beyond the chap-an', separated from it by a board partition the same height as the outside walls of the house, is the cooking room, called "cha-le-ka-nan' si mo-o'-to." It is approximately the same size as the threshing room. There are neither boards nor stones to cut this cooking room off from the open aisle of the house, but its width is determined by a low pile of stones built along its farther side from the outer house wall toward the aisle and ending at the rear left post of the four central ones. In the face of this stone wall are three concavities -- fireplaces over which cooking pots are placed. Arranged along the outer wall, and about 2 feet high, is a board shelf on which the water jars are kept.

At the right of the aisle, as one enters the building, is a broad shelf about 12 feet long; in width it extends from the side wall to the two right central posts. On this shelf, called "chuk'-so," are placed the various baskets and other utensils and implements of everyday use. Beneath it are stored the small cages or coops in which the chickens sleep at night. There are a few fay'-u in Bontoc in which the threshing room and cooking room are on the right of the aisle and the long bench is on the left, but they are very rare exceptions.

In the rear of the building is a board partition apparently extending from one side wall to the other. The bench at the right of the aisle ends against this partition, and on the left the stone fireplaces are built against it. This rear section is covered over with boards at the height of the outside wall, so that a low box is formed, 3 1/2 feet high and 4 1/4 feet wide. At the rear of the aisle a door 3 feet high and 1 foot 4 inches wide swings into this rear apartment, which, when the door is again closed, is as black as night. An examination of the inside of this section shows it to be entirely walled with stones except where the narrow door cuts it. By inside measure it is only 3 feet 6 inches wide and 6 feet 6 inches long. This is the sleeping apartment, and is called ang-an'. As one crawls into this kennel he is likely to place his hands among ashes and charred sticks which mark the place for a fire on cold nights. The left end of the ang-an' contains two boards or beds for the man and his wife. Each board is about 18 inches wide and 4 feet long; they are raised 2 or 3 inches from the earth, and the head of the bed is slightly higher than the foot. A pole is laid across the apartment at the lower end of the sleeping boards, and on this the occupants rest their feet and toast them before the small fire. At both ends of the ang-an', outside the store walls, is a small hidden secret space called "kub-kub," in which the family hides many of its choice possessions. During abundant camote[15] gathering, however, I have seen the kub-kub filled with camotes. I should probably not have discovered these spaces had there not been so great a discrepancy between the inside measure of the sleeping room and width of the building.

I know of no other primitive dwellings in the Philippines than the ones in the Bontoc culture area which are built directly on the ground. Most of them are raised on posts several feet from the earth. Some few have side walls extending to the ground, but even those have a floor raised 2, 3, or more feet from the ground and which is reached by means of a short ladder.

The second story of the Bontoc dwelling is supported on the four central posts. On all sides it projects beyond them, so that it is about 7 feet square; it is about 5 feet high. A door enters the second story directly from the aisle, and is reached by an 8-foot ladder. This second story is constructed, floor and side walls, of boards. The side walls cease at about the height of 2 feet where a horizontal shelf is built on them extending outside of them to the roof. It is about 2 feet wide and is usually stored with unthreshed rice and millet or with jars of preserved meats. Just at the left on the floor, as one enters the second story, is an earth-filled square corner walled in by two poles. On this earth are three stones -- the fireplace, where each year a chicken is cooked in a household ceremony at the close of rice harvests.

Rising above the second story is a third. In the smaller dwellings this third story is only an attic of the second, but in the larger buildings it is an independent story. To be sure, it is entered through the floor, but a ladder is used, and its floor is of strong heavy boards. It is at all times a storeroom, usually only for cereals. In the smaller houses it amounts simply to a broad shelf about the height of one's waist as he stands on the floor of the second story and his head and upper body rise through the hole in the floor. In the larger houses a person may climb into the third story and work there with practically as much freedom as in the second.

The 5-foot ridgepole of the steep, heavy, grass roof is supported by two posts rising from the basal timbers of the third story. The roof falls away sharply from the ridgepole not only at the sides but at the ends, so that, except at the ridge, the roof appears square. Immediately beneath both ends of the ridgepole there is a small opening in the grass through which the smoke of the cooking fires is supposed to escape. However, I have scarcely ever seen smoke issue from them, and, since the entire inner part of the building from the floor of the second story to the ridgepole is thickly covered with soot, it seems that little unconsumed carbon escapes through the smoke holes. The lower part of the roof, for 3 1/2 feet, descends at a less steep angle, thus forming practically an awning against sun and rain. Its lower edge is about 4 feet from the ground and projects some 4 feet beyond the side walls of the lower story.

The kat-yu'-fong, the dwelling of the poor, consists of a one-story structure built on the ground with the earth for the floor. Some such buildings have a partition or partial partition running across them, beyond which are the sleeping boards, and there are shelves here and there; but the kat-yu'-fong is a makeshift, and consequently is not so fixed a type of dwelling as the fay'-u.

Piled close around the dwellings is a supply of firewood in the shape of pine blocks 3 or 4 feet long, usually cut from large trees. These blocks furnish favorite lounging places for the women. The people live most of the time outside their dwellings, and it is there that the social life of the married women is. Any time of day they may be seen close to the a'-fong in the shade of the low, projecting roof sitting spinning or paring camotes; often three or four neighbors sit thus together and gossip. The men are seldom with them, being about the ato buildings in the daytime when not working. A few small children may be about the dwelling, as the little girls frequently help in preparing food for cooking.

During the day the dwelling is much alone. When it is so left one and sometimes two runo stalks are set up in the earth on each side of the door leaning against the roof and projecting some 8 feet in the air. This is the pud-i-pud', the "ethics lock" on an Igorot dwelling. An Igorot who enters the a'-fong of a neighbor when the pud-i-pud' is up is called a thief -- in the mind of all who see him he is such.

<u>The family</u>

Bontoc families are monogamous, and monogamy is the rule throughout the area, though now and then a man has two wives. The presidente of Titipan has five wives, for each of whom he has a separate house, and during my residence in Bontoc he was building a sixth house for a new wife; but such a family is the exception -- I never heard of another.

Many marriage unions produce eight and ten children, though, since the death rate is large, it is probable that families do not average more than six individuals.

<u>Childbirth</u>

A woman is usually about her daily labors in the house, the mountains, or the irrigated fields almost to the hour of childbirth. The child is born without feasting or ceremony, and only two or three friends witness the birth. The father of the child is there, if he is the woman's husband; the girl's mother is also with her, but usually there are no others, unless it be an old woman.

The expectant woman stands with her body bent strongly forward at the waist and supported by the hands grasping some convenient house timber about the height of the hips; or she may take a more animal-like position, placing both hands and feet on the earth.

The labor, lasting three or four hours, is unassisted by medicines or baths; but those in attendance -- the man as well as the woman -- hasten the birth by a gently downward drawing of the hands about the woman's abdomen.

During a period of ten days after childbirth the mother frequently bathes herself about the hips and abdomen with hot water, but has no change of diet. For two or three days she keeps the house closely, reclining much of the time.

The Igorot woman is a constant laborer from the age of puberty or before, until extreme incapacity of old age stays the hands of toil; but for two or three months following the advent of each babe the mother does not work in the fields. She busies herself about the house and with the new-found duties of a mother, while the husband performs her labors in the fields.

The Igorot loves all his children, and says, when a boy is born, "It is good," and if a girl is born he says it is equally "good" -- it is the fact of a child in the family that makes him happy. People in the Igorot stage of culture have little occasion to prize one sex over the other. The Igorot neither, even in marriage. One is practically as capable as the other at earning a living, and both are needed in the group.

Six or seven days after birth a chicken is killed and eaten by the family in honor of the child, but there is no other ceremony -- there is not even a special name for the feast.

If a woman gives birth to a stillborn child it is at once washed, wrapped in a bit of cloth, and buried in a camote sementera close to the dwelling.

<u>Twins</u>

The Igorot do not understand twins, -- na-a-pik', as they say. Carabaos have only one babe at a birth, so why should women have two babes? they ask. They believe that one of the twins, which unfortunate one they call "a-tin-fu-yang'," is an anito child; it is the offspring of an anito.[16] The anito father is said to have been with the mother of the twins in her unconscious slumber, and she is in no way criticised or reproached.

The most quiet babe, or, if they are equally quiet, the larger one, is said to be "a-tin-fu-yang'," and is at once placed in an olla[17] and buried alive in a sementera near the dwelling.

On the 13th of April, 1903, the wife of A-li-koy', of Samoki, gave birth to twin babies. Contrary to the advice and solicitations of the old men and the universal custom of the people, A-li-koy' saved both children, because, as he pointed out, an Ilokano of Bontoc had twin children, now 7 years old, and they are all right. Thus the breaking down of this peculiar form of infanticide may have begun.

Abortion

Both married and unmarried women practice abortion when for any reason the prospective child is not desired. It is usual, however, for the mother of a pregnant girl to object to her aborting, saying that soon she would become "po'-ta" -- the common mate of several men, rather than the faithful wife of one.

Abortion is accomplished without the use of drugs and is successful only during the first eight or ten weeks of pregnancy. The abdomen is bathed for several days in hot water, and the body is pressed and stroked downward with the hands. The foetus is buried by the woman. Only the woman herself or her mother or other near female friend is present at the abortion, though no effort is made at secrecy and its practice is no disgrace.

Child

Care of child in parents' dwelling

All male babes are called "kil-lang'" and all girl babes "gna-an'." All live practically the same life day after day. Their sole nourishment is their mother's milk, varied now and then by that of some other woman, if the mother is obliged to leave the babe for a half day or so. When the babe's first teeth appear it has a slight change of diet; its attendant now and then feeds it cooked rice, thoroughly masticated and mixed with saliva. This food is passed to the child's mouth directly from that of the attendant by contact of lips -- quite as the domestic canary feeds its young. The babes are always unclothed, and for several months are washed daily in cold water, usually both morning and night. It is a common sight at the river to see the mother, who has come down with her babe on her back for an olla of water, bathe the babe, who never seems at all frightened in the process, but to enjoy it -- this, too, at times when the water would seem to be uncomfortably cold. One often sees the father or grandmother washing the older babes at the river.

But in spite of these baths the Igorot babe, at least after it has reached the age of six or eight months, when seen in the pueblo is almost without exception very dirty; a child of a year or a year and a half is usually repulsively so. Its head has received no attention since birth, and is scaly and dirty if not actually full of sores. Its baths are now relatively infrequent, and its need of them as it plays on the dirt floor of the dwelling or pabafunan even more urgent than when it spent most of its time in the carrying blanket.

Babes have no cradles or stationary places for rest or sleep. A babe, slumbering or awake, is never laid down alone because of the fear that an anito will injure it. At night the babe sleeps between its parents, on its mother's arm. It spends its days almost without exception sitting in a blanket which is tied over the shoulder of one of its parents, its brother, or its sister. There it hangs, awake or asleep, sitting or sprawling, often a pitiable little object with the sun in its eyes and the flies hovering over its dirty face. Frequently a child of only 5 or 6 years old may be seen with a babe on its back, and older children are constant baby tenders. Babes may be found in the fawi and pabafunan where the men are lounging (Pl. XXXII), and the old men and women also care for their grandchildren. Grown people quite as commonly carry the babe astride one hip if they have an empty hand which they can put around it, and often a mother along the trail carries it at her breast where it seemingly nurses as contentedly as when in the shade of the dwelling.

Children are generally weaned long before they are 2 years old, but twice I have seen a young pillager of 5 years, while patting and stroking his mother's hips and body as she transplanted rice, yield to his early baby instinct and suckle from her pendant breasts.

After the child is about 2 years of age it is not customary for it to sleep longer at the home of the parents; the girl goes nightly to the olag, and the boy to the pabafunan or the fawi. However, this is not a hard-and-fast rule, and the age at which the child goes to the olag or fawi depends much on circumstances. The length of time it sleeps with the parents doubtless depends upon the advent or nonadvent of another child. If a little girl has a widowed grandmother or aunt she may sleep for a few years with her. During the warmer months one or two children may sleep on the stationary broad bench, the chukso, in the open part of the parents' house. It is safe to say that after the ages of 6 or 7 all children are found nightly in the olag, pabafunan, or fawi. I have seen a group of little girls from 4 to 10 years old, immediately after supper and while some families were still eating, sitting around a small blaze of fire just outside the door of their olag. The Igorot child as a rule knows its parents' home only as a place to eat. There is almost an entire absence of anything which may be called home life.

Naming

The Igorot has no definite system of naming. Parents may frequently change the name of a child, and an individual may change his during maturity. There are several reasons why names are changed, but there is no system, nor is it ever necessary to change them.

A child usually receives its first personal name between the years of 2 and 5. This first name is always that of some dead ancestor, usually only two or three generations past. The reason for this is the belief that the anito of the ancestor cares for and protects its descendants when they are abroad. If the name a child bears is that of a dead ancestor it will receive the protection of the anito of the ancestor; if the child does not prosper or has accidents or ill health, the parents will seek a more careful or more benevolent protector in the anito of some other ancestor whose name is given the child.

To illustrate this changing of names: A boy in Tukukan, two hours from Bontoc, was first named Sa-pang' when less than a year old. At the end of a year the paternal grandfather, An-ti'-ko, died in Tukukan, and the babe was named An-ti'-ko. In a few years the boy's father died, and the mother married a man in Bontoc, the home of her childhood. She moved to Bontoc with her boy, and then changed his name to Fa-li-kao', her dead father's name. The reason for this last change was because the anito of An-ti'-ko, always in or about Tukukan, could not care for the child in Bontoc, whereas the anito of Fa-li-kao' in Bontoc could do so.

The selection of the names of ancestors is shown by the following generations:

1. Mang-i-lot'
2. Cho-kas'
3. Kom-ling'
4. Mang-i-lot'
5 A. Kom-ling'
5 B. Ta-kay'-yeng
5 C. Teng-ab'
5 D. Ka-weng'

Mang-i-lot' (4) is the baby name of an old man now about 60 years old; it was the name of his great-grandfather (1). Numbers 5 A, 5 B, 5 C, and 5 D are the sons of Mang-i-lot' (4), all of whom died before receiving a second name. The child Kom-ling' (5 a) was given the name of his paternal grandfather (3). Ta-kay'-

yeng (5 B) bears the name of his maternal great-grandfather. Teng-ab' (5 C) and Ka-weng' (5 D) both bear the names of uncles, brothers of the boy's mother. The present name of Mang-i-lot' (4) is O-lu-wan'; this is the name of a man at Barlig whose head was the first one taken by Mang-i-lot'. A man may change his name each time he takes a head, though it is not customary to do so more than once or twice.

Girls as well as boys may receive during childhood two or three names, that they may receive the protection of an anito. In Igorot names there is no vestige of a kinship group tracing relation through either the paternal or maternal line.

The people are generally reticent about telling their names; and when they do tell, the name given is usually the one borne in childhood; an old man will generally answer " am-a'-ma," meaning simply "old man."

Circumcision

Most boys are circumcised at from 4 to 7 years of age. The act of circumcision, called "sig-i-at'," occurs privately without feasting or rite. The only formality is the payment of a few leaves of tobacco to the man who performs the operation. There are one or two old men in each ato who understand circumcision, but there is no cult for its performance or perpetuation.

The foreskin is cut lengthwise on the upper side for half an inch. Either a sharp, blade-like piece of bamboo is inserted in the foreskin which is cut from the inside, or the back point of a battle-ax is stuck firmly in the earth, and the foreskin is cut by being drawn over the sharp point of the blade.

The Igorot say that if the foreskin is not cut it will grow long, as does the unclipped camote vine. What the origin or purpose of circumcision was is not now known by the people of Bontoc. The practice is believed to have come with them from an earlier home; it is widespread in the Archipelago.

Amusements

The life of little girls is strangely devoid of games and playthings. They have no dolls and, I have never seen them play with the puppies which are scattered throughout the pueblo much of the year -- both common playthings for the girls of primitive people. It is not improbable that the instinct which compels most girls, no matter what their grade of culture, to play the mother is given full expression in the necessary care of babes -- a care in which the girls, often themselves almost babes, have a much larger part than their brothers. Girls also go to the fields with their parents much more than do the boys.

Girls and boys never play together in the same group. Time and again one comes suddenly on a romping group of chattering, naked little boys or girls. They usually run noiselessly into the nearest foliage or behind the nearest building, and there stand unmoving, as a pursued chicken pokes its head into the grass and seems to think itself hidden. They need not be afraid of one, seeing him every day, yet the instinct to flee is strong in them -- they do exactly what their mothers do when suddenly met in the trail -- they run away, or start to.

Several times I have found little girls building tiny sementeras with pebbles, and it is probable they play at planting and harvesting the crops common to their pueblo. They have one game called "I catch your ankle," which is the best expression of unfettered childplay and mirth I have ever seen.

After the sun had dropped behind the mountain close to the pueblo, from six to a dozen girls ranging from 5 to 10 or 11 years of age came almost nightly to the smooth grass plat in front of our house to play "sis-sis'-ki" (I catch your ankle). They laid aside their blankets and lined up nude in two opposing lines twelve or fifteen feet apart. All then called: "Sis-sis'-ki ad wa'-ni wa'-ni!" (which is, "I catch your ankle, now! now!"). Immediately the two lines crouched on their haunches, and, in half-sitting posture, with feet side by side, each girl bounced toward her opponent endeavoring to catch her ankle. After the two attacking parties met they intermingled, running and tumbling, chasing and chased, and the successful girl rapidly dragged her victim by the ankle along the grass until caught and thrown by a relief party or driven away by the approach of superior numbers. They lined up anew every five or ten minutes.

During the entire game, lasting a full half hour or until night settled on them or a mother came to take home one of the little, romping, wild things -- just as the American child is called from her games to an early bed -- peal after peal of the heartiest, sweetest laughter rang a constant chorus. The boys have at least two systematic games. One is fug-fug-to', in imitation of a ceremonial of the men after each annual rice harvest. The game is a combat with rocks, and is played sometimes by thirty or forty boys, sometimes by a much smaller number. The game is a contest -- usually between Bontoc and Samoki -- with the broad, gravelly river bed as the battle ground. There they charge and retreat as one side gains or loses ground; the rocks fly fast and straight, and are sometimes warded off by small basket-work shields shaped like the wooden ones of war. They sometimes play for an hour and a half at a time, and I have not yet seen them play when one side was not routed and driven home on the run amid the shouts of the victors.

The other game is kag-kag-tin'. It is also a game of combat and of opposing sides, but it is not so dangerous as the other and there are no bruises resulting. Some half-dozen or a dozen boys play kag-kag-tin' charging and retreating, fighting with the bare feet. The naked foot necessitates a different kick than the one shod with a rigid leather shoe; the stroke from an unshod foot is more like a blow from the fist shot out from the shoulder. The foot lands flat and at the side of or behind the kicker, and the blow is aimed at the trunk or head -- it usually lands higher than the hips. This game in a combat between individuals of the opposing sides, though two often attack a single opponent until he is rescued by a companion. The game is over when the retreating side no longer advances to the combat.

The boys are constantly throwing reed spears, and they are fairly expert spearmen several years before they have a steel-bladed spear of their own. Frequently they roll the spherical grape fruit and throw their reeds at the fruit as it passes.

Here, there, and everywhere, singly or in groups, boys perform the Igorot dance step. A tin can in a boy's hands is irresistibly beaten in rhythmic time, and the dance as surely follows the peculiar rhythmic beating as the beating follows the possession of the can. As the boys come stringing home at night from watching the palay fields, they come dancing, rhythmically beating a can, or two sticks, or their dinner basket, or beating time in the air -- as though they held a gangsa[18]. The dance is in them, and they amuse themselves with it constantly.

Both boys and girls are much in the river, where they swim and dive with great frolic.

During the months of January and February, 1903, when there was much wind, the boys were daily flying kites, but it is a pastime borrowed of the Ilokano in the pueblo. Now and then a little fellow may be seen with a small, very rude bow and arrow, which also is borrowed from the Ilokano since the arrival of the Spaniard.

Puberty

Puberty is reached relatively late, usually between the fourteenth and sixteenth years. No notice whatever is taken of it by the social group. There is neither feast nor rite to mark the event either for the individual or the group.

This nonobservance of the fact of puberty would be very remarkable, since its observance is so widespread among primitive people, were it not for the fact that the Igorot has developed the olag -- an institution calculated to emphasize the fact and significance of puberty.

Life in olag

Though the o'-lag is primarily the sleeping place of all unmarried girls, in the mind of the people it is, with startling consistency, the mating place of the young people of marriageable age.

A common sight on a rest day in the pueblo is that of a young man and woman, each with an arm around the other, loitering about under the same blanket, talking and laughing, one often almost supporting the other. There seems at all times to be the greatest freedom and friendliness among the young people. I have seen both a young man carrying a young woman lying horizontally along his shoulders, and a young woman carrying a young man astride her back. However, practically all courtship is carried on in the o'-lag.

The courtship of the Igorot is closely defined when it is said that marriage never takes place prior to sexual intimacy, and rarely prior to pregnancy. There is one exception. This is when a rich and influential man marries a girl against her desires, but through the urgings of her parents.

It is customary for a young man to be sexually intimate with one, two, three, and even more girls at the same time. Two or more of them may be residents of one o'-lag, and it is common for two or three men to visit the same o'-lag at one time.

A girl is almost invariably faithful to her temporary lover, and this fact is the more surprising in the face of the young man's freedom and the fact that the o'-lag is nightly filled with little girls whose moral training is had there.

Young men are boldly and pointedly invited to the o'-lag. A common form of invitation is for the girl to steal a man's pipe, his pocket hat, or even the breechcloth he is wearing. They say one seldom recovers his property without going to the, o'-lag for it.

When a girl recognizes her pregnancy she at once joyfully tells her condition to the father of the child, as all women desire children and there are few permanent marriages unblessed by them. The young man, if he does not wish to marry the girl, may keep her in ignorance of his intentions for two or three months. If at last he tells her he will not marry her she receives the news with many tears, it is said, but is spared the gossip and reproach of others, and she will later become the wife of some other man, since her first child has proved her power to bear children.

When the mother notices her condition she asks who the father of the child is, and on being told that the man will not marry her the mother often tries to exert a rather tardy influence for better morals. She says, "That is bad. Why have you done this?" (when the chances are that the unfortunate, girl was born into a family of but one head); "it will be well for him to give the child a sementera to work." About the same time the young man informs his mother of his relations with the girl, and of her condition, and again the maker of a people's morals seems to attempt to mold the already hardened clay. She says, "My son, that is bad. Why have you done it? Why do you not marry her?" And the son answers simply and truthfully, "I have another girl." Without attempt at remonstrance the father gives a rice sementera to the child when it is 6 or 7 years old, for that is the price fixed by the group conscience for deserting a girl with a child.

It is not usual for a married man to go to the o'-lag, though a young man may go if one of his late mates is still alone. He is usually welcomed by the girl, for there may yet be possibilities of her becoming his permanent wife. A man whose wife is pregnant, however, seldom visits the o'-lag, because he fears that, if he does, his wife's child will be prematurely born and die.

The o'-lag is built where the girls desire it and is said to be commonly located in places accessible to the men; this appears true to one going over the pueblo with this statement in mind.

The life in the o'-lag does not seem to weaken the boys or girls or cause them to degenerate, neither does it appear to make them vicious. Whereas there is practically no sense of modesty among the people, I have never seen anything lewd. Though there is no such thing as virtue, in the modern sense of the word, among the young people after puberty, children before puberty are said to be virtuous, and the married woman is said always to be true to her husband.

According to a recent translator of Blumentritt[19] that author is made to say (evidently speaking of the o'-lag):

Amongst most of the tribes [Igorot] the chastity of maidens is carefully guarded, and in some all the young girls are kept together till marriage in a large house where, guarded by old women, they are taught the industries of their sex, such as weaving, pleating, making cloth from the bark of trees, etc.

There is no such institution in Bontoc Igorot society. The purpose of the o'-lag is as far from enforcing chastity as it well can be. The old women never frequent the o'-lag, and the lesson the girls learn there is the necessity for maternity, not the

"industries of their sex" -- which children of very primitive people acquire quite
as a young fowl learns to scratch and get its food.

Marriage

The ethics of the group forbid certain unions in marriage. A man may not marry
his mother, his stepmother, or a sister of either. He may not marry his daughter,
stepdaughter, or adopted daughter. He may not marry his sister, or his brother's
widow, or a first cousin by blood or adoption. Sexual intercourse between persons
in the above relations is considered incest, and does not often occur. The line of
kin does not appear to be traced as far as second cousin, and between such there
are no restrictions.

Rich people often pledge their small children in marriage, though, as elsewhere in
the world, love, instead of the plans of parents, is generally the foundation of the
family. In February, 1903, the rich people of Bontoc were quite stirred up over
the sequel to a marriage plan projected some fifteen years before. Two families
then pledged their children. The boy grew to be a man of large stature, while the
girl was much smaller. The man wished to marry another young woman, who
fought the first girl when visited by her to talk over the matter. Then the blind
mother of the pledged girl went to the dwelling, accompanied by her brother, one
of the richest men in the pueblo, whereupon the father and mother of the successful girl knocked them down and beat them. To all appearances the young
lovers will marry in spite of the early pledges of parents. They say such quarrels
are common.

If a man wishes to marry a woman and she shares his desire, or if on her becoming pregnant he desires to marry her, he speaks with her parents and with his. If
either of her parents objects, no marriage occurs; but he does not usually falter,
even though his parents do object. They say the advent of a babe seldom fails to
win the good will of the young man's parents. In the case of the girl's pregnancy,
marriage is more assured, and her father builds or gives her a house. The olag is
no longer for her. In her case it has served its ultimate purpose -- it has announced
her puberty and proved her powers of womanhood. In the case of a desire of marriage before the girl is pregnant she usually sleeps in the olag, as in the past, and
the young man spends most of his nights with her. It is customary for the couple
to take their meals with the parents of the girl, in which case the young man gives
his labors to the family. The period of his labors is usually less than a year, since
it is customary for him to give his affections to another girl within a year if the
first one does not become pregnant.

In other words their union is a true trial union. If the trial is successful the girl's father builds her a dwelling, and the marriage ceremony occurs immediately upon occupation of the dwelling. The ceremony is in two parts. The first is called "in-pa-ke'," and at that time a hog or carabao is killed, and the two young people start housekeeping. The kap'-i-ya ceremony follows -- among the rich this marriage ceremony occupies two days, but with the poor only one day. The kap'-i-ya is performed by an old man of the ato in which the couple is to live. He suggestively places a hen's egg, some rice, and some tapui[20] in a dish before him while he addresses Lumawig, the one god, as follows:

Thou, Lumawig! now these children desire to unite in marriage. They wish to be blessed with many children. When they possess pigs, may they grow large. When they cultivate their palay, may it have large fruitheads. May their chickens also grow large. When they plant their beans may they spread over the ground, May they dwell quietly together in harmony. May the man's vitality quicken the seed of the woman.

The two-day marriage ceremony of the rich is very festive. The parents kill a wild carabao, as well as chickens and pigs, and the entire pueblo comes to feast and dance. It is customary for the pueblo to have a rest day, called "fo-sog'," following the marriage of the rich, so the entire period given to the marriage is three days. Each party to the, marriage receives some property at the time from the parents. There are no women in Bontoc pueblo who have not entered into the trial union, though all have not succeeded in reaching the ceremony of permanent marriage. However, notwithstanding all their standards and trials, there are several happy permanent marriages which have never been blessed with children. There are only two men in Bontoc who have never been married and who never entered the trial stage, and both are deaf and dumb.

Divorce

The people of Bontoc say they never knew a man and woman to separate if a child was born to the pair and it lived and they had recognized themselves married. But, as the marriage is generally prompted because a child is to be born, so an unfruitful union is generally broken in the hope that another will be more successful.

If either party desires to break the contract the other seldom objects. If they agree to separate, the woman usually remains in their dwelling and the man builds himself another. However, if either person objects, it is the other who relinquishes the dwelling -- the man because he can build another and the woman because she seldom seeks separation unless she knows of a home in which she will be welcome.

Nothing in the nature of alimony, except the dwelling, is commonly given by either party to a divorce. There are two exceptions -- in case a party deserts he forfeits to the other one or more rice sementeras or other property of considerable value; and, again, if the woman bore her husband a child which died he must give her a sementera if he leaves her.

The widowed

If either party to a marriage dies the other does not remarry for one year. There is no penalty enforced by the group for an earlier marriage, but the custom is firmly fixed. Should the surviving person marry within a year he would die, being killed by an anito whose business it is to punish such sacrilege. The widowed frequently remarry, as there are certain advantages in their married life. It is quite impossible for a man or woman alone to perform the entire round of Igorot labors. The hours of labor for the lone person must usually be long and tiresome.

Most of the widowed live in the katyufong, the smaller dwelling of the poor. The reason for this is that even if one has owned the better class of dwelling, the fayu, it is generally given to a child at marriage, the smaller house being sufficient and suitable for the lone person, especially as the widowed very frequently take their meals with some married child.

Orphans

Orphans without homes of their own become members of the household of an uncle or aunt or other near relative. The property they received from their parents is used by the family into whose home they go. Upon marriage the children receive the property as it was left them, the annual increase having gone to the family which cared for them.

If there are no relatives, orphans with property readily find a home; if there are neither relatives nor property, some family receives the children more as servants than as equals. When they are married they are usually not given more than a dwelling.

The aged

There are few old and infirm persons who have not living relatives. Among these relatives are usually descendants who have been materially benefited by property accumulated or kept intact by their aged kin. It is the universal custom for relatives to feed and otherwise care for the aged. Not much can be done for the infirm, and infirmity is the beginning of the end with all except the blind.

The chances are that the old who have no relatives have at least a little property. Such persons are readily cared for by some family which uses the property at the time and falls heir to it when the owner dies. There are a very few blind persons who have neither relatives nor property, and these are cared for by families which offer assistance, and two of these old blind men beg rice from dwelling to dwelling.

<u>Sickness, disease, and remedies</u>

All disease, sickness, or ailment, however serious or slight, among the Bontoc Igorot is caused by an a-ni'-to. If smallpox kills half a dozen persons in one day, the fell work is that of an a-ni'-to; if a man receives a stone bruise on the trail an a-ni'-to is in the foot and must be removed before recovery is possible. There is one exception to the above sweeping charge against the a-ni'-to -- the Igorot says that toothache is caused by a small worm twisting and turning in the tooth.

Igorot society contains no person who is so malevolent as to cause another sickness, insanity, or death. So charitable is the Igorot's view of his fellows that when, a few years ago, two Bontoc men died of poison administered by another town, the verdict was that the administering hands were directed by some vengeful or diabolical a-ni'-to.

As a people the Bontoc Igorot are healthful. It is seldom that an epidemic reaches them; bubonic plague and leprosy are unknown to them.

By far the majority of deaths among them is due to what the Igorot calls fever -- as they say, "im-po'-os nan a'-wak," or "heat of the body" -- but they class as "fever" half a dozen serious diseases, some almost always fatal.

The men at times suffer with malaria. They go to the low west coast as cargadors or as primitive merchants, and they return to their mountain country enervated by the heat, their systems filled with impure water, and their blood teeming with mosquito-planted malaria. They get down with fever, lose their appetite, neither know the value of nor have the medicines of civilization, their minds are often poisoned with the superstitious belief that they will die -- and they do die in from three days to two months. In February, 1903, three cargadors died within two weeks after returning from the coast.

Measles, chicken pox, typhus and typhoid fevers, and a disease resulting from eating new rice are undifferentiated by the Igorot -- they are his "fever." Measles and chicken pox are generally fatal to children. Igorot pueblos promptly and effectually quarantine against these diseases. When a settlement is afflicted with either of them it shuts its doors to all outsiders -- even using force if necessary; but force is seldom demanded, as other pueblos at once forbid their people to enter the afflicted settlement. The ravages of typhus and typhoid fever may be imagined among a people who have no remedies for them. The diseased condition resulting each year from eating new rice has locally been called "rice cholera." During the months of June, July, and August -- the two harvest months of rice and the one following -- considerable rice of the new crop is annually eaten. If rice has been stored in the palay houses until it is sweated it is in every way a healthful, nutritious food, but when eaten before it sweats it often produces diarrhea, usually leading to an acute bloody dysentery which is often followed by vomiting and a sudden collapse -- as in Asiatic cholera.

In 1893 smallpox, ful-tang', came to Bontoc with a Spanish soldier who was in the hospital from Quiangan. Some five or six adults and sixty or seventy children died. The ravage took half a dozen in a day, but the Igorot stamped out the plague by self-isolation. They talked the situation over, agreed on a plan, and were faithful to it. All the families not afflicted moved to the mountains; the others remained to minister or be ministered to, as the case might be. About thirty-five years ago smallpox wiped out a considerable settlement of Bontoc, called La'-nao, situated nearer the river than are any dwellings at present.

About thirty years ago cholera, pish-ti', visited the people, and fifty or more deaths resulted.

Some twelve years ago ka-lag'-nas, an unidentified disease, destroyed a great number of people, probably half a hundred. Those afflicted were covered with small, itching festers, had attacks of nausea, and death resulted in about three days.

Two women died in Bontoc in 1901 of beri-beri, called fu-tut. These are the only cases known to have been there.

About ten years ago a man died from passing blood -- an ailment which the Igorot named literally "in-is'-fo cha'-la or in-tay'-es cha'-la." It was not dysentery, as the person at no time had a diarrhea. He gradually weakened from the loss of small amounts of blood until, in about a year, he died.

The above are the only fatal diseases now in the common memory of the pueblo of Bontoc.

It is believed 95 per cent of the people suffer at some time, probably much of the time, with some skin disease. They say no one has been known to die of any of these skin diseases, but they are weakening and annoying. Itch, ku'-lid, is the most common, and it takes an especially strong hold on the babes in arms. This ku'-lid is not the ko'-lud or gos-gos, the white scaly itch found among the people surrounding those of the Bontoc culture area but not known to exist within it.

Two or three people suffer with rheumatism, fig-fig, but are seldom confined to their homes.

One man has consumption, o'-kat. He has been coughing five or six years, and is very thin and weak.

Diarrhea, or o-gi'-ak, frequently makes itself felt, but for only one or two days at a time. It is most common when the locusts swarm over the country, and the people eat them abundantly for several days. They say no one, not even a babe, ever died of diarrhea.

Two of the three prostitutes of Bontoc, the cast-off mistresses of Spanish soldiers, have syphilis, or na-na. Formerly one civilian was afflicted, and at present four or five of the Constabulary soldiers have contracted the disease.

Lang-ing'-i, a disease of sores and ulcers on the lips, nostrils, and rectum, afflicted a few people three or four years ago. This disease is very common in the pueblo of Ta-kong', but is reported as never causing death.

Goiter, fi-kek' or fin-to'-kel, is quite common with adults, and is more common with women than men.

Varicose veins, o'-pat, are not uncommon on the calves of both men and women.

Many old people suffer greatly with toothache, called "pa-tug' nan fob-a'." They say it is caused by a small worm, fi'-kis, which wriggles and twists in the tooth. When one has an aching tooth extracted he looks at it and inquires where "fi'-kis" is.

They suffer little from colds, mo-tug', and one rarely hears an Igorot cough.

Headache, called both sa-kit' si o'-lo and pa-tug' si o'-lo, rarely occurs except with fever.

Sore eyes, a condition known as in-o'-ki, are very frequently seen; they doubtless precede most cases of blindness.

The Igorot bears pain well, but his various fatalistic superstitions make him often an easy victim to a malady that would yield readily to the science of modern medicine and from which, in the majority of cases, he would probably recover if his mind could only assist his body in withstanding the disease.

One is surprised to find that sores from bruises do not generally heal quickly.

The Igorot attempts no therapeutic remedies for fevers, cholera, beri-beri, rheumatism, consumption, diarrhea, syphilis, goiter, colds, or sore eyes.

Some effort, therapeutic in its intent, is made to assist nature in overcoming a few of the simplest ailments of the body.

For a cut, called "na-fa'-kag," the fruit of a grass-like herb named la-lay'-ya is pounded to a paste, and then bound on the wound.

Burns, ma-la-fub-chong', are covered over with a piece of bark from a tree called ta-kum'-fao.

Kay-yub', a vegetable root, is rubbed over the forehead in cases of headache.

Boils, fu-yu-i', and swellings, nay-am-an' or kin-may-yon', are treated with a poultice of a pounded herb called ok-ok-ong'-an.

Millet burned to a charcoal, pulverized, and mixed with pig fat is used as a salve for the itch.

An herb called a-kum' is pounded and used as a poultice on ulcers and sores.

For toothache salt is mixed with a pounded herb named ot-o'-tek and the mass put in or around the aching tooth.

Leaves of the tree kay'-yam are steeped, and the decoction employed as a bath for persons with smallpox.

Death and burial

It must be said that the Bontoc Igorot does not take death very sorrowfully, and he does not take it at all passionately. A mother weeps a day for a dead child or her husband, but death is said not to bring tears from any man. Death causes no long or loud lamentation, no tearing of the hair or cutting the body; it effects no somber colors to deaden the emotions; no earth or ashes for the body -- all widespread mourning customs among primitive peoples. However, when a child or mature man or woman dies the women assemble and sing and wail a melancholy dirge, and they ask the departed why he went so early. But for the aged there are neither tears nor wailings -- there is only grim philosophy. "You were old," they say, "and old people die. You are dead, and now we shall place you in the earth. We too are old, and soon we shall follow you."

All people die at the instance of an anito. There have been, however, three suicides in Bontoc. Many years ago an old man and woman hung themselves in their dwellings because they were old and infirm, and a man from Bitwagan hung himself in the Spanish jail at Bontoc a few years ago.

The spirit of the person who dies a so-called natural death is called away by an anito. The anito of those who die in battle receive the special name "pin-teng'"; such spirits are not called away, but the person's slayer is told by some pin-teng', "You must take a head." So it may be said that no death occurs among the Igorot (except the rare death by suicide) which is not due directly to an anito.

Since they are warriors, the men who die in battle are the most favored, but if not killed in battle all Igorot prefer to die in their houses. Should they die elsewhere, they are at once taken home.

On March 19, 1903, wise, rich Som-kad', of ato Luwakan, and the oldest man of Bontoc, heard an anito saying, "Come, Som-kad'; it is much better in the mountains; come." The sick old man laboriously walked from the pabafunan to the house of his oldest son, where he had for nearly twenty years taken his food, and there among his children and friends he died on the night of March 21. Just before he died a chicken was killed, and the old people gathered at the house, cooked the chicken, and ate, inviting the ancestral anitos and the departing spirit of Som-kad' to the feast. Shortly after this the spirit of the live man passed from the body searching the mountain spirit land for kin and friend. They closed the old man's eyes, washed his body and on it put the blue burial robe with the white "anito" figures woven in it as a stripe. They fashioned a rude, high-back chair with a low seat, a sung-a'-chil (Pl. XLI), and bound the dead man in it, fastening him

by bands about the waist, the arms, and head -- the vegetal band entirely covering the open mouth. His hands were laid in his lap. The chair was set close up
before the door of the house, with the corpse facing out. Four nights and days it
remained there in full sight of those who passed.

One-half the front wall of the dwelling and the interior partitions except the
sleeping compartment were removed to make room for those who sat in the
dwelling. Most of these came and went without function, but day and night two
young women sat or stood beside the corpse always brushing away the flies which
sought to gather at its nostrils.

During the first two days few men were about the house, but they gathered in
small groups in the vicinity of the fawi and pabafunan, which were only three or
four rods distant. Much of the time a blind son of the dead man, the owner of
the house where the old man died, sat on his haunches in the shade under the low
roof, and at frequent intervals sang to a melancholy tune that his father was dead,
that his father could no longer care for him, and that he would be lonely without
him. On succeeding days other of the dead man's children, three sons and five
daughters, all rich and with families of their own, were heard to sing the same
words. Small numbers of women sat about the front of the house or close in the
shade of its roof and under its cover. Now and then some one or more of them
sang a low-voiced, wordless song -- rather a soothing strain than a depressing
dirge. During the first days the old women, and again the old men, sang at different times alone the following song, called "a-na'-ko" when sung by the women,
and "e-ya'-e" when by the men:

Now you are dead; we are all here to see you. We have given you all things necessary, and have made good preparation for the burial. Do not come to call away
[to kill] any of your relatives or friends.

Nowhere was there visible any sign of fear or awe or wonder. The women sitting
about spun threads on their thighs for making skirts; they talked and laughed and
sang at will. Mothers nursed their babes in the dwelling and under its projecting
roof. Budding girls patted and loved and dimpled the cheeks of the squirming
babes of more fortunate young women, and there was scarcely a child that passed
in or out of the house, that did not have to steady itself by laying a hand on the
lap of the corpse. All seemed to understand death. One, they say, does not die
until the anito calls -- and then one always goes into a goodly life which the old
men often see and tell about.

In a well-organized and developed modern enterprise the death of a principal man
causes little or no break. This is equally true in Igorot life. The former is so

because of perfected organization -- there are new men trained for all machines; and the latter is true because of absence of organization -- there is almost no machinery to be left unattended by the falling of one person.

On the third day the numbers increased. There were twenty-five or thirty men in the vicinity of the house, on the south side of which were half a dozen pots of basi,[21] from which men and boys drank at pleasure, though not half a dozen became intoxicated. Late in the afternoon a double row of men, the sons and sons-in-law of the deceased, lined up on their haunches facing one another, and for half an hour talked and laughed, counted on their fingers and gesticulated, diagrammed on their palms, questioned, pointed with their lips and nodded, as they divided the goodly property of the dead man. There was no anger, no sharp word, or apparent dissent; all seemed to know exactly what was each one's right. In about half an hour the property was disposed of beyond probable future dispute.

There were more women present the third day than on the second, and at all times about one-third more women than men; and there were usually as many children about as there were grown persons. In all the group of, say, 140 people, nowhere could one detect a sign of the uncanny, or even the unusual. The apparent everydayness of it all to them was what struck the observer most. The young women brushing away the flies touched and turned the fast-blackening hands of the corpse to note the rapid changes. Almost always there were small children standing in the doorway looking into that blackened, swollen face, and they turned away only to play or to loll about their mothers' necks. Always there were women bending over other women's heads, carefully parting the hair and scanning it. Women lay asleep stretched in the shade; they talked, and droned, and laughed, and spun.

During the second day men had succeeded in catching in the mountains one of the half-wild carabaos -- property of the deceased -- and this was killed. Its head was placed in the house tied up by the horns above and facing Som-kad', so the faces of the dead seemed looking at each other, while on the third day the flesh, bones, intestines, and hide were cooked for the crowd. During the third and fourth days one carabao, one dog, eight hogs, and twenty chickens were killed, cooked, and eaten.

On the fourth day the crowd increased. Custom lays idle all field tools of an ato on the burial day of an adult of that ato; but the day Som-kad' was buried the field work of the entire pueblo stood still because of common respect for this man, so old and wise, so rich and influential, and probably 200 people were about the house all the day. By noon two well-defined groups of chanting old women had formed -- one sitting in the house and the other in front of it. Wordless, melancholy chants were sung in response between the groups. The spaces surrounding the house became almost packed -- so much so that a dog succeeded in getting into the doorway, and the threatenings and maledictions that drove it away were the loudest, most disturbed expressions noted during the four days.

Before the house, which faced the west, lay the large pine coffin lid, while to the south of it, turned bottom up, was the coffin with fresh chips beside it hewn out that morning in further excavation. Children played around the coffin and people lounged on its upturned bottom. Near the front of the house a pot of water was always hot over a smoldering, smoking fire. Now and then a chicken was brought, light wood was tossed under the pot, the chicken was beaten to death -- first the wings, then the neck, and then the head. The fowl was quickly sprawled over the blaze, its feathers burned to a crisp, and rubbed off with sticks. Its legs were severed from the body with the battle-ax and put in the pot. From its front it was then cut through its ribs with one gash. The back and breast parts were torn apart, the gall examined and nodded over; the intestines were placed beneath a large rock, and the gizzard, breast of the chicken, and back with head attached dropped in the pot. During the killing and dressing neither of the two men who prepared the feast hurried, yet scarcely five minutes passed from the time the first blow was struck on the wing of the squawking fowl until the work was over and the meat in the boiling pot. The cooking of a fowl always brought a crowd of boys who hung over the fragrant vessel, and they usually got their share when, in about twenty minutes, the meat came forth. Three times in the afternoon a fowl was thus distributed. Cooked pork was passed among the people, and rice was always being brought. Twice a man went through the crowd with a large winnowing tray of cooked carabao hide cut in little blocks. This food was handed out on every side, people tending children receiving double share. The people gathered and ate in the congested spaces about the dwelling. The heat was intense -- there was scarcely a breath of air stirring. The odor from the body was heavy and most sickening to an American, and yet there was no trace of the unusual on the various faces.

New arrivals came to take their last look at Som-kad', now a black, bloated, inhuman-looking thing, and they turned away apparently unaffected by the sight.

The sun slid down behind the mountain ridge lying close to the pueblo, and a dozen men armed with digging sticks and dirt baskets filed along the trail some fifteen rods to the last fringe of houses. There they dug a grave in a small, unused sementera plat where only the old, rich men of the pueblo are buried. A group of twenty-five old women gathered standing at the front of the house swaying to the right, to the left, as they slowly droned in melancholy cadence:

You were old, and old people die. You are dead, and now we shall place you in the earth. We too are old, and soon we shall follow you.

Again and again they droned, and when they ceased others within the house took up the strain. During the singing the carabao head was brought from the house, and the horns, with small section of attached skull, chopped out, and the head returned to the ceiling of the dwelling.

Presently a man came with a slender stick to measure the coffin. He drove a nursing mother, with a woman companion and small child, from comfortable seats on the upturned wood. The people, including the group of old women, were driven away from the front of the house, the coffin was laid down on the ground before the door, and an unopened 8-gallon olla of "preserved" meat was set at its foot. An old woman, in no way distinguishable from the others by paraphernalia or other marks, muttering, squatted beside the olla. Two men untied the bands from the corpse, and one lifted it free from the chair and carried it in his arms to the coffin. It was most unsightly, and streams of rusty-brown liquid ran from it. It was placed face up, head elevated even with the rim, and legs bent close at the knees but only slightly at the hips. The old woman arose from beside the olla and helped lay two new breechcloths and a blanket over the body. The face was left uncovered, except that a small patch of white cloth ravelings, called "fo-ot'," was laid over the eyes, and a small white cloth was laid over the hair of the head. The burden was quickly caught up on men's shoulders and hurried without halting to the grave. Willing bands swarmed about the coffin. At all times as many men helped bear it as could well get hold, and when they mounted the face of a 7-foot sementera wall a dozen strong pairs of hands found service drawing up and supporting the burden. Many men followed from the house one brought the coffin cover and another the carabao horns -- but the women and children remained behind, as is their custom at burials.

At the grave the coffin rested on the earth a moment[22] while a few more basketfuls of dirt were thrown out, until the grave was about 5 feet deep. The coffin was then placed in the grave, the cover laid on, and with a joke and a laugh the pair of horns was placed facing it at the head. Instantly thirty-two men sprang on the piles of fresh, loose dirt, and with their hands and the half dozen digging sticks filled and covered the grave in the shortest possible time, probably not over one minute and a half. And away they hurried, most of them at a dogtrot, to wash themselves in the river.

From the instant the corpse was in the coffin until the grave was filled all things were done in the greatest haste, because cawing crows must not fly over, dogs must not bark, snakes or rats must not cross the trail -- if they should, some dire evil would follow.

Shortly after the burial a ceremony, called "kap-i-yan si na-tu'," is performed by the relatives in the dwelling wherein the corpse sat. It is said to be the last ceremony given for the dead. Food is eaten and the one in charge addresses the anito of the dead man as follows:

We have fixed all things right and well for you. When there was no rice or chicken for food, we got them for you -- as was the custom of our fathers -- so you will not come to make us sick. If another anito seeks to harm us, you will protect us. When we make a feast and ask you to come to it, we want you to do so; but if another anito kills all your relatives, there will be no more houses for you to enter for feasts.

This last argument is considered to be a very important one, as all Igorot are fond of feasting, and it is assumed that the anito has the same desire.

The night following the burial all relatives stay at the house lately occupied by the corpse.

On the day after the burial all the men relatives go to the river and catch fish, the small kacho. The relatives have a fish feast, called "ab-a-fon'," at the hour of the evening meal. To this feast all ancestral anito are invited.

All relatives again spend the night at the house, from which they return to their own dwellings after breakfast of the second day and each goes laden with a plate of cooked rice.

In this way from two to eight days are given to the funeral rite, the duration being greater with the wealthier people.

Only heads of families are buried in the large pine coffins, which are kept ready stored beside the granaries everywhere about the pueblo. As in the case of Som-kad', all old, rich men are buried in a plat of ground close to the last fringe of dwellings on the west of the pueblo, but all other persons except those who lose their heads are buried close to their dwellings in the camote sementeras.

The burial clothes of a married man are the los-a'-dan, or blue anito-figured burial robe, and a breechcloth of beaten bark, called "chi-nang-ta'." In the coffin are placed a fa'-a, or blue cotton breechcloth made in Titipan, the fan-cha'-la, a striped blue-and-white cotton blanket, and the to-chong', a foot-square piece of beaten bark or white cloth which is laid on the head.

A married woman is buried in a kay-in', a particular skirt made for burial in Titipan, and a white blue-bordered waistcloth or la-ma. In the coffin are placed a burial girdle, wa'-kis, also made in Titipan, a blue-and-white-striped blanket called bay-a-ong', and the to-chong', the small cloth or bark over the hair.

The unmarried are buried in graves near the dwelling, and these are walled up the sides and covered with rocks and lastly with earth; it is the old rock cairn instead of the wooden coffin. The bodies are placed flat on their backs with knees bent and heels drawn up to the buttocks. With the men are buried, besides the things interred with the married men, the basket-work hat, the basket-work sleeping hat, the spear, the battle-ax, and the earrings if any are possessed. These additional things are buried, they say, because there is no family with which to leave them, though all things interred are for the use of the anito of the dead.

In addition to the various things buried with the married woman, the unmarried has a sleeping hat.

Babes and children up to 6 or 7 years of age are buried in the sementera wrapped in a crude beaten-bark mantle. This garment is folded and wrapped about the body, and for babes, at least, is bound and tied close about them.

Babies are buried close to the dwelling where the sun and storm do not beat, because, as they say, babes are too tender to receive harsh treatment.

For those beheaded in battle there is another burial, which is described in a later chapter.

PART 4

Economic Life

Production

Under the title "Economic life" are considered the various activities which a political economist would consider if he studied a modern community -- in so far as they occur in Bontoc. This method was chosen not to make the Bontoc Igorot appear a modern man but that the student may see as plainly as method will allow on what economic plane the Bontoc man lives. The desire for this clear view is prompted by the belief that grades of culture of primitive peoples may be determined by the economic standard better than by any other single standard.

Natural production

It would be impossible for the Bontoc Igorot at present to subsist themselves two weeks by natural production. It is doubtful whether at any time they could have depended for even as much as a day in a week on the natural foods of the Bontoc culture area. The country has wild carabaos, deer, hogs, chickens, and three animals which the Igorot calls "cats," but all of these, when considered as a food supply for the people, are relatively scarce, and it is thought they were never much more abundant than now. Fish are not plentiful, and judging from the available waters there are probably as many now as formerly. It is believed that no nut foods are eaten in Bontoc, although an acorn is found in the mountains to the south of Bontoc pueblo. The banana and pineapple now grow wild within the area, but they are not abundant. Of small berries, such as are so abundant in the wild lands of the United States, there are almost none in the area. On the outside, near Suyak of Lepanto, there is a huckleberry found so plentifully that they claim it is gathered for food in its season.

Hunting

A large pile of rocks stands like a compact fortress on the mountain horizon to the north of Bontoc pueblo. Here a ceremony is observed twice annually by rich men for the increase of ay-ya-wan', the wild carabao. It is claimed that there are now seventeen wild carabaos in Ma-ka'-lan Mountain near the pueblo. There are others in the mountains farther to the north and east, and the ceremony has among its objects that of inducing these more distant herds to migrate to the public lands surrounding the pueblo.

The men go to the great rock, which is said to be a transformed anito, and there they build a fire, eat a meal, and have the ceremony called "mang-a-pu'-i si ay-ya-wan'," freely, "fire-feast for wild carabaos." The ceremony is as follows:

> Ay-ya-wan ad Sa-ka'-pa a-li-ka is-na ma-am'-mung is-na.
> Ay-ya-wan ad O-ki-ki a-li-ka is-na ma-am'-mung is-na.
> Fay-cha'-mi ya'-i nan a-pu'-i ya pa'-tay.

This is an invitation addressed to the wild carabaos of the Sakapa and Okiki Mountains to come in closer to Bontoc. They are also asked to note that a fire-feast is made in their honor.

The old men say that probably 500 wild carabaos have been killed by the men of the pueblo. There is a tradition that Lumawig instructed the people to kill wild carabaos for marriage feasts, and all of those killed -- of which there is memory or tradition -- have been used in the marriage feasts of the rich. The wild carabao is extremely vicious, and is killed only when forty or fifty men combine and hunt it with spears. When wounded it charges any man in sight, and the hunter's only safety is in a tree.

The method of hunting is simple. The herd is located, and as cautiously as possible the hunters conceal themselves behind the trees near the runway and throw their spears as the desired animal passes. No wild carabaos have been killed during the past two years, but I am told that the numbers killed three, four, six, seven, and eight years ago were, respectively, 5, 8, 7, 10, and 8.

Seven men in Bontoc have dogs trained to run deer and wild boar. One of the men, Aliwang, has a pack of five dogs; the others have one or two each. The hunting dogs are small and only moderately fleet, but they are said to have great courage and endurance. They hunt out of leash, and still-hunt until they start their prey, when they cry continually, thus directing the hunter to the runway or the place where the victim is at bay.

Not more than one deer, og'-sa, is killed annually, and they claim that deer were always very scarce in the area. A large net some 3 1/2 feet high and often 50 feet long is commonly employed in northern Luzon and through the Archipelago for netting deer and hogs, but no such net is used in Bontoc. The dogs follow the deer, and the hunter spears it in the runway as it passes him or while held at bay.

The wild hog, la'-man or fang'-o, when hunted with dogs is a surly fighter and prefers to take its chances at bay; consequently it is more often killed then by the spearman than in the runway. The wild hog is also often caught in pitfalls dug in the runways or in its feeding grounds. The pitfall, fi'-to, is from 3 to 4 feet across, about 4 feet deep, and is covered over with dry grass.

In the forest feeding grounds of Polus Mountains, between the Bontoc culture area and the Banawi area to the south, these pitfalls are very abundant, there frequently being two or three within a space one rod square.

A deadfall, called "il-tib'," is built for hogs near the sementeras in the mountains. These deadfalls are quite common throughout the Bontoc area, and probably capture more hogs than the pitfall and the hunter combined. The hogs are partial to growing palay and camotes, and at night circle about a protecting fence anxious to take advantage of any chance opening. The Igorot leaves an opening in a low fence built especially for that purpose, as he does not commonly fence in the sementeras. The il-tib' is built of two sections of heavy tree trunks, one imbedded in the earth, level with the ground, and the other the falling timber. As the hog enters the sementera, the weight of his body springs the trigger which is covered in the loose dirt before the opening, and the falling timber pins him fast against the lower timber firmly buried in the earth. From half a dozen to twenty wild hogs are annually killed by the people of the pueblo. They are said to be as plentiful as formerly.

Bontoc pueblo does not catch many wild fowls. Fowl catching is an art she never learned to follow, although two or three of her boys annually catch half a dozen chickens each. The surrounding pueblos, as Tukukan, Sakasakan, Mayinit, and Maligkong, secure every year in the neighborhood of fifty to one hundred fowl each. The sa'-fug, or wild cock, is most commonly caught in a snare, called "shi'-ay," to which it is lured by another cock, a domestic one, or often a half-breed or a wild cock partially domesticated, which is secured inside the snare set up in the mountains near the feeding grounds of the wild fowls.

The shi'-ay when set consists of twenty-four si'-lu, or running loops, attached to a cord forming three sides of an open square space. As the snare is set the open side is placed against a rock or steep base of a rise. The shi'-ay is made of braided bejuco, and when not in use. is compactly packed away in a basket for the pur-pose (see Pl. XLIV). There are also five pegs fitted into loops in the basket, four of which are employed in pegging out the three sides of the snare, and the other for securing the lure cock within the square. Only cocks are caught with the shi'-ay, and they come to fight the intruder who guides them to the snare by crowing his challenge. As the wild cock rushes at the other he is caught by one of the loops closing about him. The hunter, always hiding within a few feet of the snare, rush-es upon the captive, and at once resets his snare for another possible victim.

A spring snare, called kok-o'-lang, is employed by the Igorot in catching both wild cocks and hens. It is set in their narrow runways in the heavy undergrowth. It consists of two short uprights driven into the ground one on either side of the path. These are bound together at the tops with two crosspieces. Near the lower ends of these uprights is a loose crosspiece, the trigger, which the fowl in passing knocks down, thus freeing the short upright, marked C, in fig. 1. When this is freed the loop, E, at once tightens around the victim, as the cord is drawn taut by the releasing of the spring -- a shrub bent over and secured by the upper end of the cord. This spring is not shown in the drawing.

Bontoc has two or three quadrupeds which it names "cats." One of these is a true cat, called in'-yao. It is domesticated by the Ilokano in Bontoc and becomes a good mouser.[23] The kok-o'-lang is used to catch this cat. Pl. XLVI shows with what success this spring snare may be employed. The cat shown was caught in the night while trying to enter a chicken coop. He was a wild in'-yao, was beautiful-ly striped like the American "tiger cat," and measured 35 inches from tip to tip. The in'-yao is plentiful in the mountains, and is greatly relished by the Igorot, though Bontoc has no professional cat hunters and probably not a dozen of the animals are captured annually.

The Igorot claim to have two other "cats," one called "co'-lang," as large as in'-yao, with large legs and very large feet. A Spaniard living near Sagada says this ani-mal eats his coffee berries. The other so-called "cat" is named "si'-le" by the Igorot. It is said to be a long-tailed, dark-colored animal, smaller than the in'-yao. It is claimed that this si'-le is both carnivorous and frugivorous. These two ani-mals are trapped at times, and when caught are eaten.

During the year the boys catch numbers of small birds, all of which are eaten. Probably not over 200 are captured, however, during a year.

The ling-an', a spring snare, is the most used for catching birds. I saw one of them catch four shrikes, called ta'-la, in a single afternoon, and a fifth one was caught early the next morning. Pl. XLVII shows the ling-an' as it is set, and also shows ta'-la as he is caught.

The kok-o'-lang is also employed successfully for such birds as run on the ground, especially those which run in paths. The si-sim' is another spring snare set on the open ground. Food is scattered about leading to it, and is placed abundantly in an inclosure, the entrance to which is through the fatal noose which tightens when the bird perches on the trigger at the opening to the inclosure.

When the palay is in the milk a great many birds which feed upon it are captured by means of a broom-like bundle of runo. As the birds fly over the sementeras a boy sweeps his broom, the ka-lib', through the flock, and rarely fails to knock down a bird. The ka-lib' is about 7 feet long, 2 1/2 inches in diameter at the base, and flattened and broadened to 14 or 15 inches in width at the outer end. What the ka-lib' really does for the boy is to give him an arm about 9 feet long and a long open hand a foot and a quarter wide.

Fishing

The only water available to Bontoc pueblo for fishing purposes is the river passing between it and her sister pueblo, Samoki. In the dry season, where it is not dammed, the river is not over six and eight rods across in its widest places, and is from a few inches to 3 feet deep. All the water would readily pass, at the ordinary velocity of the stream, in a channel 20 feet wide and 6 feet deep.

Three methods are employed in fishing in this river -- the first, catching each fish in the hand; the second, driving the fish upstream by fright into a receptacle; a third, a combined process of driving the fish downstream by fright and by water pressure into a receptacle.

The Igorot seems not to have a general word for fish, but he has names for the three varieties found in the river. One, ka-cho', a very small, sluggish fish, is captured during the entire year. In February these fish were seldom more than 2 inches in length, and yet they were heavy with spawn. The ka-cho' is the fish most commonly captured with the hands. It is a sluggish swimmer and is provided with an exterior suction valve on its ventral surface immediately back of the gill opening. This valve seems to enable the fish to withstand the ordinary current of the river which, in the rainy season, becomes a torrent. This valve is also one of the causes of the Igorot's success in capturing the fish, which is not readily frightened, but clings to the bed of the stream until almost brushed away, and then ordinarily swims only a few inches or feet. Small boys from 6 to 10 years old capture by hand a hundred or more ka-cho' during half a day, simply by following them in the shallow water.

The ka-cho' is also caught in great numbers by the second or driving method. Twenty to forty or more men fish together with a large, closely woven, shovel-like trap called ko-yug', and the operation is most interesting to witness. At the river beach the fishermen remove all clothing, and stretch out on their faces in the warm, sun-heated sand. Three men carry the trap to the middle of the swift stream, and one holds it from floating away below him by grasping the side poles which project at the upper end for that purpose. The two other men, below the trap at its mouth, put large stones on their backs between the shoulder blades, so they will not float downstream, and disappear beneath the water. As quickly as possible, coming up a dozen times to breathe during the process, they clear away the rocks below the trap, piling them in it over its floor, until it finally sinks and remains stationary on the cleared spot of sandy bed. Their task being ended, the three trap setters come to shore, and sprawl on the hot sands to warm their dripping skins, while the sun dries and toasts their backs.

Then the drivers or beaters enter the river and stretch in a line from shore to shore about 75 feet below the trap. Each fellow squats in the water and places a heavy stone on his back. One of the men calls, and the row of strange, hump-backed creatures disappears beneath the water. There the men work swiftly, and, as later appears, successfully. Each turns over all the bowlders within his reach as large or larger than his two fists, and he works upstream 4 to 6 feet. They come up blowing, at first a head here and there, but soon all are up with renewed breath, waiting the next call to beat up the prey. This process is repeated again and again, and each time the outer ends of the line bend upstream, gradually looping in toward the trap. When the line of men has become quite circular and is contracting rapidly, a dozen other men enter the river from the shore and line up on each side of the mouth of the trap, a flank movement to prevent the fish running upstream outside the snare. From the circle of beaters a few now drop out; the others are in a bunch, the last stone is turned, and the prey seeks covert under the rocks in the trap, which the flankers at once lift above the water. The rocks are thrown out and the trap and fish carried to the shore.

In each drive they catch about three quarts of fish. These are dumped into baskets, usually the carrying basket of the man, and when the day's catch is made and divided each man receives an equal share, usually about 1 pound per household.

A procession of men and boys coming in from the river, each carrying his share of fish in his basket hat in his hand and the last man carrying the fish trap, is a sight very frequently seen in the pueblo.

The ka-cho' is also caught in a small trap, called ob-o'-fu, by the third method mentioned above. A small strip of shallow water along the shore is quite effectually cut off from the remainder of the stream by a row of rocks. The lower end of this strip is brought to a point where the water pours out and into the upturned ob-o'-fu, carrying with it the ka-cho' which happen to be in the swift current, the fish having been startled from their secure resting places by the fishermen who have gradually proceeded downstream overturning the stones.

A fish called "li'-ling," which attains a length of about 6 inches, is also caught by the last-described method. It is not nearly so plentiful as the ka-cho'.

One man living in Bontoc may be called a fisherman. He spends most of his time with his traps in the river, and sells his fish to the Ilokano and Igorot residents of the pueblo. He places large traps in the deep parts of the stream, adjusts them, and revisits them by swimming under the water, and altogether is considered by the Igorot boys as quite a "water man." He catches each year many ka-cho' and li'-ling, and one or more large fish, called "cha-lit." The cha-lit is said to acquire a length of 3, 4, or 5 feet.

Women and small children wade about the river and pick up quantities of small crabs, called "ag-ka'-ma," and also a small spiral shell, called "ko'-ti." It is safe to say that every hour of a rainless day one or more persons of Bontoc is gathering such food in the river. Immediately after the first rain of the season of 1903, coming April 5, there were twenty-four persons, women and small children, within ten rods of one another, searching the river for ag-ka'-ma and ko'-ti.

The women wear a small rump basket tied around the waist in which they carry their lunch to the rice sementeras, and once or twice each week they bring home from a few ounces to a pound of small crustaceans. One variety is named song'-an, another is kit-an', a third is fing'-a, and a fourth is lis'-chug. They are all collected in the mud of the sementeras.

Vegetal production

All materials for timbers and boards for the dwellings, granaries, and public buildings, all wood for fires, all wood for shields, for ax and spear handles, for agricultural implements, and for household utensils, and all material for splints employed in various kinds of basket work, and for strings (warp and woof) employed in the weaving of Bontoc girdles and skirts, are gathered wild with no effort at cultural production. There are three exceptions to this statement, however. One small shrub, called "pu-ug'," is planted near the house as a fiber plant, and is no longer known to the Igorot in the wild state. Much of the bamboo from which the basket-work splints are made is purchased from people west of Bontoc. And, lastly, there is no doubt that a certain care is taken in preserving pine trees for large boards and timbers and for coffins; there is a cutting away of dead and small branches from these trees. Moreover, the cutting of other trees and shrubs for firewood certainly has a beneficial effect upon the forest trees left standing. In fact, all persons preserve the small pitch-pine trees on private lands, and it is a crime to cut them on another's land, although a poor man may cut other varieties on private lands when needed.

Cultural production

Agriculture

In all of Igorot culture the most apparent and strikingly noteworthy fact is its agriculture. In agriculture the Igorot has reached his highest development. On agriculture hangs his claim to the rank of barbarian -- without it he would be a savage.

Igorot agriculture is unique in Luzon, and, so far as known, throughout the Archipelago, in its mountain terraces and irrigation.

There are three possible explanations of the origin of Philippine rice terraces. First, that they (and those of other islands peopled by primitive and modern Malayans, and those of Japan and China) are indigenous -- the product of the mountain lands of each isolated area; second, that most of them are due to cultural influences from one center, or possibly more than one center, to the north of Luzon -- as influences from China or Japan spreading southward from island to island; third, that they, especially all those of the Islands -- excluding only China -- are due to influences originating south of the Philippines, spreading northward from island to island.

Terracing may be indigenous to many isolated areas where it is found, and doubtless is to some; it is found more or less marked wherever irrigation is or was practiced in ancient or modern agriculture. However, it is believed not to be an original production of the Philippines. Certain it is that it is not a Negrito art, nor does it belong to the Moro or to the so-called Christian people.

Different sections of China have rice terraces, and as early as the thirteenth century Chinese merchants traded with the Philippines, yet there is no record that they traded north of Manila -- where terracing is alone found. Besides, the Chinese record of the early commerce with the Islands -- written by Chao Jukua about 1250 it is claimed -- specifically states that the natives of the Islands were the merchants, taking the goods from the shore and trading them even to other islands; the Chinese did not pass inland. Even though the Chinaman brought phases of his culture to the Islands, it would not have been agriculture, since he did not practice it here. Moreover, whatever culture he did leave would not be found in the mountains three or four days inland, while the people with whom he traded were without the art. The same arguments hold against the Japanese as the inspirers of Igorot terraces. There is no record that they traded in the Islands as early as did the Chinese, and it is safe to say, no matter when they were along the coasts of Luzon, that they never penetrated several days into the mountains, among a wild, head-hunting people, for what the agricultural Igorot had to sell.

The historic cultural movements in Malaysia have been not from the north southward but from Sumatra and Java to the north and east; they have followed the migrations of the people. It is believed that the terrace-building culture of the Asiatic islands for the production of mountain rice by irrigation during the dry season has drawn its inspiration from one source, and that such terraces where found to-day in Java, Lombok, Luzon, Formosa, and Japan are a survival of very early culture which spread from the nest of the primitive Malayan stock and left its marks along the way -- doubtless in other islands besides these cited. If Japan, as has Formosa, had an early Malayan culture, as will probably be proved in due time, one should not be surprised to find old rice terraces in the mountains of Batanes Islands and the Loo Choo Islands which lie between Luzon and Japan.

Building the sementera

It must be noted here that all Bontoc agricultural labors, from the building of the sementera to the storing of the gathered harvest, are accompanied by religious ceremonials. They are often elaborate, and some occupy a week's time. These ceremonials are left out of this chapter to avoid detail; they appear in the later chapter on religion.

There are two varieties of sementeras -- garden patches, called "pay-yo'" -- in the Bontoc area, the irrigated and the unirrigated. The irrigated sementeras grow two crops annually, one of rice by irrigation during the dry season and the other of camotes, "sweet potatoes," grown in the rainy season without irrigation. The unirrigated sementera is of two kinds. One is the mountain or side-hill plat of earth, in which camotes, millet, beans, maize, etc., are planted, and the other is the horizontal plat (probably once an irrigated sementera), usually built with low terraces, sometimes lying in the pueblo among the houses, from which shoots are taken for transplanting in the distant sementeras and where camotes are grown for the pigs. Sometimes they are along old water courses which no longer flow during the dry season; such are often employed for rice during the rainy season.

The unirrigated mountain-side sementera, called "fo-ag'," is built by simply clearing the trees and brush from a mountain plat. No effort is made to level it and no dike walls are built. Now and then one is hemmed in by a low boundary wall.

The irrigated sementeras are built with much care and labor. The earth is first cleared; the soil is carefully removed and placed in a pile; the rocks are dug out; the ground shaped, being excavated and filled until a level results. This task for a man whose only tools are sticks is no slight one. A huge bowlder in the ground means hours -- often days -- of patient, animal-like digging and prying with hands and sticks before it is finally dislodged. When the ground is leveled the soil is put back over the plat, and very often is supplemented with other rich soil. These irrigated sementeras are built along water courses or in such places as can be reached by turning running water to them. Inasmuch as the water must flow from one to another, there are practically no two sementeras on the same level which are irrigated from the same water course. The result is that every plat is upheld on its lower side, and usually on one or both ends, by a terrace wall. Much of the mountain land is well supplied with bowlders and there is an endless water-worn supply in the beds of all streams. All terrace walls are built of these undressed stones piled together without cement or earth. These walls are called "fa-ning'." They are from 1 to 20 and 30 feet high and from a foot to 18 inches wide at the top. The upper surface of the top layer of stones is quite flat and becomes the path among the sementeras. The toiler ascends and descends among the terraces on stone steps made by single rocks projecting from the outside of the wall at regular intervals and at an angle easy of ascent and descent (see Pl. LIII).

These stone walls are usually weeded perfectly clean at least once each year, generally at the time the sementera is prepared for transplanting. This work falls to the women, who commonly perform it entirely nude. At times a scanty front-and-back apron of leaves is worn tucked under the girdle.

In the Banawi district, south of the Bontoc area, there are terrace walls certainly 75 feet in height, though many of these are not stoned, since the earth is of such a nature that it does not readily crumble.

It is safe to say that nine-tenths of the available water supply of the dry season in the Bontoc area is utilized for irrigation. In some areas, as about Bontoc pueblo, there is practically not a gallon of unused water where there is space for a sementera.

A single area consisting of several thousand acres of mountain side is frequently devoted to sementeras, and I have yet to behold a more beautiful view of cultivated land than such an area of Igorot rice terraces. Winding in and out, following every projection, dipping into every pocket of the mountain, the walls ramble along like running things alive. Like giant stairways the terraces lead up and down the mountain side, and, whether the levels are empty, dirt-colored areas, fresh, green-carpeted stairs, or patches of ripening, yellow grain, the beholder is struck with the beauty of the artificial landscape and marvels at the industry of an otherwise savage people.

Irrigating

By irrigation is meant the purposeful distribution of water over soil by man by means of diverting streams or by the use of canals in the shape of ditches or troughs for conveying and directing part of a water supply, or by means of some other man-directed power to raise water to the required level.

The Igorot employ three methods of irrigation: One, the simplest and most natural, is to build sementeras along a small stream which is turned into the upper sementera and passes from one to another, falling from terrace to terrace until all water is absorbed, evaporated, or all available or desired land is irrigated. Usually such streams are diverted from their courses, and they are often carried long distances out of their natural way. The second method is to divert a part of a river by means of a stone dam. The third method is still more artificial than the preceding -- the water is lifted by direct human power from below the sementera and poured to run over the surface.

The first method is the most common, since the mountains in Igorot land are full of small, usually perpetual, streams. There are practically no streams within reach of suitable pueblo sites which are not exhausted by the Igorot agriculturist. Everywhere small streams are carefully guarded and turned wherever there is a square yard of earth that may be made into a rice sementera. Small streams in some cases have been wound for miles around the sides of a mountain, passing deep gullies and rivers in wooden troughs or tubes.

Much land along the river valleys is irrigated by means of dams, called by the Igorot "lung-ud'." During the season of 1903 there was one dam (designated the main dam in Pl. LVII -- see also Pls. LV and LVI) across the entire river at Bontoc, throwing all the water which did not leak through the stones into a large canal on the Bontoc side of the valley. Half a mile above this was another dam (called the upper dam in Pl. LVII) diverting one-half the stream to the same valley, only onto higher ground. Immediately below the main dam were two low piles of stones (designated weirs) jutting into the shallow stream from the Bontoc side, and each gathering sufficient water for a few sementeras. Within a quarter of a mile below the main dam were three other loose, open weirs of rocks, two of which began on a shallow island, throwing water to the Samoki side of the river. In the stream a short distance farther down a shallow row of rocks and gravel turned water into three new sementeras constructed early in the year on a gravel island in the river.

The main dam is about 12 feet high, 2 feet broad at the top, 8 or 10 at the bottom, and is about 300 feet long. It is built each year during November and December, and requires the labor of fifteen or twenty men for about six weeks. It is constructed of river-worn bowlders piled together without adhesive. The top stones are flat on the upper surface, and the dam is a pathway across the river for the people from the time of its completion until its destruction by the freshets of June or July.

The upper dam is a new piece of primitive engineering. It, with its canal, has been in mind for at least two years; but it was completed only in 1903. The dam is small, extending only half way across the river, and beginning on an island. This dam turns water into a canal averaging 3 feet wide and carrying about 5 inches of water. The canal, called "a'-lak," is about 3,000 feet long from the dam at A in Pl. LVII to the place of discharge into the level area at B. For about 530 feet of this distance it was impossible for the primitive engineer to construct a canal in the earth, as the solid rock of the mountain dips vertically into the river. About fifty sections of large pine trees were brought and hollowed into troughs, called "ta-la'-kan," which have been secured above the water by means of buttresses, by wooden scaffolding, called "to-kod'," and by attachment to the overhanging rocks, until there is now a continuous artificial waterway from the dam to the tract of irrigated land.

Considerable engineering sense has been shown and no small amount of labor expended in the construction of this last irrigating scheme. The pine logs are a foot or more in diameter, and have a waterway dug in them about 10 or 12 inches deep and wide. These trees were felled and the troughs dug with the wasay, a short-handled tool with an iron blade only an inch or an inch and a half wide, and convertible alike into ax and adz.

There seems to be a fall of about 22 feet between A at the upper dam and B at the discharge from the troughs.[24] This fall in a distance of about 3,000 feet seems needlessly great; however, the primitive engineer has shown excellent judgment in the matter. First, by putting the dam (upper dam) where it is, only half the stream had to be built across. Second, there is a rapids immediately below the dam, and, had the Igorot built his dam below the rapids, a dam of the same height would have raised the water to a much lower level; this would have necessitated a canal probably 10 or 12 feet deep instead of three. Third, the height of the water at the upper dam has enabled him to lay the log section of the waterway above the high-water mark of the river, thus, probably, insuring more or less permanence. Had the dam been built much lower down the stream the troughs would have been near the surface of the river and been torn away annually by the freshets, or the people would be obliged each year to tear down and reconstruct that part of the canal. As it now is it is probable that only the short dam will need to be rebuilt each year.

All dams and irrigating canals are built directly by or at the expense of the persons benefited by the water. Water is never rented to persons with sementeras along an artificial waterway. If a person refuses to bear his share of the labor of construction and maintenance his sementeras must lie idle for lack of water.

All sementera owners along a waterway, whether it is natural or artificial, meet and agree in regard to the division of the water. If there is an abundance, all open and close their sluice gates when they please. When there is not sufficient water for this, a division is made -- usually each person takes all the water during a certain period of time. This scheme is supposed to be the best, since the flow should be sufficient fully to flood the entire plat -- a 100-gallon flow in two hours is considered much better than an equal flow in two days.

During the irrigating season, if there is lack of water, it becomes necessary for each sementera owner to guard his water rights against other persons on the same creek or canal. If a man sleeps in his house during the period in which his sementeras are supposed to receive water, it is pretty certain that his supply will be stolen, and, since he was not on guard, he has no redress. But should sleep chance to overtake him in his tiresome watch at the sementeras, and should some one turn off and steal his water, the thief will get clubbed if caught, and will forfeit his own share of water when his next period arrives.

The third method of irrigation -- lifting the water by direct human power -- is not much employed by the Igorot. In the vicinity of Bontoc pueblo there are a few sementeras which were never in a position to be irrigated by running water. They are called "pay-yo' a kao-u'-chan," and, when planted with rice in the dry season, need to be constantly tended by toilers who bring water to them in pots from the river, creeks, or canals. On the Samoki side of the valley during a week or so of the driest weather in May, 1903, there were four "well sweeps," each with a 5-gallon kerosene-oil can attached, operating nearly all day, pouring water from a canal into sementeras through 60 or 80 feet of small, wooden troughs.

Turning the soil

Since rice, called "pa-ku'." is the chief agricultural product of the Igorot it will be considered in the following sections first, after which data of other vegetable products will be given.

Turning the soil for the annual crop of irrigated rice begins in the middle of December and continues nearly two months. The labor of turning and fertilizing the soil and transplanting the young rice is all in progress at the same time -- generally, too, in the same sementera. Since each is a distinct process, however, I shall consider each separately. Before the soil is turned in a sementera it has given up its annual crop of camotes, and the water has been turned on to soften the earth. From two to twenty adults gather in a sementera, depending on the size of the plat, of which there are relatively few containing more than 10,000 square feet. They commonly range from 30 square feet to 1,500 or 2,000. The following description is one of several made in detail while watching the rice industry of the Bontoc Igorot.

The sementera is about 20 by 50 feet, or about 1,000 square feet, and lies in the midst of the large valley area between Bontoc and Samoki. It is on the Samoki side of the river, but is the property of a Bontoc family. There are two groups of soil turners in the sementera -- three men in one, and two unmarried women, an older married woman, and a youth in the other. At one end of the plat two, and part of the time three, women are transplanting rice. Four men are bringing fertilizer for the soil. Strange to say, each of the men in the group of three is "clothed" -- one wears his breechcloth as a breechcloth, and the other two wear theirs simply as aprons, hanging loose in front. Three of the men bringing fertilizer are entirely nude except for their girdles, since they ford the river with their loads between the sementera and Bontoc and do not care to wet their breechcloths; the other man wears a bladder bag hanging from his girdle as an apron. One of the young women turning the soil wears a skirt; the other one and the old woman wear front-and-back aprons of camote vines; the youth with them is nude. The three transplanters wear skirts, and one of them wears an open jacket.

Besides these there are three children in and about the sementera; one is a pretty, laughing girl of about 9 years; one is a shy, faded-haired little girl of 3 or 4 years; and the other is a fat chunk of a boy about 5 years. All three are perfectly naked. It is impossible to say what clothing these toilers wore before I went among them to watch their work, but it is certain they were not more clothed.

Let us watch the typical group of the three women and the youth: Each has a sharpened wooden turning stick, the kay-kay, a pole about 6 feet long and 2 inches in diameter. The four stand side by side with their kay-kay stuck in the earth, and, in unison, they take one step forward and push their tools from them, the earth under which the tools are thrust falling away and crumbling in the water before them. While it is falling away the toilers begin to sing, led by the elder woman. The purport of the most common soil-turning song is this: "It is hard work to turn the soil, but eating the rice is good." The song continues while the implements are withdrawn from the earth and jabbed in again in a new place, while the syllable pronounced at that instant is also noticeably jabbed into the air. Again they withdraw their implements and, singing and working in rhythmic unison, again jab kay-kay and syllable. The implements are now thrust about 8 inches below the surface; the song ceases; each toiler pries her section of the soil loose and, in a moment, together they push their tools from them, the mass of soil -- some 2 feet long, 1 foot wide, and 8 inches deep -- falls away in the water, and the song begins again. As the earth is turned a camote, passed by in the camote harvest, is discovered; the old woman picks it up and lays it on the dry ground beside her. The little girl shyly comes for it and stores it in a basket on the terrace wall with a few dozen others found during the morning.

After a section of earth 10 or 15 feet square has been turned the rhythmic labor and song ceases. Each person now grasps her kay-kay with one hand at the middle and the other near the sharpened end and with it rapidly crumbles and spreads about the new-turned soil. Now they trample the bed thoroughly, throwing out any stones or pebbles discovered by their feet, and frequently using the kay-kay further to break up some small clod of earth. Finally a large section of the sementera is prepared, and the toilers form in line abreast and slowly tread back and forth over the plat, making the bed soft and smooth beneath the water for the transplanting.

It is a delightful picture in the soil-turning season to see the acres of terraces covered by groups of toilers, relieving their labors with almost constant song.

I saw only one variation from the above methods in the Bontoc area. In some of the large sementeras in the flat river bottom near Bontoc pueblo a herd of seventeen carabaos was skillfully milled round and round in the water, after the soil was turned, stirring and mixing the bed into a uniform ooze. The animals were managed by a man who drove them and turned them at will, using only his voice and a long switch. It is impossible to get carabaos to many irrigated sementeras because of the high terrace walls, but this herd is used annually in the Bontoc river bottom.

After each rice harvest the soil of the irrigated sementera is turned for planting camotes, but this time it is turned dry. More effort is needed to thrust the kay-kay deep enough into the dry soil, and it is thrust three or four times before the earth may be turned. Only one-half the surface of a sementera is turned for camotes. Raised beds are made about 2 feet wide and 8 to 12 inches high. The spaces between these beds become paths along which the cultivator and harvester walks. The soil is turned from the spaces used as paths over the spaces which become beds, but the earth under the bed is not turned or loosened.

Bontoc beds are almost invariably constructed like parallel-sided, square-cornered saw teeth standing at right angles to the blade of the saw, which is also a camote bed, and are well shown in Pl. LXII. In Tulubin this saw-tooth bed also occurs, but the continuous spiral bed and the broken, parallel, straight beds are equally as common; they are shown in figs. 2 and 3.

The mountain-side sementera for camotes, maize, millet, and beans is prepared simply by being scratched or picked an inch or two deep with the woman's camote stick, the su-wan'. If the plat is new the grass is burned before the scratching occurs, but if it is cultivated annually the surface seldom has any care save the shallow work of the su-wan'; in fact, the surface stones are seldom removed.

In the season of 1903, the first rains came April 5, and the first mountain sementera was scratched over for millet April 10, after five successive daily rains.

Fertilizing

Much care is taken in fertilizing the irrigated sementeras. The hog of a few pueblos in the Bontoc area, as in Bontoc and Samoki, is kept confined all its life in a walled, stone-paved sty dug in the earth (see Pl. LXXVII). Into this inclosure dry grasses and dead vines are continually placed to absorb and become rotted by the liquids. As the soil of the sementera is turned for the new rice crop these pigsties are cleaned out and the rich manure spread on the beds.

The manure is sometimes carried by women though generally by men, and the carriers in a string pass all day between the sementeras and the pueblo, each bearing his transportation basket on his shoulder containing about 100 pounds of as good fertilizer as agricultural man ever thought to employ.

The manure is gathered from the sties with the two hands and is dumped in the sementera in 10-pound piles about 5 feet apart after the soil has been turned and trod soft and even.

It is said that in some sections of Igorot land dry vegetable matter is burned so that ash may be had for fertilizing purposes.

I have seen women working long, dry grass under the soil in camote sementeras at the time the crop was being gathered (Pl. LXIV), but I believe fertilizers are seldom employed, except where rice is grown. Mountain-side sementeras are frequently abandoned after a few years' service, as they are supposed to be exhausted, whereas fertilization would restore them.

Seed planting

Pad-cho-kan' is the name of the sementera used as a rice seed bed. One or more small groups of sementeras in every pueblo is so protected from the cold rains and winds of November and December and is so exposed to the warm sun that it answers well the purposes of a primitive hotbed; consequently it becomes such, and anyone who asks permission of the owner may plant his seed there (see Pl. LXV).

The seed is planted in the beds after they have been thoroughly worked and softened, the soil usually being turned three times. The planting in Bontoc occurs the first part of November. November 15, 1902, the rice had burst its kernel and was above water in the Bontoc beds. The seed is not shelled before planting, but the full fruit heads, sin-lu'-wi, are laid, without covering, on the soft ooze, under 3 or 4 inches of water. They are laid in rows a few inches apart, and are so close together that by the time the young plants are 3 inches above the surface of the water the bed is a solid mass of green.

Bontoc pueblo has six varieties of rice. Neighboring pueblos have others; and it is probable that fifty, perhaps a hundred, varieties are grown by the different irrigating peoples of northern Luzon. In Bontoc, ti'-pa is a white beardless variety. Ga'-sang is white, and cha-yet'-it is claimed to be the same grain, except it is dark colored; it is the rice from which the fermented beverage, tapui, is made. Pu-i-a-pu'-i and tu'-peng are also white; tu'-peng is sowed in unirrigated mountain sementeras in the rainy season. Gu-mik'-i is a dark grain.

Camotes, or to-ki', are planted once in a long period in the sementeras surrounding the buildings in the pueblo. There is nothing to kill them, the ground has no other use, so they are practically perpetual.

The average size of all the eight varieties of Bontoc camotes is about 2 by 4 inches in diameter. Six of the varieties are white and two are red. The white ones are the following: Li-no'-ko, pa-to'-ki, ki'-nub fa-fay'-i, pi-i-nit', ki-weng', and tang-tang-lab'. The red ones are si'-sig and pit-ti'-kan.

To illustrate the many varieties which may exist in a small area I give the names of five other camotes grown in the pueblo of Balili, which is only about four hours from Bontoc. The Balili white camotes are bi-tak'-no, a-go-bang'-bang, and la-ung'-an and the red are gis-gis'-i and ta-mo'-lo.

Millet, called "sa'-fug," is sowed on the surface of the earth. The sowing is "broadcast," but in a limited way, as the fields are usually only a few rods square. The seed is generally sowed by women, who carry a small basket or dish of it in one hand and scatter the seed from between the thumb, forefinger, and middle finger of the free hand.

There are said to be four varieties of millet in Bontoc. Mo-di' and poy-ned' are light-colored seeds; pi-ting'-an is a darker seed -- the Igorot says "black;" and si-nang'-a is the fourth. I have never seen it but I am told it is white.

Maize, or pi'-ki, and beans, practically the only other seeds planted, are planted annually in "hills." The rows of "hills" are quite irregular. Maize, as is also millet, is planted immediately after the first abundant rains, occurring early in April.

The Bontoc man has three varieties of beans. One is called ka'-lap; the kernel is small, being only one-fifth of an inch long. Usually it is pale green in color, though a few are black; both have an exterior white germ. I'-tab is about one-third of an inch long. It is both gray and black in color, and has a long exterior white germ. The third variety is black with an exterior white germ. It is called ba-la'-tong, and is about one-fourth of an inch in length.

Transplanting

Transplanting is always the work of women, since they are recognized as quicker and more dexterous in most work with the hands than are the men.

The women pull up the young rice plants in the seed beds and tie them in bunches about 4 inches in diameter. They transport them by basket to the newly prepared sementera and dump them in the water so they will remain fresh.

As has been said, the manure fertilizer is placed about the sementera in piles. The women thoroughly spread this fertilizer with their hands and feet when they transplant (see Pl. LIX). When the soil is ready the transplanter grasps a handful of the plants, twists off 3 or 4 inches of the blades, leaving the plant about 6 inches long, and, while holding the plants in one hand, with the other she rapidly thrusts them one by one into the soft bed. They are placed in fairly regular rows, and are about 5 inches apart. The planter leans enthusiastically over her work, usually resting one elbow on her knee -- the left elbow, since most of the women are right-handed -- and she sets from forty to sixty plants per minute.

When the sementeras are planted they present a clean and beautiful appearance -- even the tips of the rice blades twisted off are invariably crowded into the muddy bed to assist in fattening the crop.

As many as a dozen women often work together in one sementera to hasten the planting. There are usually two or three little girls with their mothers, who while away the hours playing work. They stuff up the chinks of the stone walls with dirt and vegetable matter; they carry together the few camotes discovered in this last handling of the old camote bed; and they quite successfully and industriously play at transplanting rice, though such small girls are not obliged to work in the field.

Camotes are also transplanted. The women cut or pick off the "runners" from the perpetual vines in the sementeras near the dwellings. These they transplant in the unirrigated mountain sementeras after the crops of millet and maize have been gathered.

The irrigated sementeras are also planted to camotes by transplanting from these house beds. This transplanting lasts about six weeks in Bontoc, beginning near the middle of July.

Some little sugar cane is grown by the Igorot of the Bontoc area. It is claimed to grow up each year from the roots left at the preceding harvest. At times new patches of cane are started by transplanting shoots from the parent plants. It is said that in January the stalks are cut and set in a rich mud, and that in the season of Baliling, from about July 15 until early in September, the rooted shoots are transplanted to the new beds.

Cultivating

The chief cultivation given to Igorot crops is bestowed on rice, though all cultivated lands are remarkably free from weeds. The rice sementeras are carefully weeded, "suckers" are pulled out, and the beds are thinned generally, so that each plant will have all needful chance to develop fruit. This weeding and thinning is the work of women and half-grown children. Every day for nearly two months, or until the fruit heads appear, the cultivators are diligently at work in the sementeras. No tools or agricultural implements other than bare hands are used in this work.

The men keep constant watch of the sementera walls and the irrigating canals, repairing all, thus indirectly assisting the women in their cultivation by directing water to the growing crop and by conserving it when it is obtained.

Protecting

The rice begins to fruit early in April, at which time systematic effort to protect the new grain from birds, rats, monkeys, and wild hogs commences. This effort continues until the harvest is completed, practically for three months. Much of this labor is performed by water power, much by wind power, and about all the children and old people in a pueblo are busied from early dawn until twilight in the sementera as independent guards. Besides, throughout the long night men and women build fires among the sementeras and guard their crop from the wild hog. It is a critical time with the Igorot.

The most natural, simplest, and undoubtedly the most successful protection of the grain is the presence of a person on the terrace walls of the sementera, whether by day or night. Hundreds of fields are so guarded each day in Bontoc by old people and children, who frequently erect small screens of tall grass to shade and protect themselves from the sun.

The next simplest method is one followed by the boys. They employ a hollow section of carabao horn, cut off at both ends and about 8 inches in length; it is called "kong-ok'." This the boys beat when birds are near, producing an open, resonant sound which may readily be heard a mile.

The wind tosses about over the growing grain various "scarecrows." The pa-chek' is one of these. It consists of a single large dry leaf, or a bunch of small dry leaves, suspended by a cord from a heavy, coarse grass 6 or 8 feet high; the leaf, the sa-gi-kak', hangs 4 feet above the fruit heads. It swings about slightly in the breeze, and probably is some protection against the birds. I believe it the least effective of the various things devised by the Igorot to protect his rice from the multitudes of ti-lin' -- the small, brown ricebird[25] found broadly over the Archipelago.

The most picturesque of these wind-tossed bird scarers is the ki'-lao. The ki'-lao is a basket-work figure swung from a pole and is usually the shape and size of the distended wings of a large gull, though it is also made in other shapes, as that of man, the lizard, etc. The pole is about 20 feet high, and is stuck in the earth at such an angle that the swinging figure attached by a line at the top of the pole hangs well over the sementera and about 3 or 4 feet above the grain (see Pl. LXVII). The bird-like ki'-lao is hung by its middle, at what would be the neck of the bird, and it soars back and forth, up and down, in a remarkably lifelike way. There are often a dozen ki'-lao in a space 4 rods square, and they are certainly effectual, if they look as bird-like to ti-lin' as they do to man. When seen a short distance away they appear exactly like a flock of restless gulls turning and dipping in some harbor.

The water-power bird scarers are ingenious. Across a shallow, running rapids in the river or canal a line, called "pi-chug'," is stretched, fastened at one end to a yielding pole, and at the other to a rigid pole. A bowed piece of wood about 15 inches long and 3 inches wide, called "pit-ug'," is suspended by a line at each end from the horizontal cord. This pit-ug' is suspended in the rapids, by which it is carried quickly downstream as far as the elasticity of the yielding pole and the pi-chug' will allow, then it snaps suddenly back upstream and is ready to be carried down and repeat the jerk on the relaxing pole. A system of cords passes high in the air from the jerking pole at the stream to other slender, jerked poles among the sementeras. From these poles a low jerking line runs over the sementeras, over which are stretched at right angles parallel cords within a few feet of the fruit heads. These parallel cords are also jerked, and their movement, together with that of the leaves depending from them, is sufficient to keep the birds away. One such machine may send its shock a quarter of a mile and trouble the birds over an area half an acre in extent.

Other Igorot, as those of the upper Abra River in Lepanto Province, employ this same jerking machine to produce a sharp, clicking sound in the sementera. The jerking cord repeatedly raises a series of hanging, vertical wooden fingers, which, on being released, fall against a stationary, horizontal bamboo tube, producing the sharp click. These clicking machines are set up on two supporting sticks a few feet above the grain every three or four yards about the sementeras.

There are many rodents, rats and mice, which destroy the growing grain during the night unless great care is taken to cheek them. The Igorot makes a small dead fall which he places in the path surrounding the sementera. I have seen as many as five of these traps on a single side of a sementera not more than 30 feet square. The trap has a closely woven, wooden dead fall, about 10 or 15 inches square; one end is set on the path and the other is supported in the air above it by a string. One end of this string is fastened to a tall stick planted in the earth, the lower end is tied to a short stick -- a part of the "spring" held rigid beneath the dead fall until the trigger is touched. The dead fall drops when the rat, in touching the trigger, releases the lower end of the cord. The animal springs the trigger either by nibbling a bait on it or by running against it, and is immediately killed, since the dead fall is weighted with stones.

Sementeras near some forested mountains in the Bontoc area are pestered with monkeys. Day and night people remain on guard against them in lonely, dangerous places -- just the kind of spot the head-hunter chooses wherein to surprise his enemy.

All border sementeras in every group of fields are subject to the night visits of wild hogs. In some areas commanding piles of earth for outlooks are left standing when the sementeras are constructed. In other places outlooks are erected for the purpose. Permanent shelters, some of them commodious stone structures, are often erected on these outlooks where a person remains on guard night and day (Pl. LXVIII), at night burning a fire to frighten the wild hogs away.

At this season of the year when practically all the people of the pueblo are in the sementeras. it is most interesting to watch the homecoming of the laborers at night. At early dusk they may be seen coming in over the trails leading from the sementeras to the pueblo in long processions. The boys and girls 5 or 6 years old or more, most of them entirely naked, come playing or dancing along -- the boys often marking time by beating a tin can or two sticks -- seemingly as full of life as when they started out in the morning. The younger children are toddling by the side of their father or mother, a small, dirty hand smothered in a large, labor-cracked one; or else are carried on their father's back or shoulder, or perhaps astride their mother's hip. The old men and women, almost always unsightly and ugly, who go to the sementera only to guard and not to toil, come slowly and feebly home, often picking their way with a staff. There is much laughing and coquetting among the young people. A boy dashes by with several girls in laughing pursuit, and it is not at all likely that he escapes them with all his belongings. Many of the younger married women carry babies; some carry on their heads baskets filled with weeds used as food for the pigs, and all have their small rump baskets filled with "greens" or snails or fish.

A man may carry on his shoulder a huge short log of wood cut in the mountains, the wood partially supported on the shoulder by his spear; or he perhaps carries a large bunch of dry grass to be thrown into the pigpen as bedding; or he comes swinging along empty handed save for his spear used as a staff. Most of the returning men and boys carry the empty topil, the small, square, covered basket in which rice for the noon meal is carried to the sementera; sometimes a boy carries a bunch of three or four, and he dangles them open from their strings as he dances along.

For an hour or more the procession continues -- one almost-naked figure following another -- all dirty, most of them doubtless tired, and yet seemingly happy and content with the finish of their day of toil. It is long after dark before the last straggler is in.

Harvesting

Rice harvesting in Bontoc is a delightful and picturesque sight to an American, and a most serious religious matter to the Igorot.

Though ceremonials having to do with agriculture have purposely been omitted from this chapter, yet, since one of the most striking and important features of the harvesting is the harvest ceremonial, it is thought best to introduce it here.

Sa-fo'-sab is the name of the ceremony. It is performed in a pathway adjoining each sementera before a single grain is gathered. In the path the owner of the field builds a tiny fire beside which he stands while the harvesters sit in silence. The owner says:

"So-mi-ka-ka' pa-ku' ta-mo i-sa'-mi sik'-a kin-po-num' nan a-lang',"

which, freely rendered, means, "Palay, when we carry you to the granary, increase greatly so that you will fill it."

As soon as the ceremonial is said the speaker harvests one handful of the grain, after which the laborers arise and begin the harvest.

In the trails leading past the sementera two tall stalks of runo are planted, and these, called "pud-i-pud'," warn all Igorot that they must not pass the sementera during the hours of the harvest. Nor will they ignore the warning, since if they do they are liable to forfeit a hog or other valuable possession to the owner of the grain.

I spent half a day trying to get close enough to a harvesting party to photograph it. All the harvesters were women, and they scolded our party long and severely while we were yet six or eight rods distant; my Igorot boys carrying the photographic outfit -- boys who had lived four months in my house -- laughingly but positively refused to follow me closer than three or four rods to the sementera. No photographs were obtained at that time. It was only after the matter was talked over by some of the men of the pueblo that photographs could be willingly obtained, and the force of the warning pud-i-pud' withdrawn for our party. Even during the time my Igorot boys were in the trail by a harvest party all other Igorot passed around the warning runo. The Igorot says he believes the harvest will be blasted even while being gathered should one pass along a pathway skirting any side of the sementera.

Several harvesters, from four to a dozen, labor together in each sementera. They begin at one side and pass across the plat, gathering all grain as they pass. Men and women work together, but women are recognized the better harvesters, since their hands are more nimble. Each fruited stalk is grasped shortly below the fruit head, and the upper section or joint of the stalk, together with the fruit head and topmost leaf, is pulled off. As most Bontoc Igorot are right-handed, the plucked grain is laid in the left hand, the fruit heads projecting beyond between the thumb and forefinger while the leaf attached to each fruit head lies outside and below the thumb. When the proper amount of grain is in hand (a bunch of stalks about an inch in diameter) the useless leaves, all arranged for one grasp of the right hand, are stripped off and dropped; the bunch of fruit heads, topping a 6-inch section of clean stalk or straw is handed to a person who may be called the binder. This person in all harvests I have seen was a woman. She binds all the grain three, four, or five persons can pluck; and when there is one binder for every three gatherers the binder finds some time also to gather.

The binder passes a small, prepared strip of bamboo twice around the palay stalks, holds one end between her teeth and draws the binding tight; then she twists the two ends together, and the bunch is secure. The bunch, the manojo of the Spaniard, the sin fing-e' of the Igorot, is then piled up on the binder's head until a load is made. Before each bunch is placed on the pile the fruitheads are spread out like an open fan. These piles are never completed until they are higher than the woman's arm can reach -- several of the last bunches being tossed in place, guided only by the tips of the fingers touching the butt of the straw. The women with their heads loaded high with ripened grain are striking figures -- and one wonders at the security of the loads.

When a load is made it is borne to the transportation baskets in some part of the harvested section of the sementera, where it is gently slid to the earth over the front of the head as the woman stoops forward. It is loaded into the basket at once unless there is a scarcity of binders in the field, in which case it awaits the completion of the harvest.

In all agricultural labors the Igorot is industrious, yet his humor, ever present with him, brings relief from continued toil. The harvest field is no exception, since there is much quiet gossip and jest during the labors.

In 1903 rice was first harvested May 2. The harvest continued one month, the crop of a sementera being gathered here and there as it ripened. The Igorot calls this first harvest month the "moon of the small harvest." During June the crop is ripened everywhere, and the harvest is on in earnest; the Igorot speaks of it as the "moon of the all harvest."

I had no view of the harvest of millet or maize; however, I have seen in the pueblo much of each grain of some previous harvest. The millet I am told, is harvested similarly to the rice, and the clean-stalked bunches are tied up in the same way - - only the bunches are four or five times larger.

The fruit head, or ears, of the maize is said to be plucked off the stalks in the fields as the American farmer gathers green corn or seed corn. It is stored still covered with its husks.

The camote harvest is continued fairly well throughout the year. Undoubtedly some camotes are dug every day in the year from the dry mountain-side sementeras, but the regular harvest occurs during November and December, during which time the camotes are gathered from the irrigated sementeras preparatory to turning the soil for the transplanting of new rice.

Women are the camote gatherers. I never saw men, nor even boys, gathering camotes. At no other time does the Igorot woman look so animal like as when she toils among the camote vines, standing with legs straight and feet spread, her body held horizontal, one hand grasping the middle of her short camote stick and the other in the soil picking out the unearthed camotes. She looks as though she never had stood erect and never would stand erect on two feet. Thus she toils day after day from early morning till dusk that she and her family may eat.

Storing

No palay is carried to the a-lang', the separate granary building, or to the dwelling for the purpose of being stored until the entire crop of the sementera is harvested. It may be carried part way, but there it halts until all the grain is ready to be carried home.

It is spread out on the ground or on a roof in the sun two or three days to dry before storing. When the grain is to be stored away an old man -- any man -- asks a blessing on it that it may make men, hogs, and chickens well, strong, and fat when they consume it. This ceremony is called "ka-fo'-kab," and the man who performs it is known by the title of "in-ka-fa'."

The Igorot granary, the a-lang', is a "hip-roofed" structure about 8 feet long, 5 wide, 4 feet high at the sides and 6 at the ridgepole. Its sides are built of heavy pine planks, which are inserted in grooved horizontal timbers, the planks being set up vertically. The floor is about a foot from the earth. The roof consists of a heavy, thick cover of long grass securely tied on a pole frame. It is seldom that a granary stands alone -- usually there are two or more together, and Bontoc has several groups of a dozen each, as shown in Pl. LXXII. When built together they are better protected from the rain storms. The roofs also are made so they extend close to the earth, thus almost entirely protecting the sides of the structure from the storms. All cracks are carefully filled with pieces of wood wedged and driven in. Even the door, consisting of two or three vertical planks set in grooved timbers, is laboriously wedged the same way. The building is rodent proof, and, because of its wide, projecting roof and the fact that it sets off the earth, it is practically moisture proof.

Most palay is stored in the granaries in the small bunches tied at harvest. The a-lang' is carefully closed again after each sementera crop has been put in. There are granaries in Bontoc which have not been opened, it is said, in eight or more years, except to receive additional crops of palay, and yet the grain is as perfectly preserved as when first stored. Some palay, especially that needed for consumption within a reasonable time, is stored in the upper part of the family dwelling.

Maize and millet are generally stored in the dwelling, in the second and third stories, since not enough of either is grown to fill an a-lang', it is said.

Camotes are sometimes stored in the granary after the harvest of the irrigated fields. Often they are put away in the kubkub, the two compartments at either end of the sleeping room on the ground floor of the dwelling. At other times one sees bushels of camotes put away on the earth under the broad bench extending the full length of the dwelling. In the poorer class of dwellings the camotes are frequently dumped in a corner.

Beans are dried and shelled before storing and are set away in a covered basket, usually in the upper part of the dwelling. Only one or two cargoes are grown by each family, so little space is needed for storage.

Since rice is the staple food and may be preserved almost indefinitely. the Igorot has developed a means and place to care for it. Maize and millet, while probably capable of as long preservation, are generally not grown in sufficient quantity to require more storage space than the upper part of the dwelling affords. The Igorot has not developed a way to preserve his camotes long after harvest; they are readily perishable, consequently no place has been differentiated as a storehouse.

Expense and profit

An irrigated sementera 60 by 100 feet, having 6,000 square feet of surface, is valued at two carabaos, or, in money, about 100 pesos. It produces an average annual crop of ten cargoes of palay, each worth 1 peso. Thus there is an annual gross profit of ten per cent on the value of the permanent investment.

It requires ten men one day to turn the soil and fertilize the plat. The wage paid in palay is equivalent to 5 cents per laborer, or 50 cents. Five women can transplant the rice in one day; cost, 25 cents. Cultivating and protecting the crop falls to the members of the family which owns the sementera, so the Igorot say; he claims never to have to pay for such labor. Twenty people can harvest the crop in a day; cost, 1 peso.

The total annual expense of maintaining the sementera as a productive property is, therefore, equivalent to 1.75 pesos. This leaves 8.25 pesos net profit when the annual expense is deducted from the annual gross profit. A net profit of 8.25 per cent is about equivalent to the profit made on the 10,000-acre Bonanza grain farms in the valley of the Red River of the North, and the 5,000-acre corn farm of Iowa.

Zooculture

The carabao, hog, chicken, and dog are the only animals domesticated by the Igorot of the Bontoc culture area.

Cattle are kept by Benguet Igorot throughout the extent of the province. Some towns, as Kabayan, have 300 or 400 head, but the Bontoc Igorot has not yet become a cattle raiser.

In Benguet, Lepanto, and Abra there are pueblos with half a hundred brood mares. Daklan, of Benguet, has such a bunch, and other pueblos have smaller herds.

In Bontoc Province between Bontoc pueblo and Lepanto Province a few mares have recently been brought in. Sagada and Titipan each have half a dozen. Near the east side of the Bontoc area there are a few bunches of horses reported among the Igorot, and in February, 1903, an American brought sixteen head from there into Bontoc. These horses are all descendants of previous domestic animals, and an addition of half a hundred is said to have been made to the number by horses abandoned by the insurgents about three years past. Some of the sixteen brought out in 1903 bore saddle marks and the brands common in the coastwise lands. These eastern horses are not used by the Igorot except for food, and no property right is recognized in them, though the Igorot brands them with a battle-ax brand. He exercises about as much protecting control over them as the Bontoc man does over the wild carabao.

Carabao

The people of Bontoc say that when Lumawig came to Bontoc they had no domestic carabaos -- that those they now have were originally purchased, before the Spaniards came, from the Tinguian of Abra Province.

There are in the neighborhood of 400 domestic carabaos owned in Bontoc and Samoki. Most of them run half wild in the mountains encircling the pueblos. Such as are in the mountains receive neither herding, attention in breeding, feed, nor salt from their owners. The young are dropped in February and March, and their owners mark them by slitting the ear, each person recognizing his own by the mark.

A herd of seventeen, consisting of animals belonging to five owners, ranges in the river bottom and among the sementeras close to Bontoc. These animals are more tame than those of the mountains, but receive little more attention, except that they are taught to perform a certain unique labor in preparing the sementeras for rice, as has been noted in the section on agriculture. This is the only use to which the Bontoc carabao is put as a power in industry. He is seldom sold outside the pueblo and is raised for consumption, chiefly on various ceremonial occasions.

Four men in Bontoc own fifty carabaos each. Three others have a herd of thirty in joint ownership. Others own five and six each, and again a single carabao may be the joint property of two and even six individuals. Carabaos are valued at from 40 to 70 pesos.

Hog

Bontoc has no record of the time or manner of first acquiring the hog, chicken, or dog. The people say they had all three when Lumawig came.

Sixty or 70 per cent of the pigs littered in Bontoc are marked lengthwise with alternate stripes of brick-red or yellowish hair, the other hair being black or white; the young of the wild hog is marked the same. All the pigs, both domestic and wild, outgrow this red or yellow marking at about the age of six months, and when they are a year old become fine-looking black hogs with white marking not unlike the Berkshire of the States. There is no chance to doubt that the Igorot domestic hog was the wild hog in the surrounding mountains a few generations ago.

The Bontoc hog is bred, born, and raised in a secure pen, yet wild blood is infused direct, since pigs are frequently purchased by Bontoc from surrounding pueblos, most of whose hogs run half wild and intermingle with the wild ones of the mountains. That the domestic hog in some places in northern Luzon does thus interbreed with the wild ones is a proved fact. In the Quiangan area I was shown a litter of half-breeds and was told that it was customary for the pueblo sows to breed to the wild boar of the mountains.

The Bontoc hog in many ways is a pampered pet. He is at all times kept in a pen and fed regularly three times each day with camote vines when in season, with camote parings, and small camotes available, and with green vegetal matter, including pusleys, gathered by the girls and women when there are no camote vines. All of his food is carefully washed and cooked before it is given to him.

The pigsty consists of a pit in the earth about 4 feet deep, 5 or 6 feet wide, and 8 or 12 feet long. It is entirely lined with bowlders, and the floor space consists of three sections of about equal size. One end is two or more feet deeper than the other, and it is into this lower space that the washings of the pen are stored in the rotted straw and weeds, and from which the manure for fertilizer is taken. The other end is covered over level with the outside earth with timbers, stones, and dirt; it is the pig's bed and is entered by a doorway in the stone wall. Most of these "beds" have a low, grass roof about 30 inches high over them. Underneath the roof is an opening in the earth where the people defecate. Connecting the "bed" section and the opposite lower section of the sty is an incline on which the stone "feed" troughs are located.

As soon as a pig is weaned he is kept in a separate pen, and one family may have in its charge three or four pens. The sows are kept mainly for breeding, and there are many several years old. The richest man in Bontoc owns about thirty hogs, and these are farmed out for feeding and breeding -- a common practice. When one is killed it is divided equally between the owner and the feeder. When a litter of pigs is produced the bunch is divided equally, the sow remaining the property of the owner and counting as one in the division. Throughout the Island of Luzon it is the practice to leave most male animals uncastrated. But in Bontoc the boar not intended for breeding is castrated.

Hogs are raised for ceremonial consumption. They are commonly bought and sold within the pueblo, and are not infrequently sold outside. A pig weighing 10 pounds is worth about 3 pesos, and a hog weighing 60 or 70 pounds is valued at about 12 pesos.

Chicken

The Bontoc domestic chickens were originally the wild fowl, found in all places in the Archipelago, although some of them have acquired varied colorings and markings, largely, probably, from black and white Spanish fowl, which are still found among them. The markings of the wild fowl, however, are the most common, and practically all small chickens are marked as are their wild kin. The wild fowl bears markings similar to those of the American black-breasted red game, though the fowls are smaller than the American game fowl. Each of the twelve wild cocks I have had in my hands had perfect five-pointed single combs, and the domestic cock of Bontoc also commonly has this perfect comb. I know of no people within the Bontoc area who now systematically domesticate the wild fowl, though this was found to be the custom of the Ibilao southeast of Dupax in the Province of Nueva Vizcaya. Those people catch the young wild fowl for domestication.

The Bontoc domestic fowl are not confined in a coop except at night, when they sleep in small cages placed on the ground in the dwelling houses. In the daytime they range about the pueblo feeding much in the pigpens, though they are fed a small amount of raw rice each morning. Their nests are in baskets secured under the eaves of the dwelling, and in those baskets the brooding hens hatch their chicks, from eight to twenty eggs being given a hen. The fowl is raised exclusively for ceremonial consumption, and is frequently sold in the pueblo for that purpose, being valued at from half a peso to a peso each. A wild fowl sells for half a peso.

In Banawi of the Quiangan area, south of Bontoc, one may find large capons, but Bontoc does not understand caponizing.

Dog

The dog of the Bontoc Igorot is usually of a solid color, black, white, or yellow, really "buckskin" color. Where he originated is not known. He has none of the marks of the Asiatic dog which has left its impress everywhere in the lowlands of the west coast of Luzon -- called in the Islands the "Chino" dog, and in the States the "Eskimo" dog. The Igorot dog is short-haired, sharp-eared, gaunt, and sinewy, with long legs and body. In height and length he ranges from a fair-sized fox terrier to a collie. I fail to see anything in him resembling the Australian dingo or the "yellow cur" of the States. The Ibilao have the same dog in two colors, the black and the "brindle" -- the brown and black striped. In fact, a dog of the same general characteristics occurs throughout northern Luzon. No matter what may be his origin, a dog so widely diffused and so characteristically molded and marked must have been on the island long enough to have acquired its typical features here. The dog receives little attention from his owners. Twice each day he is fed sparingly with cooked rice or camotes. Except in the case of the few hunting dogs, he does nothing to justify his existence. He lies about the dwelling most of the time, and is a surly, more or less evil-tempered cur to strangers, though when a pueblo flees to the mountains from its attacking enemies the dog escapes in a spiritless way with the women and children. He is bred mainly for ceremonial consumption.

In Benguet the Igorot eats his dog only after it has been reduced to skin and bones. I saw two in a house so poor that they did not raise their heads when I entered, and the man of the house said they would be kept twenty days longer before they would be reduced properly for eating. No such custom exists in Bontoc, but dogs are seldom fat when eaten. They are not often bought or sold outside the pueblo. A litter of pups is generally distributed about the town, and dogs are constantly bought and sold within the pueblo for ceremonial purposes. They are valued at from 2 to 4 pesos.

Clothing production

Man's clothing

Up to the age of 6 or 7 years the Igorot boys are as naked as when born. At that time they put on the suk'-lang, the basket-work hat worn on the back of the head, held in place by a cord attached at both sides and passing across the forehead and usually hidden by the front hair. The suk'-lang is made in nearly all pueblos in the Bontoc culture area. It does not extend uninterruptedly to the western border, however, since it is not worn at all in Agawa, and in some other pueblos near the Lepanto border, as Fidelisan and Genugan, it has a rival in the headband. The beaten-bark headband, called "a-pong'-ot," and the headband of cloth are worn by short-haired men, while the long-haired man invariably wears the hat. The suk'-lang varies in shape from the fez-like ti-no-od' of Bontoc and Samoki, through various hemispherical forms, to the low, flat hats developing eastward and perfected in the last mountains west of the Rio Grande de Cagayan. Barlig makes and wears a carved wooden hat, either hemispherical or slightly oval. It goes in trade to Ambawan.

The men of the Bontoc area also have a basket-work, conical rain hat. It is water-proof, being covered with beeswax. It is called "seg-fi'," and is worn only when it rains, at which time the suk'-lang is often not removed.

About the age of 10 the boys frequently affect a girdle. These girdles are of four varieties. The one most common in Bontoc and Samoki is the song-kit-an', made of braided bark-fiber strings, some six to twelve in number and about 12 feet long. They are doubled, and so make the girdle about 6 feet in length. The strings are the twisted inner bark of the same plants that play a large role in the manu-facture of the woman's skirt. This girdle is usually worn twice around the body, though it is also employed as an apron, passing only once around the body and hanging down over the genitals (see Pl. XXI). Another girdle worn much in Tukukan, Kanyu, and Tulubin is called the "i-kit'." It is made of six to twelve braided strings of bejuco (see Pl. LXXX). It is constructed to fit the waist, has loops at both ends, passes once around the body, and fastens by a cord passing from one loop to the other. Both the sang-ki-tan' and the i-kit' are made by the women. A third class of girdles is made by the men. It is called ka'-kot, and is worn and attached quite as is the i-kit'. It is a twisted rope of bejuco, often an inch in diameter, and is much worn in Mayinit. A fourth girdle, called "ka'-ching," is a chain, frequently a dog chain of iron purchased on the coast, oftener a chain manufactured by the men, and consisting of large, open links of commercial brass wire about one-sixth of an inch in diameter.

At about the age of puberty, say at 15, it is usual for the boy to possess a breech-cloth, or wa'-nis. However, the cloth is worn by a large per cent of men in Bontoc and Samoki, not as a breechcloth but tucked under the girdle and hanging in front simply as an apron. Within the Bontoc area fully 50 per cent of the men wear the breechcloth simply as an apron.

There are several varieties of breechcloths in the area. The simplest of these is of flayed tree bark. It is made by women in Barlig, Tulubin, Titipan, Agawa, and other pueblos. It is made of white and reddish-brown bark, and sometimes the white ones are colored with red ocher. The white one is called "so'-put" and the red one "ti-nan'-ag." Some of the other breechcloths are woven of cotton thread by the women. Much of this cotton is claimed by the Igorot to be tree cotton which they gather, spin and weave, but much also comes in trade from the Ilokano at the coast. Some is purchased in the boll and some is purchased after it has been spun and colored. Many breechcloths are now bought ready made from the Ilokano.

Men generally carry a bag tucked under the girdle, and very often indeed these bags are worn in lieu of the breechcloth aprons -- the girdle and the bag apron being the only clothing (see Pl. CXXV and also Frontispiece, where, from left to right, figs. 1, 2, 3, 5, and 7 wear simply a bag). One of the bags commonly worn is the fi-chong', the bladder of the hog; the other, cho'-kao, is a cloth bag some 8 inches wide and 15 inches long. These cloth bags are woven in most of the pueblos where the cotton breechcloth is made.

Old men now and then wear a blanket, pi'-tay, but the younger men never do. They say a blanket is for the women.

Some few of the principal men in many of the pueblos throughout the area have in late years acquired either the Army blue-woollen shirt, a cotton shirt, or a thin coat, and these they wear during the cold storms of January and February, and on special social occasions.

During the period of preparing the soil for transplanting palay the men frequently wear nothing at the middle except the girdle. In and out of the pueblo they work, carrying loads of manure from the hogpens to the fields, apparently as little concerned or noticed as though they wore their breechcloths.

All Igorot -- men, women, and children -- sleep without breechcloth, skirt, or jacket. If a woman owns a blanket she uses it as a covering when the nights are cold. All wear basket-work nightcaps, called "kut'-lao." They are made to fit closely on the head, and have a small opening at the top. They may be worn to keep the hair from snarling, though I was unable to get any reason from the Igorot for their use, save that they were worn by their ancestors.

Woman's clothing

From infancy to the age of 8 and very often 10 years the little girls are naked; not unfrequently one sees about the pueblo a girl of a dozen years entirely nude.

However, practically all girls from about 5 years, and also all women, have blankets which are worn when it is cold, as almost invariably after sundown, though no pretense is made to cover their nakedness with them. During the day this pi'-tay, or blanket, is seldom worn except in the dance. I have never seen women or girls dance without it. The blankets of the girls are usually small and white with a blue stripe down each side and through the middle; they are called "kud-pas'." Those of the women are of four kinds -- the ti-na'-pi, the fa-yi-ong', the fan-che'-la, and the pi-nag-pa'-gan. In Barlig, Agawa, and Tulubin the flayed tree-bark blanket is worn; and in Kambulo, east of Barlig, woven bark-fiber blankets are made which sometimes come to Bontoc.

Before a girl puts on her lu-fid', or woven bark-fiber skirt, at about 8 or 10 years of age, she at times wears simply the narrow girdle, later worn to hold up the skirt. The skirt is both short and narrow. It usually extends from below the navel to near the knees. It opens on the side, and is frequently so scant and narrow that one leg is exposed as the person walks, the only part of the body covered on that side being under the girdle, or wa'-kis -- a woven band about 4 inches wide passing twice around the body (see Pl. XXIII). The women sometimes wear the braided-string bejuco belt, i-kit', worn by the men.

The lu-fid' and the wa'-kis are the extent of woman's ordinary clothing. For some months after the mother gives birth to a child she wears an extra wa'-kis wrapped tightly about her, over which the skirt is worn as usual. During the last few weeks of pregnancy the woman may leave off her skirt entirely, wearing simply her blanket over one shoulder and about her body. Women wear breechcloths during the three or four days of menstruation.

During the period when the water-soaked soil of the sementera is turned for transplanting palay the women engaged in such labor generally lay aside their skirts. Sometimes they retain a girdle and tuck an apron of camote leaves or of weeds under it before and behind. I have frequently come upon women entirely naked climbing up and down the steep, stone dikes of their sementeras while weeding them, and also at the clay pits where Samoki women get their earth for making pottery. In May, 1903, it rained hard every afternoon for two or three hours in Bontoc pueblo, and at such times the women out of doors uniformly removed their clothing. They worked in the fields and went from the fields to their dwellings nude, wearing on their heads while in the trail either their long, basket rain protector or a head covering of camote vines, under which reposed their skirts in an effort to keep them dry. Sometimes while passing our house en route from the field to the pueblo the women wore the girdle with the camote-vine apron, called pay-pay. Often no girdle was worn, but the women held a small bunch of leaves against the body in lieu of an attached apron. Sometimes, however, their hands were occupied with their burdens, and their nudity seemed not to trouble them in the least. The women remove their skirts, they say, because they usually possess only one at a time, and they prefer to go naked in the rain and while working in the wet sementeras rather than sit in a wet skirt when they reach home.

Few women in the Bontoc area wear jackets or waists. Those to the west, toward the Province of Lepanto, frequently wear short ones, open in front without fastening, and having quarter sleeves. Those women also wear somewhat longer skirts than do the Bontoc women.

In Agawa, and near-by pueblos to the west, and in Barlig and vicinity to the east, the women make and wear flayed-bark jackets and skirts. From Barlig bark jackets for women come in trade to Tulubin. They are not simply sheets of bark, but the bark is strengthened by a coarse reinforcement of a warp sewed or quilted.

Many of the women's skirts and girdles woven west of Bontoc pueblo are made also of the Ilokano cotton. The skirts and girdles of Bontoc pueblo and those found commonly eastward are entirely of Igorot production. Four varieties of plants yield the threads; the inner bark is gathered and then spun or twisted on the naked thigh under the palm of the hand (see Pl. LXXXIII).

All weaving in Igorot land is done by the woman with the simplest kind of loom, such as is scattered the world over among primitive people. It is well shown in Pl. LXXXIV, which is a photograph of a Lepanto Igorot loom.

Implement and utensil production

Introduction

It is only after one has brought together all the implements and utensils of an Igorot pueblo that he realizes the large part played in it by basket work. Were basketry and pottery cut from the list of his productions the Igorot's everyday labors would be performed with bare hands and crude sticks.

Where is the Igorot's "stone age"? There are stone hammers and stones used as anvils in the ironsmith's shop. There are stone troughs or bowls in most pigpens in which the animal's food is placed. Very rarely, as in the Quiangan area, one sees a large, flat stone supported a foot or two from the earth by other stones. It is used as a bench or table, but has no special purpose. There are whetstones for sharpening the steel spear and battle-ax; there is the stone of the "flint-and-steel" fire machine; and of course stones are employed as seats, in constructing terrace walls, in dams, and in the building of various inhabited structures, but that is all. There is no "stone age" -- no memory of it -- and, if the people were swept away to-day, to-morrow would reveal no trace of it. It is believed that the Igorot is to-day as much in the "stone age" as he ever has been in his present land. He had little use for stone weapons, implements, or utensils before he manufactured in iron.

Before he had iron he was essentially a user and maker of weapons, implements, utensils, and tools of wood. There are many vestiges of the wood age to-day; several show the use of wood for purposes usually thought of as solely within the sphere of stone and metal. Among these vestiges may be noted the bamboo knife used in circumcision; the sharp stick employed in the ceremonial killing of domestic hogs in Benguet; the bamboo instrument of ten or a dozen cutting blades used to shape and dress the hard, wooden spear shafts and battle-ax handles; the use of bamboo spearheads attached to hard-wood shafts; and the bamboo spikes stuck in trails to impale the enemy.

In addition to the above uses of wood for cutting flesh and working wood there follow, in this and subsequent chapters, enough data regarding the uses of wood to demonstrate that the wood age plays a large part in the life of a primitive people prior to the common use of metals. Without metals there was practically no occasion for the development of stone weapons and tools in a country with such woods as the bamboo; so in the Philippines we find an order of development different from that widespread in the temperate zones -- the "stone age" appears to be omitted.

Wooden implements and utensils

The kay-kay (Pl. LXI) is one of the most indispensable wooden tools in Igorot land. It is a hard-wood implement from 5 to 7 feet long, sharpened to a dull, flat edge at one end; this end is fire tempered to harden and bind the fibers, thus preventing splitting and excessive wear. The kay-kay is obtained in the mountains in the vicinity of most pueblos, so it is seldom bought or sold. It is the soil-turning stick, used by both men and women in turning the earth in all irrigated sementeras for rice and camotes. It is also employed in digging around and prying out rocks to be removed from sementeras or needed for walls. It is spade, plow, pickax, and crowbar. A small per cent of the kay-kay is shod with an iron point, rendering them more efficient, especially in breaking up new or sod ground.

The su-wan', the woman's camote stick, is about 2 feet long and an inch in diameter (Pl. LXXV). It is a heavy, compact wood, and is used by the woman until worn down 6 or 8 inches, when it usually becomes the property of a small girl for gathering wild plants for the family pigs. The su-wan' of the woman of Bontoc and Samoki comes, mostly in trade, from the mountains near Tulubin. It is employed in picking the earth loose in all unirrigated sementeras, as those for camotes, millet, beans, and maize. It is also used to pick over the earth in camote sementeras when the crop is gathered. Perhaps 1 per cent of these sticks is shod with an iron point. Such an instrument is of genuine service in the rough, stony mountain lands, but is not so serviceable as the unshod stick in the irrigated sementeras, because it cuts and bruises the vegetables.

The most common wooden vessel in the Bontoc area is the kak-wan', a vessel, or "pail" holding about six or eight quarts. In it the cooked food of the pigs is mixed and carried to the animals. Every household has two or more of them.

A few small, poorly made wooden dishes, called "chu'-yu," are found in each dwelling, from which the people eat broth of fish or other meats. All are of inferior workmanship and, in common with all things of wood made by the Igorot, are the product of the man's art. Both the knife and fire are used to hollow out these bowls.

A long-handled wooden dipper, called "ka-od'," is found in every dwelling. It belongs with the kak-wan', the pig-food pail.

Tug-on' is a large, long-handled spoon used exclusively as a drinking dipper for the fermented liquor called "sa-fu-eng'."

Fa'-nu is a wooden ladle employed in cooking foods.

A few very crude eating spoons, about the size of the dessert spoon of America, are found in most dwellings. They are usually without ornament, and are called "i-chus'."

Metal implements and utensils

The wa'-say is the only metal implement employed at all commonly in the area; it is found in each family. It consists of an iron, steel-bitted blade from an inch to an inch and a half in width and about 6 inches in length. It is attached to the short, wooden handle by a square haft inserted into the handle. Since the haft is square the implement may be instantly converted into either an "ax" with blade parallel to the handle or an "adz" with blade at right angle to the handle.

This is the tool used in felling and cutting up all trees, and in getting out and dressing all timbers and boards. It is the sole carpenter tool, unless the man by chance possess a bolo.

There are no metal agricultural implements in common use. As was noted earlier in the chapter, the soil-turning stick and the woman's camote stick are now and then shod with iron, but they are rare.

There are a few large, shallow Chinese iron boilers in the area, used especially for boiling sugar, evaporating salt in Mayinit, and for cooking carabao or large quantities of hog on ceremonial occasions. There are probably not more than two or three dozen such boilers in Bontoc pueblo, though they are becoming much more plentiful during the past three years -- since the Igorot has more money and goes more often to Candon on the coast, where he buys them.

Pottery

Most of the pottery consumed in the Bontoc area is the product of Samoki, the sister pueblo of Bontoc. Samoki pottery meets no competition down the river to the north until in the vicinity of Bitwagan, which makes and vends similar ware both up and down the river. To the south there is also competition, since Data makes and sells an excellent pot to Antedao, Fidelisan, Sagada, Titipan, and other near-by pueblos. It is probable, also, that Lias and Barlig, to the east, are supplied with pottery, and, if so, that their source is Bitwagan. But Bitwagan and Data pots are really not competitors with those of Samoki; they rather supply areas which the Samoki potters can not reach because of distance and the hostility of the people.

There are no traditions clustering around pottery making in Samoki. The potters say they taught themselves, and have always made earthenware.

To-day Samoki pottery is made of two clays -- one a reddish-brown mineral dug from pits several feet deep on the hillside, shown in Pl. LXXXII, and the other a bluish mineral gathered from a shallow basin situated on the hillside nearer the river than the pits, and in which a little water stands much of the year.

Formerly Samoki made pottery of only the brown clay, and she used cut grass intermixed for a temper, but she claims those earlier pots were too porous to glaze well. Consequently the experiment was made of adding the blue surface clay, in which there is a considerable amount of fresh and decaying vegetable matter -- probably sufficient to give temper, although the potters do not recognize it as such.

Samoki consists of eight ato, one of which is I-kang'-a. occupying the outer fringe of dwellings on the northwest side of the pueblo. It is claimed that all of the women of I-kang'-a, whether married or single, are potters. Even women who marry men of the I-kang'-a ato, and who come to that section of the pueblo to live, learn and follow the potter's art. A few married women in other ato also manufacture pottery. They seem to be married daughters of I-kang'-a ato.

A fine illustration of community industry is presented by the ato potters of Samoki. It could not be learned that there are any definite regulations, other than custom, demanding that all women of I-kang'-a manufacture pots, or any regulation which forces daughters of that ato to discontinue the art when they marry outside. But custom has fixed quite rigidly such a regulation, and though, as just stated, a few I-kang'-a women married into other ato of Samoki do manufacture pottery, yet no I-kang'-a women married into other pueblos carry on the art. It may be argued that a lack of suitable clay has thwarted manufacture in other pueblos, but clay is common in the mountains of the area, and the sources of the materials used in Samoki are readily accessible to at least the pueblo of Bontoc, where also there are many Samoki women living.

The clay pits lie north of Samoki, between a quarter and a half of a mile distant, and the potters go to them in the early morning while the earth is moist, and dig and bring home the clays. The woman gathers half a transportation basket of each of the clays, and while at the pits crudely works both together into balls 4 or 5 inches in diameter. In this form the clay is carried to the pueblo.

All the pottery is manufactured in the shade of the potter's dwelling, and the first process is a thorough mixing of the two clays. The balls of the crudely mixed material are put into a small, wooden trough, are slightly moistened, and then thoroughly worked with a wooden pestle, the potter crouching on her haunches or resting on her knees during the labors. She is shown in Pl. LXXXIX A. After the clay is mixed it is manipulated in small handfuls, between the thumb and fingers, in order that all stones and coarse pieces of vegetable matter may be removed. When the mortarful has thus been handled it is ready for making pots.

A mass of this clay, thoroughly mixed and plastic, is placed on a board on the earth before the kneeling or crouched potter. She pokes a hole in the top of this mass with thumbs and fingers, and quickly enlarges it. As soon as the opening is large enough to admit one hand it is dug out and enlarged by scraping with the ends of the fingers, and the clay so gathered is immediately built onto the upper rim of the mass. The inside is next further scraped and smoothed with the side of the forefinger. At this juncture a small mass of clay is rolled into a strip between the hands and placed on the upper edge of the shaping mass, completely encircling it. This roll is at once shaped by the hands into a crude, flaring rim. A few swift touches on the outer face of the crude pot removes protruding masses and roughly shapes the surface. The rim is moistened with water and smoothed inside and out by the hand and a short, round stick. This process is well illustrated in Pl. XC. The first stage of manufacture is completed and the vessel is set in the sun with the rim of an old broken pot for a supporting base.

In the course of a few hours the shaped and nearly completed rim of the pot becomes strong and set by the heat of the sun. However, the rough and irregular bowl has apparently retained relatively a larger amount of moisture and is in prime condition to be thinned, expanded, and given final form. The pot is now handled by the rim, which is sufficiently rigid for the purpose, and is turned about on its supporting base as is needed, or the base is turned about on the earth like a crude "potter's wheel." A smooth discoidal stone, some 4 or 5 inches in diameter, and a wooden paddle are the instruments used to shape the bowl. The paddle is first dipped in water and rubbed over one of the flattish surfaces of the stone slightly to moisten it, and is then beaten against the outer surface of the bowl, while the stone, tapped against the inner surface, prevents indenting or cracking, and, by offering a more or less nonresisting surface, assists in thinning and expanding the clay. After the upper part of the bowl has been thus completed the potter sits on her feet and haunches, with her knees thrust forward from her. Again and again she moistens her paddle and discoidal stone, and continues the spanking process until the entire bowl of the pot is shaped. It is then set in the sun to dry -- this time usually bottom side up.

After it has thoroughly dried, both the inner and outer surfaces are carefully and patiently smoothed and polished with a small stone, commonly a ribbon agate. During this process all pebbles found protruding from the surface are removed and the pits are filled with new clay thoroughly smoothed in place, and the thickness of the pot is made more uniform. The vessel is again placed on its supporting base in the sun, and kept turned and tilted until it has become well dried and set. Two and sometimes three days are required to bring a pot thus far toward completion, though during the same time there are several equally completed by each potter.

There remains yet the burning and glazing. Samoki burns her pots in the morning before sunrise. Immediately on the outskirts of the pueblo there is a large, gravelly place strewn with thin, black ash where for generations the potters coming and going have completed their primitive ware. Usually two or more firings occur each week, and several women combine and burn their pots together. On the earth small stones are laid upon which one tier of vessels is placed, each lying upon its side. Tier upon tier of pots is then placed above the first layer, each on its side and each supported by and supporting other pots. The heat is supplied by pine bark placed beneath and around the lower layer. The pile is entirely blanketed with dead grass tied in small bunches which has been gathered, prepared, and kept in the houses of the potters for the purpose. The grass retains its form long after the blaze and glow have ceased, and clings about the pile as a blanket, checking the wasteful radiation of heat and cutting out the drafts of air that would be disastrous to the heated clay. As this blanket of grass finally gives way here and there the attending potters replenish it with more bunches. The pile is fired about one hour; when sufficiently baked the pots are lifted from the fire by inserting in each a long pole. Each potter then takes a vessel at a time, places it red hot on its supporting base on the earth before her, and immediately proceeds, with much care and labor, to glaze the rim and inside of the bowl. The glaze is a resin obtained in trade from Barlig. It is applied to the vessel from the end of a glazing stick -- sometimes a pole 6 or 7 feet long, but usually about a yard in length. After the rim and inner surface of the bowl have been thoroughly glazed the potter begins on another vessel -- turning the last one over to one or two little girls, from 4 to 6 years of age, who find great happiness in smearing the outer surface of the now cooling and dull-brown pot with resin held in bunches in the hands. This outer glaze, applied by the young apprentices, who, in play, are learning an art of their future womanhood, is neither so thick nor so carefully laid as is the glaze of the rim and inner surface of the vessel. When the glazing is completed the pot is still too hot to be borne in the hands; however, the glaze has become rigid and hard.

Analyses made at the Bureau of Government Laboratories, Manila, show that the clays used in the Samoki pots contain the following mineral:

Analyses of Samoki pottery clays

Minerals.	Brown pit clay	Blue surface clay
	Per cent	PER CENT
Silica	54.46	60.99
Oxide of aluminum	16.77	17.71
Ferric oxide of iron	11.14	9.53

Oxide of calcium	0.53	0.59
Loss by ignition	16.81	10.65

Oxide of magnesium Trace Trace

Oxide of potassium Trace --

Oxide of sodium -- Trace

Carbon dioxide -- Trace

The botanist of the Bureau of Government Laboratories[26] says in the report of his analysis of the resin used to glaze these pots:

This gum is known as Almaciga (Sp.). It is produced by some species of the dipterocarpus or shorea -- which it is impossible to determine. ... It should not be confounded with the other common almaciga from the trees of the genus Agathis.

The Government analyst[27] who analyzed the clays and examined the finished and glazed pots says of the Samoki pot that about two-thirds of the organic matter in the clay is consumed in the baking or burning of the pot. The organic matter in the middle one-third of the wall of the pot is not consumed. The clay is a remarkably hard one and is difficult of ignition; this is the reason it makes good cooking vessels. He further says that the glaze is not a true glaze. It seems that the resin does nothing except lose its oils when applied to the red-hot pots, and there is left on the surface the unconsumed carbon.

Basket work

All basket work is done by the men. Much of the time when they are in the fawi or pabafunan, gossiping and smoking, they are busied making the ordinary and necessary utensils of the field and dwelling. The basket work is all crude, with the possible exception of some of the hats worn by the men.

As is brought forth later under the head of "Commerce," much basket work is done by only one or two communities, and from them passes in trade over a large area. Most of the basket work of the area is of bejuco or bamboo. There are two varieties of bamboo used in the area -- a'-nis and fi'-ka. A'-nis is found in the area and fi'-ka is brought in in trade from the southwest.

The most important piece of basket work is the ki-ma'-ta, the man's transportation basket, made of a'-nis bamboo; it is shown in Pl. CXX. It is made by many pueblos, and is found throughout the area. It consists of two baskets joined firmly to a light, wooden crossbar called "pa'-tang." The entire ki-ma'-ta weighs about 5 pounds, and with it the Igorot carries loads weighing as much as 100 pounds.

The man has another basket called "ko-chuk-kod'," which is used frequently by him, also sometimes by women, for carrying earth when building the sementeras. The ko-chuk-kod' is made in Bontoc and Samoki. It is not shown in any of the illustrations, but is quite similar to the tay-ya-an', or large transportation basket of the woman, yet is slimmer. It is also similar in shape and size to the woman's transportation basket in Benguet which is worn on the back supported by a head-band.

The woman has two important a'-nis bamboo transportation baskets, which are constantly employed. One called "lu'-wa," the shallow lower basket shown in Pl. LXXV, is made only in Samoki; the other tay-ya-an', shown in Pl. XCIII, holds about three pecks. It is made only in Bontoc and Samoki.

Ag-ka-win' is the small rump basket almost invariably worn by women when working in the irrigated sementera. It is of fi'-ka bamboo, is made commonly in Bontoc and Samoki, and occasionally in Tulubin. The field toiler often carries her lunch to the field in the ag-ka-win', and when she returns the basket is usually filled with crustaceans and mollusks picked up in the wet sementera or gathered in the river, or with weeds or grasses to be cooked as "greens."

The woman's rain protector, a scoop-shaped affair about 4 feet long, called "tug-wi'," is said to be made only in Ambawan and Barlig. It consists of a double weave of coarse splints, between which is a waterproof layer of a large palm leaf. It is worn over the head, and is an excellent protection from the rain. It may well have been suggested to primitive man by the banana leaf, which I have repeatedly seen carried over the head and back by the Igorot in many sections of northern Luzon during the rains. I have also seen it used many times in Manila by Tagalog who were caught out in a storm without an umbrella. The rain protector is shown lying in front of the house in Pl. XXXVII.

Tak-o-chug' is the man's dirt scoop made of a'-nis bamboo. It resembles the tug-wi' in shape, but is only about 1 1/2 feet long. It is employed in handling earth, and conveying the dirt to the ko-chuk-kod', or dirt transportation basket.

A basket very similar to tak-o-chug', but called "sug-fi'," is employed by the woman in her housework in handling vegetables. It is shown in Pl. XCIV, containing camote parings.

The to'-pil is the man's "dinner pail." It is made of a'-nis bamboo, is a covered basket, and is constructed to contain from one and a half to three quarts of solid food. In it men and boys carry their lunch to the fields. All the pueblos make the to'-pil.

Another basket, called "sang'-i," is generally employed in carrying the man's food. It is used for long trips from home, although I have seen it used simply for carrying the field lunch. It is made of bejuco in Ambawan, Barlig, and Tulubin, and passes widely in the area through commerce. It is worn on the back, secured by bejuco straps passing in front of the shoulders.

Fang'-ao is the sang'-i with a waterproof bejuco covering. As it is worn on the back, the man appears to be wearing a cape made of hanging vegetable threads. This is the basket commonly known as the "head basket," but it is used for carrying food, blankets, anything, on the trail. It is made in Ambawan, Barlig, and Kanyu, and is found pretty well scattered throughout the area. It is shown, front and back view, in Pl. XCV.

Fa'-i si gang'-sa is an open-work bejuco basket, in shape very similar to the sang'-i, used to carry the gang'-sa, or metal drum. It is worn slung on the back as is the sang'-i.

A house basket holding about a peck, called "fa-lo'-ko," is made of a'-nis bamboo. It is used in various capacities, for vegetables and cereals, in and about the house. It is made in all the pueblos and is shown in Pl. XCIV. A few other household baskets are often found. Among these are the large, bottle-shaped locust basket, i-wus', a smaller basket, ko'-lug, of the same shape used to hold threshed rice, and the open-work spoon basket, so'-long, which usually hangs over the fireplace in each dwelling.

The large winnowing tray, lig-o', shown bottom up in Pl. XCIII, is made in Samoki and Kanyu of a'-nis bamboo. There are two sizes of winnowing trays, both of which are employed everywhere in the area.

Several small a'-nis bamboo eating trays, called "ki'-ug," are shown in Pl. XCIV. These food dishes are used on ceremonial occasions, and some of them can not be purchased. They are made in all pueblos.

Samoki alone is said to make the rice sieve, called "a-ka'-ug. It passes widely in the pueblo.

Aside from these various basket utensils and implements there are the three kinds of fish traps described in the section on fishing.

There are also three varieties of basket-work hats. The rain hat called "seg-fi'," is made in Bontoc, and may be in imitation of those worn nearer the western coast. This with the suk-lang, the pocket hat always worn by the men and boys, and the kut'-lao. or sleeping hat, worn by children and adults of both sexes, are described under the head of "Clothing."

Weapon production

Igorot weapons are few and relatively simple. The bow and arrow, used wherever the Negrito is in Luzon, is not known to the Igorot warrior of the Bontoc culture area. Small boys in Bontoc pueblo make for themselves tiny bows 1 1/2 or 2 feet long with which they snap light arrows a few feet. But the instrument is of the crudest, merely a toy, and is a thing of the day, being acquired from the culture of the Ilokano who live in the pueblo. The Igorot claim they never employed the bow and arrow, and, to-day at least, consider the question as to their ever using it as very foolish, since, they say, pointing to the child's toy, "It is nothing."

In 1665 -- 1668 Friar Casimiro Diaz wrote of the Igorot that they used arrows,[28] but it is believed his statement did not apply to the Bontoc man. Igorot-like people throughout northern Luzon commonly do not have this weapon, yet the large Tinguian group of Abra, west and north of Bontoc, and the Ibilao of southeastern Nueva Vizcaya, Nueva Ecija, and adjacent Isabela employ the bow constantly.

The natural projectile weapon of the Negrito is the bow and arrow; that of the Malayan seems to be the blowgun -- at present, however, largely replaced by the spear, though in some southern islands, especially in Paragua, it has held its own.

Wooden weapons

Shields are universally made and used by the Igorot. They are made by the men of each pueblo, and are seldom bought or sold. They are cut from single pieces of wood, and are generally constructed of very light wood, though some are heavy. The hand grip is cut in the solid timber. is almost invariably made for the left hand, and will usually accommodate only three fingers -- the thumb and little finger remaining outside the grip and free to press forward the upper and lower ends of the shield, respectively, slanting it to glance a blow of a spear.

Within the present boundary of Bontoc Province there are three distinct patterns of wooden shields in use in three quite distinct culture areas. There is still another shield immediately beyond the western border of the province but which is believed to be produced also in the Bontoc area.

First, is the shield of the Bontoc culture area. It is usually about 3 feet long and 1 foot wide, is blackened with a greasy soot, though now and again one in original wood is seen. The upper part or "chief" of the shield is cut, leaving three points projecting several inches above the solid field; the lower end or "base" is cut, leaving two points. Across both ends of the shield is a strengthening lace of bejuco, passing through perforations from front to back. The front surface of the shield is most prominent over the deep-cut hand grip at the boss or "fess point," toward which a wing approaches on both the dexter and sinister sides of the front of the shield, being carved slightly on the field. This is the usual Bontoc shield, but some few have meaningless straight-line decorations cut in the field.

In the Tinglayan culture area, immediately north of Bontoc, the usual shield is very similar to the above, except that various sections of both the face and back of the shield are of natural wood or are colored dull red. The strengthening of bejuco lacings and the raised wings are also found.

Still farther north is the Kalinga shield -- a slim, gracefully formed shield, differing from the typical Bontoc weapon chiefly in its more graceful outline. It is of a uniform black color and has the bejuco lacings the same as the others.

The fourth variety, made at Bagnen, immediately across the Bontoc border, in Lepanto, and probably also made and certainly used near at hand in Bontoc, is quite similar to the Bontoc type but is smaller and cruder. It is uncolored, and on its front has crude drawings of snakes and frogs (or perhaps men) drawn with soot paint.

Banawi area, south of the Bontoc area. has a shield differing markedly from the others. It is longer, usually somewhat wider, and not cut at either end. The lower end is straight across at right angles to the sides; the upper end rises to a very obtuse angle at the middle. The front is usually much plainer than is that of the other shields mentioned.

Throughout the Bontoc area there is a spear with a bamboo blade, entirely a wooden weapon. The spear is employed in warfare, and is losing its place only as iron becomes plentiful enough and cheap enough to substitute for the bamboo blades or heads. Even in sections in which iron spears are relatively common the wooden spear is used much in warfare, since spears thrown at an enemy are frequently lost.

Sharp-pointed bamboo spikes are often stuck in the trails of war parties when they are returning from some foray in which they have been successful. These spikes are from about 6 inches in length, as among the people of the Bontoc area, to 3 or more feet, as among the Ibilao of southeastern Nueva Vizcaya. The latter people nightly place these long spikes, called "luk'-dun," in the trails leading to their dwellings. They are placed at a considerable angle, and would impale an intruder in the groin or upper thigh, inflicting a cruel and disabling wound. The shorter spikes either cut through the bottom of the foot or stab the instep or leg near the ankle. They are much dreaded, and, though crude, are very effective weapons.

Metal weapons

The metal spear blade or head is a product of Igorot workmanship. Baliwang, situated about six hours north of Bontoc, makes most of the metal spear blades used in the Bontoc area. Sapao, located about a day and a half to the south, makes excellent metal blades, but they seldom reach the Bontoc culture area, although blades of inferior production from Sapao are found in Ambawan, the southernmost pueblo of the area.

Baliwang has four smithies, in each of which two or three men labor, each man in a smithy performing a separate part of the work. One operates the bellows, another feeds the fire and does the heavy striking during the initial part of the work, and the other -- the real blade maker, the artist -- directs all the labor, and performs the finer and finishing parts of the blade production.

The smithies are about 12 feet square without side walls. They have a grass roof sloping to within 3 feet of the earth, enlarging the shaded area to near 20 feet square. Near one side of the room is the bellows, called "op-op'," consisting of two vertical, parallel wooden tubes about 5 feet long and 10 inches in diameter, standing side by side. Each tube has a piston or plunger, called "dot-dot';" the packing ring of the piston is of wood covered with chicken feathers, making it slightly flexible at the rim, so it fits snugly in the tube. The lower end of the bellows tubes rests in the earth, 4 inches above which a small bamboo tube leads the compressed air to the fireplace from each bellows tube. These small tubes, called "to-bong'," end near an opening through a brick at the back of the fire, and the air forced through them passes on through the brick to the burning charcoal. The outer end of the to-bong' is cut at an angle, and as the tubes end outside the opening in the brick, the air inbreathed by the bellows, as the plungers are raised, is drawn from back of the fireplace -- thus the fire is not disturbed.

The fuel is an inferior charcoal prepared by the Igorot from pine. This bellows is found throughout the Archipelago and is evidently a Malayan product. It is believed that it came to Bontoc with the Igorot from their earlier home and is not, as some say, a Chinese invention.[29] The Igorot manufacturer of metal pipes uses exactly the same kind of bellows, except that it is very much smaller, and so appears like a toy. It is poorly shown in Pl. CIX.

Much of the iron now employed in the manufacture of Igorot weapons is Chinese bar iron coming from China to the Islands at Candon, in Ilokos Sur. However, the people readily make weapons from any iron they may acquire, greatly preferring the scraps of broken Chinese cast-iron pots, vessels purchased primarily for making sugar. In his choice of cast iron the Igorot exhibits a practical knowledge of metallurgy, since cast iron makes better steel than wrought iron -- that is, as he has to work.

Ironsmith's stone hammer.

The anvils of the smithy, numbering four or five, are large rocks set solidly in the earth. The hammers are nearly all stone, though some of the workmen have a small iron hammer used in finishing the weapons.

There are several varieties of stone hammers. One weighing about 30 pounds is 16 inches long, 10 inches wide, and from 4 to 6 inches thick. An inch-deep groove is cut in both edges of the hammer, and into these grooves the short, double wooden handle is attached by a withe. Another hammer, similar to the above in shape and attachment, is about one-third its size and weight. There is a still smaller hammer lashed with leather bands to a single, straight wooden handle; and there is also a round hammer stone about 3 inches in diameter without handle or attachment, which hammer, together with the larger one last mentioned, is largely superseded in some of the smithies by the metal hammer.

The bellows operator sits squatting on a slight platform the height of the bellows, and constantly works the plungers up and down with rhythmic strokes.

Two men at first handle the hot iron -- one, the real blade maker, holds the white-hot metal with long-handled iron pinchers (purchased in Candon) and his helper wields the 30-pound hammer. He stands with legs well apart, grasps the heavy hammer with both hands, and swings it back and forth between his legs. The blow is struck at the downward, backward swing.

These smiths weld iron, and also temper it to make steel. The following detailed picture of a welding observed in a Baliwang smithy may be duplicated there any day. The two pieces of iron to be welded were separately heated a dull red. One was then laid on the other and both were cooled with water. Wet earth, gathered for the occasion at the side of the smithy, was then put over them; while still covered they were inserted again in the fire. When red-hot they were withdrawn, the little mound of earth covering the two pieces of iron being still in place but having been brought also to a red heat. A few light blows fell on the red mass, and it was again returned to the fire. Four times the iron was withdrawn and received a few blows with a light hammer wielded by the master smith. On being withdrawn the fifth time half a dozen blows were struck by the helper with the 30-pound hammer. Again the iron was heated, but when removed the sixth time the welding was evidently considered finished, as the shaping of the weapon was then begun. Weldings made by these smiths seem to be complete.

The tempering done by the Igorot is crude, and is such as may be seen in any country blacksmith shop in the States. The iron is heated and is tempered by cooling in a small wooden trough of water. There is great difference in the quality of the steel turned out by the Igorot, even by the same man, though some men are recognized as more skillful than others.

There are four styles of spear blades made by Baliwang. The one most common is called "fal-feg'." It is a simple, single-barbed blade, and ranges from 2 inches to 6 inches in length. This style of blade is the most used in warfare, and the smaller, lighter blades are considered better for this purpose than the heavier ones.

The fang'-kao, or barbless lance blade, is next common in use. It is not a war blade, but is used almost entirely in killing carabaos and hogs. There is one notable exception to this statement -- Ambawan has almost no other class of spear. These blades range from 4 to 12 or 14 inches in length.

The other two blades, si-na-la-wi'-tan and kay-yan', are relatively rare. The former is quite similar to the fal-feg', except that instead of the single pair of barbs there are other barbs -- say, from one to ten pairs. This spear is not considered at all serviceable as a hunting spear, and is not used in war as much as is the fal-feg'. It is prized highly as an anito scarer. When a man passes alone in the mountains anito are very prone to walk with him; however, if the traveler carries a si-na-la-wi'-tan, anito will not molest him, since they are afraid when they see the formi-dable array of barbs.

Kay-yan' is a gracefully formed blade not used in hunting, and employed less in war than is si-na-la-wi'-tan. Though the Igorot has almost nothing in his culture for purely aesthetic purposes, yet he ascribes no purpose for the kay-yan' -- he says it looks pretty; but I have seen it carried to war by war parties.

The pueblo of Sapao makes superior-looking steel weapons, though many Igorot claim the steel of the Baliwang spear is better than that from Sapao. In Quiangan I saw a fang'-kao, or lance-shaped blade made in Sapao, having six faces on each side. The five lines separating the faces ran from the tang to the point of the blade, and were as regular and perfect as though machine made. The best class of Sapao blades is readily distinguishable by its regular lines and the smooth and perfect surface finish.

All spearheads are fastened to the wooden shaft by a short haft or tang inserted in the wood. An iron ferrule or a braided bejuco ferrule is employed to strengthen the shaft where the tang is inserted. A conical iron ferrule or cap is also placed on the butt of the shaft. This ferrule is often used, as the spear is always stuck in the earth close at hand when the warrior works any distance from home; and as he passes along the steep mountain trails or carries heavy burdens he commonly uses the spear shaft as a staff.

The spear shafts are made by the owner of the weapon, it not being customary for anyone to produce them for sale. Some of them are rather attractively decorated with brass and copper studs, and a few have red and yellow bejuco ferrules near the blade. In some pueblos of the Bontoc area, as at Mayinit, spear shafts are worked down and eventually smoothed and finished by a flexible, bamboo knife-blade machine. It consists of about a dozen blades 8 or 10 inches in length, fas-tened together side by side with string. The blades lie one overlapping the other like the slats of an American window shutter. Each projecting blade is sharpened to a chisel edge. The machine is grasped in the hand, as shown in fig. 6, and is slid up and down the shaft with a slight twisting movement obtained by bending the wrist. The machine becomes a flexible, many-bladed plane.

Baliwang alone makes the genuine Bontoc battle-ax. It is a strong, serviceable blade of good temper, and is hafted to a short, strong, straight wooden handle which is strengthened by a ferrule of iron or braided bejuco. The ax has a slender point opposed to the bit or cutting edge of the blade. This point is often thrust in the earth and the upturned blade used as a stationary knife, on which the

Igorot cuts meats and other substances by drawing them lengthwise along the sharp edge. The bit of the ax is at a small angle with the front and back edges of the blade, and is nearly a straight line. The axes are kept keen and sharp by whetstones collected and preserved solely for the purpose. Besao, near Sagada, quarries and barters a good grade of whetstone.

Bamboo spear-shaft dresser.

A slender, long-handled battle-ax now and then comes into the area in trade from the north. Balbelasan, of old Abra Province, but now in the northern part of extended Bontoc Province, is one of the pueblos which produce this beautiful ax. The blade is longer and very much slimmer than the Bontoc blade, but its marked distinguishing feature is the shape of the cutting edge. The blade is ground on two straight lines joined together by a short curved line, giving the edge the striking form of the beak of a rapacious bird. The slender, graceful handle, always fitted with a long iron ferrule, has a process on the under side near the middle. The handle is also usually fitted with a decorated metal ferrule at the tip and frequently is decorated for its full length with bands of brass or tin, or with sheets of either metal artistically incised.

The Balbelasan ax is not used by the pueblos making it, or at least by many of them, but finds its field of usefulness east and northeast of Bontoc pueblo as far as the foothills of the mountains west of the Rio Grande de Cagayan. I was told by the Kalinga of this latter region that the people in the mountain close to the Cagayan in the vicinity of Cabagan Nuevo, Isabela Province, also use this ax.

In the southern and western part of the Bontoc area the battle-ax shares place with the bolo, the sole hand weapon of the Igorot of adjoining Lepanto, Benguet, and Nueva Vizcaya Provinces.

The bolo within the Bontoc area comes from Sapao and from the Ilokano people of the west coast. The southern pueblo in the Bontoc area, Ambawan, uses the bolo of Sapao to the entire exclusion of the battle-ax. Tulubin, the next pueblo to Ambawan, and only an hour from it, uses almost solely the Baliwang battle-ax. Such pueblos as Titipan and Antedao, about three hours west of Bontoc, use both the ax and bolo, while the pueblos further west, as Agawa, Sagada, Balili, Alap, etc., use the bolo exclusively -- frequently an Ilokano weapon.

The Sapao bolo is, in appearance, superior to that of Ilokano manufacture. It is a broad blade swelling markedly toward the center, and is somewhat similar in shape to the barong of the Sulu Moro of the Sulu Archipelago. This weapon finds its chief field of use in the Quiangan and Banawi areas. In these districts the bolo is fitted with an open scabbard, and the bright blade presents a novel appearance lying exposed against the red scabbard. The Igorot manufacturer of the bolo does not make the scabbard, and most of the bolos used within the Bontoc area are sheathed in the closed wooden scabbard commonly found in Lepanto and Benguet.

Pipe production, and smoking

The Igorot of Bontoc area make pipes of wood, clay, and metal. All their pipes have small bores and bowls. In Benguet a wooden pipe is commonly made with a bowl an inch and a half in diameter; it has a large bore also. In Banawi I obtained a wooden pipe with a bowl 8 1/4 inches in circumference and 4 inches in height, but having a bore averaging only half an inch in diameter.

Nearly all pueblos make the pipes they use, but pipes of clay and metal are man-ufactured by the Igorot for Igorot trade. I never learned that wooden pipes are made by them for commercial purposes.

The wooden pipe of the area varies from simple tubular forms, exactly like a mod-ern cigar holder, to those having bowls set at right angle to the stem. All wooden pipes are whittled by the men, and some of them are very graceful in form and have an excellent polish. They are made of at least three kinds of wood -- ga-sa'-tan, la-no'-ti, and gi-gat'. Most pipes -- wooden, clay, or metal -- have separable stems.

A few men in Agawa, a pueblo near the western border of the area, make beauti-ful clay pipes, called "ki-na-lo'-sab." The clay is carefully macerated between the fingers until it is soft and fine. It is then roughly shaped by the fingers, and after-wards, when partially hardened, is finished with a set of five light, wooden tools.

The finished bowls are in three different colors. When baked about nine hours the pipes come forth gray. Those coming out red have been burned about twelve hours, usually all night. The black ones are made by reburning the red bowls about half an hour in palay straw.

Two men in Sabangan and one each in Genugan and Takong -- all western pueb-los -- manufacture metal "anito" pipes. To-day brass wire and the metal of car-tridge shells are most commonly employed in making these pipes.

The process of manufacture is elaborate and very interesting. First a beeswax model is made the exact size and shape of the finished metal pipe. All beeswax, called "a-tid'," used in pipe making comes from Barlig through Kanu, and the illustration (Pl. CVIII) shows the form in which it passes in commerce in the area. A small amount of wax is softened by a fire until it can be flattened in the palm of the hand. It is then rolled around a stick the size of the bore in the bowl. The outside of the wax bowl is next designed as is shown in the illustration (Pl. CVIII). A careful examination of the illustration will show that the design represents the sitting figure of a man. He is resting his elbows on his knees and holding his lower jaw in his hands -- eyes, ears, nose, mouth, and fingers are all represented. This design is made in the wax with a small knife. The wax for the short stem piece is flattened and folded around a stick the size of the bore of the stem. The stem piece is then set into the bowl and the design which was started on the bowl is continued over the stem.

When the wax pipe is completed a projecting point of wax is attached to the base of the pipe, and the whole is imbedded in a clay jacket, the point of wax, however, projecting from the jacket. The clay used by the pipe maker is obtained in a pit at Pingad in the vicinity of Genugan. Around the wax point a clay funnel is built. The clay mold, called "bang-bang'-a," is thoroughly baked by a fire. In less than an hour the mold is hardened and brown, and the wax pipe within it has melted and the wax been poured out of the mold through the gate or opening left by the melting point of wax, leaving the mold empty.

A small Malayan bellows, called "op-op'," the exact duplicate in miniature of the double tubular bellows described in the preceding section on "metal weapons," furnishes the draught for a small charcoal fire. The funnel of the clay mold is filled with pieces of metal, and the entire thing is buried in the fired charcoal. In fifteen minutes the metal melts and runs down through the gate at the bottom of the funnel into the hollow, wax-lined mold. Since the entire mold is hot, the metal does not cool or harden promptly, and the pipe maker taps and jars the mold in order to make the metal penetrate and fill every part.

The mold is set aside to cool and is then broken away from the metal core. Today the pipe maker possesses a file with which to smooth and clean the crude pipe. Formerly all that labor, and it is extensive, was performed with stones.

It requires two men to make the "anito" pipes -- tin-ak-ta'-go. One superintends all the work and performs the finest of it, and the second pumps the bellows and smooths and cleans the pipe after it is cast. The two men make four pipes per day, but the purchaser of an "anito" pipe puts days of toil on the metal, smoothing and perfecting it by cleaning and digging out the design until it becomes really a beautiful bit of primitive art.

When a pueblo wants a few tin-ak-ta'-go it sends for the manufacturer, and he comes to the pueblo with his helper and remains as long as necessary. Ay-o'-na, of Genugan, annually visits Titipan, Ankiling, Sagada, Bontoc, and Samoki. He usually furnishes all material, and receives a peseta for each pipe, but the pueblo furnishes the food. In this way a pipe maker is a journeyman about half the year.

Tukukan makes a smooth, cast-metal pipe, called "pin-e-po-yong'," and Baliwang makes tubular iron pipes at her smithies. They are hammered out and pounded and welded over a core. I have seen several of such excellent workmanship that the welded seam could not be detected on the surface.

In the western part of the area both men and women smoke, and some smoke almost constantly. Throughout the areas occupied by Christians children of 6 or 7 years smoke a great deal. I have repeatedly seen girls not over 6 years of age smoking rolls of tobacco, "cigars," a foot long and more than an inch in diameter, but in Bontoc area small children do not smoke. In most of the area women do not smoke at all, and boys seldom smoke until they reach maturity.

In Bontoc the tobacco leaf for smoking is rolled up and pinched off in small sections an inch or so in length. These pieces are then wrapped in a larger section of leaf. When finished for the pipe the tobacco resembles a short stub of a cigar. Only half a dozen whiffs are generally taken at a smoke, and the pipe with its tobacco is then tucked under the edge of the pocket hat. Four pipes in five as they are seen sticking from a man's hat show that the owners stopped smoking long before they exhausted their pipes.

<u>Fire making</u>

The oldest instrument for fire making used by the Bontoc Igorot is now seldom found. However, practically all boys of a dozen years know how to make and use it.

It is called "co-li'-li," and is a friction machine made of two pieces of dry bamboo. A 2-foot section of dead and dry bamboo is split lengthwise and in one piece a small area of the stringy tissue lining the tube is splintered and picked quite loose. Immediately over this, on the outside of the tube, a narrow groove is cut at right angles to it. This piece of bamboo becomes the stationary lower part of the fire machine. One edge of the other half of the original tube is sharpened like a chisel blade. This section is grasped in both hands, one at each end, and is at first slowly and heavily, afterwards more rapidly, drawn back and forth through the groove of the stationary bamboo, making a small conical pile of dry dust beneath the opening.

After a dozen strokes the sides of the groove and the edge of the friction piece burn brown, presently a smell of smoke is plain, and before three dozen strokes have been made smoke may be seen. Usually before one hundred strokes a larger volume of smoke tells that the dry dust constantly falling on the pile has grown more and more charred until finally a tiny friction-fired particle falls, carrying combustion to the already heated dust cone.

The machine is carefully raised, and, if the fire is permanently kindled, the pinch of smoldering dust is inserted in a wisp of dry grass or other easily inflammable material; in a minute or two flames burst forth, and the fire may be transferred where desired.

The pal-ting', the world-wide flint and steel-percussion fire machine, is found with all Bontoc men.

At Sagada there is a ledge of exposed and crumbling rock from which most of the men of the western part of the Bontoc culture area obtain their "flint." The "steel" is any piece of iron which may be had -- probably a part of the ferrule from the butt of a spear shaft is used more than is any other one kind of iron.

The pal-ting' is secured either in a very small basket or a leather roll which is fastened closed by a string. In this receptacle a small amount of dry tree cotton is also carried. The pal-ting' receptacle is carried about in the large bag hanging at the girdle.

Fire is made by a tiny percussion-heated particle of the stone as it flies away under the sharp, glancing blow of the "steel" and catches in the dry cotton held by the thumb nail on the upper surface of the stone.

If the fire maker wishes to light his pipe, he tucks the smoldering cotton lightly into his roll of tobacco; a few draws are sufficient to ignite the pipeful. If an out-of-door fire is desired the cotton is first used to ignite a dry bunch of grass. Should the fire be needed in the dwelling, the cotton is placed on charcoal. Blowing and care will produce a good, blazing wood fire in a few minutes.

To-day friction matches are known throughout the area, although probably not one person in one hundred has ever owned a box of matches.

The fire syringe, common west of Bontoc Province among the Tinguian, is not known in the Bontoc culture area.

Division of labor

Under this title must be grouped all forms of occupations which are considered necessary to the life of the pueblo.

Up to the age of 5 or 6 years Bontoc children do not work. As has been said in a previous chapter, during the months of April and May many little girls from 5 to 10 work and play together for long hours daily gathering a few varieties of wild plants close about the pueblo for food for the pigs. This labor is unnecessary as soon as the camote vines become large enough for gathering. During June and July these same girls gather the camote vines for pig food. About August this labor falls to the women.

Mention has also been made of the fact that during the latter half of April and May the boys and girls of all ages from 6 or 7 years to 13 or 14 guard the palay sementeras against the birds from earliest dawn till heavy twilight.

Little girls often help about the dwelling by paring camotes for the forthcoming meal.

At all times the elder children, both boys and girls, are baby tenders while their parents work.

Man is the sole hunter and warrior, and he alone fishes when traps or snares are employed.

Only men go to the mountains to cut and bring home firewood and lumber for building purposes; widowed women sometimes bring home dead fallen wood found along the trails. Only men construct the various private and public buildings. They alone build the stone dikes of the sementeras and construct the irrigating ditches and dams; they transport to the pueblo most of the harvested palay. They manufacture and vend basi, and prepare the salted meats. They make all weapons, and all implements and utensils for field and household labors. Contrary to a widespread custom among primitive people, as has been noted, the Igorot man constructs all basket work, whether hats, baskets, trays, or ornaments, and bindings of weapons and implements. Men are the workers of all metal and stone. They are the only cargadors, though in the Kiapa area of Benguet Province women sometimes go on the trails as paid burden bearers for Americans.

Only men are said to tattoo and circumcise. They determine the days of rest and of ceremony for the pueblo, and all pueblo ceremonies are in their hands; so also are the ceremonies of the ato -- only men are "priests," except for private house-hold ceremonials.

Men constitute the "control element" of the pueblo. They are the legislative, exec-utive, and judicial power for the pueblo and each ato; they are considered the wis-dom of their people, and they alone, it is said, give public advice on important matters.

The woman is the only weaver of fabrics and the only spinner of the materials of which the fabrics are made. On the west coast the Ilokano men do a great deal of the spinning, but the Igorot man has not imitated them in the industry, though he has often seen them. Women are the sole potters of Samoki, and they alone transport and vend their wares to other pueblos. In the Mayinit salt industry only the woman tends the salt house, gathering the crude salt solution.

Only the women plant the rice seed, and they alone transplant the palay; they also care for the growing plants and harvest most of the crops. In the transplanting and harvesting of palay the woman is given credit for greater dexterity than the man; men harvest palay only when sufficient women can not be found. Women plant, care for, harvest, and transport to the pueblo all camotes, millet, maize, and beans.

The men and women together construct and repair irrigated sementeras, men usually digging the earth while the women transport it. Together they prepare the soil of irrigated sementeras, and carry manure to them from the pigpens. Men at times do the women's work in harvesting, and women sometimes assist the men to carry the harvest to the pueblo. Either threshes out and hulls the rice, though the woman does more than half this work. Both prepare foods for cooking, cook the meals, and serve them. Both bring water from the river for household uses, though the woman brings the greater part. Each tends the babe while the other works in the field. Both care for the chickens and pigs, even to cooking the food for the latter. Men and women catch fish by hand in the river, manufacture tapui, and in the salt industry both evaporate the salt solution and vend the salt.

In the treatment of the sick and the driving out of afflicting anito, men and women alike serve.

Little work is demanded of the old people, though the labors they perform are of great value to the pueblo, as the strong are thus given more time for a vigorous industrial life.

Great service is rendered the pueblo by the councils of the old men, and they are the "priests" of all ceremonials, except those of the household.

The old men do practically nothing at manual labor in the field. However, numbers of old men and women guard the palay sementeras from the birds, and they frequently tend their grandchildren about the pueblo. They also bring water from the river to the dwelling.

Old women seem generally busy. They prepare and cook foods, and they spin materials for women's skirts and girdles. The blind women share in these labors, even going to the river for water.

By labor of the group is meant the common effort of two or more people whose everyday possessions and accumulations are not in common, as they are in a family, to perform some definite labor which can be better done by such effort than by the separate labors of the several members of the group.

A pueblo war probably represents the largest necessary group-occupation, because at such time all available warriors unite in a concerted effort. Next to this, though possibly coming before it, is the group assembled for the erection of a dwelling. As has been noted, all dwellings are built by a group, and when a rich man's domicile is to be put up a great many people assemble -- the men to erect the dwelling, and the women to prepare and cook the food. A great deal of agricultural labor is performed by the group. New irrigation ditches are built by, or at the instance of, all those who will benefit by them. The dam built annually across the river at Bontoc pueblo is constructed by all, or at the instance of all, who benefit from the additional irrigation water. Wild carabaos are hunted by a group of men, and the domestic carabaos can be caught only when several men surround and attack them.

All interpueblo commerce is carried on by a group of people. Almost never does a person pass from one pueblo to another alone, and commerce is the chief thing which causes the interpueblo communication. These groups of traveling merchants consist of from two or three persons to a dozen or more -- as in the case of the Samoki pottery sellers.

Wages, and exchange of labor

The woman receives the same wage as the man. There are two reasons why she should. First, all labor is by the day, so the facts of sickness and maternity never keep the woman from her labor when she is expected and is depended on; and, second, she is as efficient in the labors she performs as is the man -- in some she is recognized as more efficient. She does as much work as a man, and does it as well or better. It is worth so much to have a certain work done in a particular time, and the Igorot pays the wage to whomever does the work. The growing boy or girl who performs the same labors as an adult receives an equal wage.

Not only do the people work by the day, but they are paid daily also. Every night the laborer goes to the dwelling of his employer and receives the wage; the wages of unmarried children are paid to their parents.

To all classes of laborers dinner and sometimes supper is supplied. For weeding and thinning the sementeras of young palay and for watching the fruiting palay to drive away the birds, the only wage is these two meals. But this labor is light, and frightening away the birds is usually the work of children or very old people who can not perform hard labors. In all classes of work for which only food is given, much time is left to the laborers in which the men may weave their basket work and the women spin the bark-fiber thread for skirts.

Five manojos of palay is the daily wage for all laborers except those mentioned in the last paragraph. This is the wage of the wood gatherer in the mountains, of the builder of granaries, sementeras, irrigating ditches, and dikes, and of those who prepare soils and who plant and harvest crops.

There is much exchange of labor between individuals, and even between large groups of people, such as members of an ato. Formerly exchange of labor was practiced slightly more than at present, but to-day, as has been noted, all dwellings are built by the unpaid labor of those who come for the accompanying feast and "good time," and because their own dwellings were or will be built by such labor. A great deal of agricultural labor is now paid for in kind; practically all the available labor in an ato turns out to help a member when a piece of work is urgent. However, it is not customary for poor people to exchange their labor, since they constantly need food for those dependent on them. When the poor man desires a wage for his toil he needs only to tell some rich person that he wishes to work for him -- both understand that a wage will be paid.

Distribution

By the term "distribution" is here meant the ordinary division of the productions of Bontoc area among the several classes of Igorot in the area -- in other words, what is each person's share of that which the area produces?

It must be said that distribution is very equitable. Wages are uniform. No man or set of men habitually spoils another's accumulations by exacting from him a tax or "rake off." There is no form of gambling or winning another's earnings. There are no slaves or others who labor without wages; children do not retain their own wages until they marry, but they inherit all their parents' possessions. There is almost no usury. There is no indigent class, and the rich men toil as industriously in the fields as do the poor -- though I must say I never knew a rich man to go as cargador on the trail.

Theft

Higher forms of society, even such society as the Christianized Filipinos of the coastal cities, produce and possess a considerable number of people who live and often raise families on personal property stolen and carried away from the lawful owners. Almost no thief in the Bontoc area escapes detection -- the society is too simple for him to escape -- and when he is apprehended he restores more than he took away. There is no opportunity for a thief class to develop, consequently there is no chance for theft to distort the usual equitable division of products.

Conquest

Conquest, or the act of gaining control and acquisition of another's property by force of arms, is not operative in the Bontoc area. Moro and perhaps other southern Malayan people frequently capture people by conquest whom they enslave, and they also bring back much valuable loot in the shape of metals and the much-prized large earthen jars.

Certain Igorot, as those of Asin, make forcible conquests on their neighbors and carry away persons for slavery. Asin made a raid westward into Suyak of Lepanto Province in 1900, and some American miners joined the expedition of natives to try to recover the captives. But Bontoc has no such conquests, and, since the people have long ago ceased migration, there is no conquest of territory. In their interpueblo warfare loot is seldom carried away. There is practically nothing in the form of movable and easily controlled valuable possessions, such as domestic cattle, horses, or carabaos, so the usual equilibrium of Bontoc property distribution has little to disturb it.

The primitive agriculturist is thought of in history as the victim of warlike neighbors who make predatory forays against him, repeatedly robbing him of his hard-earned accumulations. In Igorot land this is not the case. There are no savage or barbaric people, except the Negritos who are not agriculturists. Sometimes, however, some of the Igorot groups descend to the settlements of the Christians in the lowlands and in the night bring back a few carabaos and hogs. The Igorot of Quiangan are noted for such robberies made on the pueblos of Bagabag and

Ibung to the south in central Nueva Vizcaya. Sometimes, also, one Igorot group speaks of another as Busol, or enemy, and says the Busol come to rob them in the night. I believe, however, from inquiries made, that relatively very small amounts of property pass from one Igorot group to another by robbery or conquest.

The Bontoc Igorot appears to be in a transition stage, not usually emphasized, between the communism of the savage or barbarian in which each person is said to have a share as long as necessities last, and the more advanced forms of society in which many classes are able to divert to their own advantage much which otherwise would not come to them. The Igorot is not a communist, neither in any sense does he get the monopolist's share. He is living a life of such natural production that he enjoys the fruits of his labors in a fairer way than do many of the men beneath him or above him in culture.

Consumption

Under this title will be considered simply the foods and beverages of the people. No attempt will be made to treat of consumption in its breadth as it appears to the economist.

Foods

There are few forms of animal life about the Igorot that he will not and does not eat. The exceptions are mainly insectivora, and such larger animals as the mythology of the Igorot says were once men -- as the monkey, serpent-eagle, crow, snake, etc. However, he is not wholly lacking in taste and preference in his foods. Of his common vegetable foods he frequently said he prefers, first, beans; second, rice; third, maize; fourth, camotes; fifth, millet.

Rice is the staple food, and most families have sufficient for subsistence during the year. When rice is needed for food bunches of the palay, as tied up at the harvest, are brought and laid in the small pocket of the wooden mortar where they are threshed out of the fruit head. One or two mortarsful is thus threshed and put aside on a winnowing tray. When sufficient has been obtained the grain is put again in the mortar and pounded to remove the pellicle. Usually only sufficient rice is threshed and cleaned for the consumption of one or two days. When the pellicle has been pounded loose the grain is winnowed on a large round tray by a series of dexterous movements, removing all chaff and dirt with scarcely the loss of a kernel of good rice.

The work of threshing, hulling, and winnowing usually falls to the women and girls, but is sometimes performed by the men when their women are preoccupied. At one time when an American wished two or three bushels of palay threshed, as horse food for the trail, three Bontoc men performed the work in the classic tread-mill manner. They spread a mat on the earth, covered it with palay, and then tread, or rather "rubbed," out the kernels with their bare feet. They often scraped up the mass with their feet, bunching it and rubbing it in a way that strongly suggested hands.

Rice is cooked in water without salt. An earthern pot is half filled with the grain and is then filled to the brim with cold water. In about twenty minutes the rice is cooked, filling the vessel, and the water is all absorbed or evaporated. If there is no great haste, the rice sets ten or fifteen minutes longer while the kernels dry out somewhat. As the Igorot cooks rice, or, for that matter, as the native anywhere in the Islands cooks it, the grains are not mashed and mussed together, but each kernel remains whole and separate from the others.

Cooked rice, ma-kan', is almost always eaten with the fingers, being crowded into the mouth with the back of the thumb. In Bontoc, Samoki, Titipan, Mayinit, and Ganang salt is either sprinkled on the rice after it is dished out or is tasted from the finger tips during the eating. In some pueblos, as at Tulubin, almost no salt is eaten at any time. When rice alone is eaten at a meal a family of five adults eats about ten Bontoc manojo of rice per day.

Beans are cooked in the form of a thick soup, but without salt. Beans and rice, each cooked separately, are frequently eaten together; such a dish is called "sib-fan'." Salt is eaten with sib-fan' by those pueblos which commonly consume salt.

Maize is husked, silked, and then cooked on the cob. It is eaten from the cob, and no salt is used either in the cooking or eating.

Camotes are eaten raw a great deal about the pueblo, the sementera, and the trail. Before they are cooked they are pared and generally cut in pieces about 2 inches long; they are boiled without salt. They are eaten alone at many meals, but are relished best when eaten with rice. They are always eaten from the fingers.

One dish, called "ke-le'-ke," consists of camotes, pared and sliced, and cooked and eaten with rice. This is a ceremonial dish, and is always prepared at the lis-lis ceremony and at a-su-fal'-i-wis or sugar-making time.

Camotes are always prepared immediately before being cooked, as they blacken very quickly after paring.

Millet is stored in the harvest bunches, and must be threshed before it is eaten. After being threshed in the wooden mortar the winnowed seeds are again returned to the mortar and crushed. This crushed grain is cooked as is rice and without salt. It is eaten also with the hands -- "fingers" is too delicate a term.

Some other vegetable foods are also cooked and eaten by the Igorot. Among them is taro which, however, is seldom grown in the Bontoc area. Outside the area, both north and south, there are large sementeras of it cultivated for food. Several wild plants are also gathered, and the leaves cooked and eaten as the American eats "greens."

The Bontoc Igorot also has preferences among his regular flesh foods. The chicken is prized most; next he favors pork; third, fish; fourth, carabao; and fifth, dog. Chicken, pork (except wild hog), and dog are never eaten except ceremonially. Fish and carabao are eaten on ceremonial occasions, but are also eaten at other times -- merely as food.

The interesting ceremonial killing, dressing, and eating of chickens is presented elsewhere, in the sections on "Death" and "Ceremonials." It is unnecessary to repeat the information here, as the processes are everywhere the same, excepting that generally no part of the fowl, except the feathers, is unconsumed -- head, feet, intestines, everything, is devoured.

The hog is ceremonially killed by cutting its throat, not by "sticking," as is the American custom, but the neck is cut, half severing the head. At Ambuklao, on the Agno River in Benguet Province, I saw a hog ceremonially killed by having a round-pointed stick an inch in diameter pushed and twisted into it from the right side behind the foreleg, through and between the ribs, and into the heart. The animal bled internally, and, while it was being cut up by four men with much ceremony and show, the blood was scooped from the rib basin where it had gathered, and was mixed with the animal's brains. The intestines were then emptied by drawing between thumb and fingers, and the blood and brain mixture poured into them from the stomach as a funnel. A string of blood-and-brain sausages resulted, when the intestines were cooked. The mouth of the Bontoc hog is held or tied shut until the animal is dead. The Benguet hog could be heard for fifteen minutes at least a quarter of a mile.

After the Bontoc hog is killed it is singed, cut up, and all put in the large shallow iron boiler. When cooked it is cut into smaller pieces, which are passed around to those assembled at the ceremonial.

Fish are eaten both ceremonially and privately whenever they may be obtained. The small fish, the kacho, are in no way cleaned or dressed. Two or three times I saw them cooked and eaten ceremonially, and was told they are prepared the same way for private consumption. The fish, scarcely any over 2 inches in length, were strung on twisted green-grass strings about 6 inches in length. Several of these strings were tied together and placed in an olla of water. When cooked they were lifted out, the strings broken apart, and the fish stripped off into a wooden bowl. Salt was then liberally strewn over them. A large green leaf was brought as a plate for each person present, and the fish were divided again and again until each had an equal share. However, the old men present received double share, and were served before the others. At one time a man was present with a nursing babe in his arms, and he was given two leaves, or two shares, though no one expected the babe could eat its share. After the fish food was passed to each, the broth was also liberally salted and then poured into several wooden bowls. At one fish feast platters of cooked rice and squash were also brought and set among the people. Handful after handful of solid food followed its predecessor rapidly to the always-crammed mouth. The fish was eaten as one might eat sparingly of a delicacy, and the broth was drunk now and then between mouthfuls.

Two other fish are also eaten by the Igorot of the area, the liling, about 4 to 6 inches in length -- also cooked and eaten without dressing -- and the chalit, a large fish said to acquire the length of 4 feet.

Several small animals, crustaceans and mollusks, gathered in the river and picked up in the sementeras by the women, are cooked and eaten. All these are considered similar to fish and are eaten similarly. Among these is a bright-red crab called "agkama."[30] This is boiled and all eaten except part of the back shell and the hard "pinchers." A shrimp-like crustacean obtained in the irrigated sementeras is also boiled and eaten entire. A few mollusks are eaten after being cooked. One, called kitan, I have seen eaten many times; it is a snail-like animal, and after being boiled it is sucked into the mouth after the apex of the shell has been bitten or broken off. Two other animals said to be somewhat similar are called finga and lischug.

The carabao is killed by spearing and, though also eaten simply as food, it is seldom killed except on ceremonial occasions, such as marriages, funerals, the building of a dwelling, and peace and war feasts whether actual events at the time or feasts in commemoration.

The chief occasion for eating carabao merely as a food is when an animal is injured or ill at a time when no ceremonial event is at hand. The animal is then killed and eaten. All is eaten that can be masticated. The animal is neither skinned, singed, nor scraped. All is cut up and cooked together -- hide, hair, hoofs, intestines, and head, excepting the horns. Carabao is generally not salted in cooking, and the use of salt in eating the flesh depends on the individual eater.

Sometimes large pieces of raw carabao meat are laid on high racks near the dwelling and "dried" in the sun. There are several such racks in Bontoc, and one can know a long distance from them whether they hold "dried" meat. If one pueblo, in the area exceeds another in the strength and unpleasantness of its "dried" meat it is Mayinit, where on the occasion of a visit there a very small piece of meat jammed on a stick-like a "taffy stick" -- and joyfully sucked by a 2-year-old babe successfully bombarded and depopulated our camp.

Various meats, called "it-tag'," as carabao and pork, are "preserved" by salting down in large bejuco-bound gourds, called "fa'-lay," or in tightly covered ollas, called "tu-u'-nan." All pueblos in the area (except Ambawan, which has an unexplained taboo against eating carabao) thus store away meats, but Bitwagan, Sadanga, and Tukukan habitually salt large quantities in the fa'-lay. Meats are kept thus two or three years, though of course the odor is vile.

The dog ranks last in the list of regular flesh foods of the Bontoc man. In the Benguet area it ranks second, pork receiving the first place. The Ibilao does not eat dog -- his dog is a hunter and guard, giving alarm of the approaching enemy.

In Bontoc the dog is eaten only on ceremonial occasions. Funerals and marriages are probably more often celebrated by a dog feast than are any other of their ceremonials. The animal's mouth is held closed and his legs secured while he is killed by cutting the throat. Then his tail is cut off close to the body -- why, I could not learn, but I once saw it, and am told it always is so. The animal is singed in the fire and the crisped hair rubbed off with sticks and hands, after which it is cut up and boiled, and then further cut up and eaten as is the carabao meat.

Young babies are sometimes fed hard-boiled fresh eggs, but the Igorot otherwise does not eat "fresh" eggs, though he does eat large numbers of stale ones. He prefers to wait, as one of them said, "until there is something in the egg to eat." He invariably brings stale or developing eggs to the American until he is told to bring fresh ones. It is not alone the Igorot who has this peculiar preference -- the same condition exists widespread in the Archipelago.

Locusts, or cho'-chon, are gathered, cooked, and eaten by the Igorot, as by all other natives in the Islands. They are greatly relished, but may be had in Bontoc only irregularly -- perhaps once or twice for a week or ten days each year, or once in two years. They are cooked in boiling water and later dried, whereupon they become crisp and sweet. By some Igorot they are stored away, but I can not say whether they are kept in Bontoc any considerable time after cooking.

The locusts come in storms, literally like a pelting, large-flaked snowstorm, driving across the country for hours and even days at a time. All Igorot have large scoop nets for catching them and immense bottle-like baskets in which to put them and transport them home. The locust catcher runs along in the storm, and, whirling around in it with his large net, scoops in the victims. Many families sometimes wander a week or more catching locusts when they come to their vicinity, and cease only when miles from home. The cry of "enemy" will scarcely set an Igorot community astir sooner than will the cry of "cho'-chon." The locust is looked upon by them as a very manna from heaven. Pi-na-lat' is a food of cooked locusts pounded and mixed with uncooked rice. All is salted down in an olla and tightly covered over with a vegetable leaf or a piece of cloth. When it is eaten the mixture is cooked, though this cooking does not kill the strong odor of decay.

Other insect foods are also eaten. I once saw a number of men industriously robbing the large white "eggs" from an ant nest in a tree. The nest was built of leaves attached by a web. Into the bottom of this closed pocket the men poked a hole with a long stick, letting a pint or more of the white pupae run out on a winnowing tray on the earth. From this tray the furious ants were at length driven, and the eggs taken home for cooking.

<u>Beverages</u>

The Igorot drinks water much more than any other beverage. On the trail, though carrying loads while the American may walk empty handed, he drinks less than the American. He seldom drinks while eating, though he makes a beverage said to be drunk only at mealtime. After meals he usually drinks water copiously.

Ba-si is the Igorot name of the fermented beverage prepared from sugar cane. "Ba-si," under various names, is found widespread throughout the Islands. The Bontoc man makes his ba-si in December. He boils the expressed juice of the sugar cane about six hours, at which time he puts into it a handful of vegetable ferment obtained from a tree called "tub-fig'." This vegetable ferment is gathered from the tree as a flower or young fruit; it is dried and stored in the dwelling for future use. The brewed liquid is poured into a large olla, the flat-bottom variety called "fu-o-foy'" manufactured expressly for ba-si, and then is tightly covered over and set away in the granary. In five days the ferment has worked sufficiently, and the beverage may be drunk. It remains good about four months, for during the fifth or sixth month it turns very acid.

Ba-si is manufactured by the men alone. Tukukan and Titipan manufacture it to sell to other pueblos; it is sold for about half a peso per gallon. It is drunk quite a good deal during the year, though mostly on ceremonial occasions. Men frequently carry a small amount of it with them to the sementeras when they guard them against the wild hogs during the long nights. They say it helps to keep them warm. One glass of ba-si will intoxicate a person not accustomed to drink it, though the Igorot who uses it habitually may drink two or three glasses before intoxication. Usually a man drinks only a few swallows of it at a time, and I never saw an Igorot intoxicated except during some ceremony and then not more than a dozen in several months. Women never drink ba-si.

Ta-pu-i is a fermented drink made from rice, the cha-yet'-it variety, they say, grown in Bontoc pueblo. It is a very sweet and sticky rice when cooked. This beverage also is found practically everywhere in the Archipelago. Only a small amount of the cha-yet'-it is grown by Bontoc pueblo. To manufacture ta-pu-i the rice is cooked and then spread on a winnowing tray until it is cold. When cold a few ounces of a ferment called "fu-fud" are sprinkled over it and thoroughly stirred in; all is then put in an olla, which is tied over and set away. The ferment consists of cane sugar and dry raw rice pounded and pulverized together to a fine powder. This is then spread in the sun to dry and is later squeezed into small balls some 2 inches in diameter. This ferment will keep a year. When needed a ball is pulverized and sprinkled fine over the cooked rice. An olla of rice prepared for ta-pu-i will be found in one day half filled with the beverage.

Ta-pu-i will keep only about two months. It is never drunk by the women, though they do eat the sweet rice kernels from the jar, and they, as well as the men, manufacture it. It is claimed never to be manufactured in the Bontoc area for sale. A half glass of the beverage will intoxicate. At the end of a month the beverage is very intoxicating, and is then commonly weakened with water. Ta-pu-i is much preferred to ba-si.

The Bontoc man prepares another drink which is filthy, and, even they themselves say, vile smelling. It is called "sa-fu-eng'," is drunk at meals, and is prepared as follows: Cold water is first put in a jar, and into it are thrown cooked rice, cooked camotes, cooked locusts, and all sorts of cooked flesh and bones. The resulting liquid is drunk at the end of ten days, and is sour and vinegar-like. The preparation is perpetuated by adding more water and solid ingredients -- it does not matter much what they are.

The odor of sa-fu-eng' is the worst stench in Bontoc. I never closely investigated the beverage personally -- but I have no reason to doubt what the Igorot says of it; but if all is true, why is it not fatal?

Salt

Throughout the year the pueblo of Mayinit produces salt from a number of brackish hot springs occupying about an acre of ground at the north end of the pueblo.

Mayinit has a population of about 1,000 souls, probably half of whom are directly interested in salt production. It is probable that the pueblo owes its location to the salt springs, although adjoining it to the south is an arable valley now filled with rice sementeras, which may first have drawn the people.

The hot springs slowly raise their water to the surface, where it flows along in shallow streams. Over these streams, or rather sheets of sluggish water, the Igorot have built 152 salt houses, usually about 12 feet wide and from 12 to 25 feet long. The houses, well shown in Pl. CXV, are simply grass-covered roofs extending to the earth.

There is no ownership in the springs to-day -- just as there is no ownership in springs which furnish irrigating water -- one owns the water that passes into his salt house, but has no claim on that which passes through it and flows out below. So each person has ownership of all and only all the water he can use within his plant, and the people claim there are no disputes between owners of houses -- as they look at it, each owner of a salt house has an equal chance to gather salt.

The ground space of the salt house is closely paved with cobblestones from 4 to 6 inches in diameter. The water passes among the bases of these stones, and the salt is deposited in a thin crust over their surface. (See Pl. CXVI.)

These houses are inherited, and, as a consequence, several persons may ultimately have proprietary interest in one house. In such a case the ground space is divided, often resulting in many twig-separated patches, as is shown in fig. 7.

About once each month the salt is gathered. The women of the family work naked in the stream-filled house, washing the crust of salt from the stones into a large wooden trough, called "ko-long'-ko." Each stone is thoroughly washed and then replaced in the pavement. The saturated brine is preserved in a gourd until sufficient is gathered for evaporation.

Ground plan of Mayinit salt house.

Two or more families frequently join in evaporating their salt. The brine is boiled in the large, shallow iron boilers, and from half a day to a day is necessary to effect the evaporation. Evaporation is discontinued when the salt is reduced to a thick paste.

The evaporated salt is spread in a half-inch layer on a piece of banana leaf cut about 5 inches square. The leaf of paste is supported by two sticks on, but free from, a piece of curved broken pottery which is the baking pan. The salt thus prepared for baking is set near a fire in the dwelling where it is baked thirty or forty minutes. It is then ready for use at home or for commerce, and is preserved in the square, flat cakes called "luk'-sa."

Analyses have been made of Mayinit salt as prepared by the crude method of the Igorot. The showing is excellent when the processes are considered, the finished salt having 86.02 per cent of sodium chloride as against 90.68 per cent for Michigan common salt and 95.35 for Onondaga common salt.

Table of salt composition

Constituent elements	Mayinit salt[31]	Common fine -Saturatedbrine Evaporated salt	Baked salt	Michigan salt[32]	Onondaga salt.
	PERCENT	PERCENT	PERCENT	PERCENT	PERCENT)
Calcium sulphate	0.73	1.50	0.46	0.805	1.355
Sodium sulphate	.92	6.28	10.03	--	--
Sodium chloride	7.95	72.19	86.02	90.682	95.353
Insoluble matter	2.1	4 .1	6 .45	--	--

Water	88.03	19.19	1.78	6.752	3.000
Undetermined	.23	.68	.1.26	--	--
Calcium chloride	--	--	-- .	97	4 .155
Magnesium chloride	--	--	--	.78	1 .136
Total	100	100	100	99.994	99.999

One house produces from six to thirty cakes of salt at each baking. A cake is valued at an equivalent of 5 cents, thus making an average salt house, producing, say, fifteen cakes per month, worth 9 pesos per year. Salt houses are seldom sold, but when they are they claim they sell for only 3 or 4 pesos.

Sugar

In October and November the Bontoc Igorot make sugar from cane. The stalks are gathered, cut in lengths of about 20 inches, tied in bundles a foot in diameter, and stored away until the time for expressing the juice.

The sugar-cane crusher, shown in Pl. CXVIII, consists of two sometimes of three, vertical, solid, hard-wood cylinders set securely to revolve in two horizontal timbers, which, in turn, are held in place by two uprights. One of the cylinders projects above the upper horizontal timber and has fitted over it, as a key, a long double-end sweep. This main cylinder conveys its power to the others by means of wooden cogs which are set firmly in the wood and play into sockets dug from the other cylinder. Boys commonly furnish the power used to crush the cane, and there is much song and sport during the hours of labor.

Two people, usually boys, sitting on both sides of the crusher, feed the cane back and forth. Three or four stalks are put through at a time, and they are run through thirty or forty times, or until they break into pieces of pulp not over three or four inches in length.

The juice runs down a slide into a jar set in the ground beneath the crusher.

The boiling is done in large shallow iron boilers over an open fire under a roof. I have known the Igorot to operate the crusher until midnight, and to boil down the juice throughout the night. Sugar-boiling time is known as a-su-fal'-i-wis.

A delicious brown cake sugar is made, which, in some parts of the area, is poured to cool and is preserved in bamboo tubes, in other parts it is cooked and preserved in flat cakes an inch in thickness.

There is not much sugar made in the area, and a large part of the product is purchased by the Ilokano. The Igorot cares very little for sweets; even the children frequently throw away candy after tasting it.

Meals and mealtime

The man of the family arises about 3.30 or 4 o'clock in the morning. He builds the fires and prepares to cook the family breakfast and the food for the pigs. A labor generally performed each morning is the paring of camotes. In about half an hour after the man arises the camotes and rice are put over to cook. The daughters come home from the olag, and the boys from their sleeping quarters shortly before breakfast. Breakfast, called "mang-an'," meaning simply "to eat," is taken by all members of the family together, usually between 5 and 6 o'clock. For this meal all the family, sitting on their haunches, gather around three or four wooden dishes filled with steaming hot food setting on the earth. They eat almost exclusively from their hands, and seldom drink anything at breakfast, but they usually drink water after the meal.

The members of the family who are to work away from the dwelling leave about 7 or 7.30 o'clock -- but earlier, if there is a rush of work. If the times are busy in the fields, the laborers carry their dinner with them; if not, all members assemble at the dwelling and eat their dinner together about 1 o'clock. This midday meal is often a cold meal, even when partaken in the house.

Field laborers return home about 6.30, at which time it is too dark to work longer, but during the rush seasons of transplanting and harvesting palay the Igorot generally works until 7 or 7.30 during moonlight nights. All members of the family assemble for supper, and this meal is always a warm one. It is generally cooked by the man, unless there is a boy or girl in the family large enough to do it, and who is not at work in the fields. It is usually eaten about 7 or 7.30 o'clock, on the earth floor, as is the breakfast. A light is used, a bright, smoking blaze of the pitch pine. It burns on a flat stone kept ready in every house -- it is certainly the first and crudest house lamp, being removed in development only one infinitesimal step from the Stationary fire. This light is also sometimes employed at breakfast time, if the morning meal is earlier than the sun.

Usually by 8 o'clock the husband and wife retire for the night, and the children leave home immediately after supper.

Transportation

The human is the only beast of burden in the Bontoc area. Elsewhere in northern Luzon the Christianized people employ horses, cattle, and carabaos as pack animals. Along the coastwise roads cattle and carabaos haul two-wheel carts, and in the unirrigated lowland rice tracts these same animals drag sleds surmounted by large basket-work receptacles for the palay. The Igorot has doubtless seen all of these methods of animal transportation, but the conditions of his home are such that he can not employ them.

He has no roads for wheels; neither carabaos, cattle, nor horses could go among his irrigated sementeras; and he has relatively few loads of produce coming in and going out of his pueblo. Such loads as he has can be transported by himself with greater safety and speed than by quadrupeds; and so, since he almost never moves his place of abode, he has little need of animal transportation.

To an extent the river is employed to transport boards, timbers, and firewood to both Bontoc and Samoki during the high water of the rainy season. Probably one-fourth of the firewood is borne by the river a part of its journey to the pueblos. But there is no effort at comprehensive water transportation; there are no boats or rafts, and the wood which does float down the river journeys in single pieces.

The characteristic of Bontoc transportation is that the men invariably carry all their heavy loads on their shoulders, and the women as uniformly transport theirs on their heads.

In Benguet all people carry on their backs, as also do the women of the Quiangan area.

In all heavy transportation the Bontoc men carry the spear, using the handle as a staff, or now and then as a support for the load; the women frequently carry a stick for a staff. Man's common transportation vehicle is the ki-ma'-ta, and in it he carries palay, camotes, and manure. He swings along at a pace faster than the walk, carrying from 75 to 100 pounds. He carries all firewood from the mountains, directly on his bare shoulders. Large timbers for dwellings are borne by two or more men directly on the shoulders; and timbers are now, season of 1903, coming in for a schoolhouse carried by as many as twenty-four men. Crosspieces, as yokes, are bound to the timbers with bark lashings, and two or four men shoulder each yoke.

Rocks built into dams and dikes are carried directly on the bare shoulders. Earth, carried to or from the building sementeras, in the trails, or about the dwellings, is put first in the tak-o-chug', the basket-work scoop, holding about 30 or 40 pounds of earth, and this is carried by wooden handles lashed to both sides and is dumped into a transportation basket, called "ko-chuk-kod'." This is invariably hoisted to the shoulder when ready for transportation. When men carry water the fang'-a or olla is placed directly on the shoulder as are the rocks.

When the man is to be away from home over night he usually carries his food and blanket, if he has one, in the waterproof fang'-ao slung on his back and supported by a bejuco strap passing over each shoulder and under the arm. This is the so-called "head basket," and, as a matter of fact, is carried on war expeditions by those pueblos that use it, though it is also employed in more peaceful occupations. As a cargador the man carries his burdens on the shoulder in three ways -- either double, the cargo on a pole between two men; or singly, with the cargo divided and tied to both ends of the pole; or singly, with the cargo laid directly on the shoulder.

Women carry as large burdens as do the men. They have two commonly employed transportation baskets, neither of which have I seen a man even so much as pick up. These are the shallow, pan-shaped lu'-wa and the deeper, larger tay-ya-an'. In these two baskets, and also at times in the man's ki-ma'-ta, the women carry the same things as are borne by the men. Not infrequently the woman uses her two baskets together at the same time -- the tay-ya-an' setting in the lu'-wa, as is shown in Pls. CXIX and CXXI. When she carries the ki-ma'-ta she places the middle of the connecting pole, the pal-tang on her head, with one basket before her and the other behind. At all times the woman wears on her head beneath her burden a small grass ring 5 or 6 inches in diameter, called a "ki'-kan." Its chief function is that of a cushion, though when her burden is a fang'-a of water the ki'-kan becomes also a base -- without which the round-bottomed olla could not be balanced on her head without the support of her hands.

The woman's rain protector is often brought home from the camote gardens bottom up on the woman's head full of camote vines as food for the pigs, or with long, dry grass for their bedding. And, as has been noted, all day long during April and May, when there were no camote vines, women and little girls were going about bearing their small scoop-shaped sug-fi' gathering wild vegetation for the hogs.

Almost all of the water used in Bontoc is carried from the river to the pueblo, a distance ranging from a quarter to half a mile. The women and girls of a dozen years or more probably transport three-fourths of the water used about the house. It is carried in 4 to 6 gallon ollas borne on the head of the woman or shoulder of the man. Women totally blind, and many others nearly blind, are seen alone at the river getting water.

About half the women and many of the men who go to the river daily for water carry babes. Children from 1 to 4 years old are frequently carried to and from the sementeras by their parents, and at all times of the day men, women, and children carry babes about the pueblo. They are commonly carried on the back, sitting in a blanket which is slung over one shoulder, passing under the other, and tied across the breast. Frequently the babe is shifted forward, sitting astride the hip. At times, though rarely, it is carried in front of the person. A frequent sight is that of a woman with a babe in the blanket on her back and an older child astride her hip supported by her encircling arm.

When one sees a woman returning from the river to the pueblo at sundown a child on her back and a 6-gallon jar of water on her head, and knows that she toiled ten or twelve hours that day in the field with her back bent and her eyes on the earth like a quadruped, and yet finds her strong and joyful, he believes in the future of the mountain people of Luzon if they are guided wisely -- they have the strength and courage to toil and the elasticity of mind and spirit necessary for development.

Commerce

The Bontoc Igorot has a keen instinct for a bargain, but his importance as a comerciante has been small, since his wants are few and the state of feud is such that he can not go far from home.

His bargain instinct is shown constantly. The American stranger is charged from two to ten times the regular price for things he wishes to buy. Early in April of the last two years the price of palay for the American has, on a plea of scarcity, advanced 20 per cent, although it has been proved that there is at all times enough palay in the pueblo for three years' consumption.

Rather than spoil a possible high price of a product, outside pueblos have left articles overnight with Bontoc friends to be sold to the American next day at his own price, and when those pueblos came again to vend similar wares the high prices were maintained.

Barter

Most commerce is carried on by barter. Within a pueblo naturally having neither stores nor a legalized currency people trade among themselves, but the word "barter" as here used means the systematic exchange of the products of one community for those of another.

To note the articles produced for commerce by two or three pueblos will give a fair illustration of the importance which interpueblo commerce carried on entirely by barter has assumed among the Igorot. of the Bontoc culture group, though the comerciante rarely remains from home more than one night at a time.

The luwa, the woman's shallow transportation basket, is made by the pueblo of Samoki only, and it is employed by fifteen or eighteen other pueblos. Samoki also makes the akaug, or rice sieve, which is used commonly in the vicinity. Bontoc and Samoki alone make the woman's deeper transportation basket, the tayyaan, and it is used quite as extensively as is the luwa.

The sleeping hat is made only by Bontoc and Samoki; it goes extensively in commerce. The large winnowing tray employed universally by the Igorot is said to be made nowhere in the vicinity except in Samoki and Kamyu. Bontoc and Samoki alone make the man's dirt scoop, the takochug, and it is invariably employed by all men laboring in the sementeras.

Neither Bontoc nor Samoki is within the zone of bejuco, from which a considerable part of their basket work is made, and, as a consequence, the raw material is bartered for from pueblos one or two days distant. Barlig furnishes most of the bejuco. Every manojo of Bontoc and Samoki palay is tied up at harvest time with a strip of one variety of bamboo called "fika" made by the pueblos from sections of bamboo brought in bundles from a day's journey westward to barter during April and May. The rain hat of the Bontoc man is coated with beeswax coming in trade from Barlig, as does also the clear and pure resin used by the women of Samoki in glazing their pots.

Towns to the east of Bontoc, such as Tukukan, Sakasakan, and Tinglayan, grow tobacco which passes westward in trade from town to town nearly, if not quite, through the Province of Lepanto. It doubles its value for about every day of its journey, or at each trading.

Samoki pottery and the salt of Mayinit offer as good illustrations as there are of the Igorot barter. A dozen loads of earthenware, from sixty to seventy-five pots, leave Samoki at one time destined for a single pueblo (see Pl. CXXIII). The Samoki pot is made for a definite trade. Titipan uses many of a certain kind for her commercial basi and the potters say that they make pots somewhat different for about all the two dozen pueblos supplied by them. The potter has learned the art of catering to the trade. There is not only a variety of forms made but the capacity of the fangas ranges from about one quart to ten and twelve gallons, and each variety is made to satisfy a particular and known demand. Samoki ware seldom passes as far east as Sakasakan, only four or five hours distant, because similar ware is made in Bituagan, which supplies not only Sakasakan but the pueblos farther up the river.

There are supposed to be between 280 and 290 families dwelling in Bontoc, and, at a conservative estimate, each family has eight fangas. Each dwelling of a widow has several, so it is a fair estimate to say there are 300 dwellings in the pueblo, having a total of 2,400 fangas. Samoki has about 1,200 fangas in daily use. The estimated population of the several towns that use Samoki pots is 24,000.

There is about one pot per individual in daily use in Bontoc and Samoki, and this estimate is probably fair for the other pueblos. So about 24,000 Samoki pots are daily in use, and this number is maintained by the potters. Igorot claim the average life of a fanga of Samoki is one year or less, so the pueblo must sell at least 24,000 pots per annum. At the average price of 5 centavos about the equivalent of 1,200 pesos come to the pueblo annually from this art, or about 40 pesos for each of the thirty potters, whether or not she works at her art. A few years ago, during a severe state of feud, Samoki pots increased in value about thirty-fold; it is said that the potters purchased carabao for ten large ollas each. To-day the large ollas are worth about 2 pesos, and carabaos are valued at from 40 to 70 pesos.

Mayinit salt passes in barter to about as many pueblos as do the Samoki pots, but while the pots go westward to the border of the Bontoc culture area the salt passes far beyond the eastern border, being bartered from pueblo to pueblo. It does not go far north of Mayinit, or go at all regularly far west, because those pueblos within access of the China Sea coast buy salt evaporated from sea water by the Ilokano of Candon. In April at two different times twelve loads of Candon salt passed eastward through Bontoc on the shoulders of Tukukan men, but during the rainy season and the busy planting and harvesting months Mayinit salt supplies a large demand.

In Bontoc and Samoki there are about one hundred and fifty gold earrings which came from the gold-producing country about Suyak, Lepanto Province. Carabaos are almost invariably traded for these. Sometimes one carabao, sometimes two, and again three are bartered for one gold earring. During the months of March and April the pueblo of Balili traded three of these earrings to Bontoc men for carabaos, and this particular form of barter has been carried on for generations.

Balili, Alap, Sadanga, Takong, Sagada, Titipan and other pueblos between Bontoc pueblo and Lepanto Province to the west weave breechcloths and skirts which are brought by their makers and disposed of to Bontoc and adjacent pueblos. Agawa, Genugan, and Takong bring in clay and metal pipes of their manufacture. Much of these productions is bartered directly for palay. If money is paid for the articles it is invariably turned into palay, because this is the greatest constant need of manufacturing Igorot pueblos.

Sale

The Spaniard left his impress on the Igorot of Bontoc pueblo in no realm probably more surely than in that of the appreciation of the value of money.

The sale instinct, and not the barter instinct, is foremost now in Bontoc and Samoki when an American is a party to a bargain, and this is true in all pueblos on the main trail to Lepanto and the west coast. But one has little difficulty in bartering for Igorot productions if he has things the people want -- such as brass wire, cloth for the woman's skirt, the man's breechcloth, a shirt, or coat. In many pueblos the people try to buy for money the articles the American brings in for barter, although it is true that barter will often get from them many things which money can not buy. To the northeast and south of Bontoc barter will purchase practically anything.

The conditions of peace among the pueblos since the arrival of the Americans and the money which is now everywhere within the area have been the important factors in helping to develop interpueblo commerce from barter to sale.

Most of the clothing worn in the pueblos of Lepanto Province is made from cotton purchased for money at the coast. With few exceptions the breechcloths and blankets worn by Bontoc and Samoki are purchased for money, though it is not very many years since the bark breechcloth made in Titipan and Barlig was worn, and in Tulubin, only two hours distant, Barlig blankets and breechcloths of whole bark are worn to-day.

One week in April a Bontoc Igorot traded a carabao to an Ilokano of Lepanto Province for a copper ganza, the customary way of purchasing ganzas, and the following week another Bontoc man sold a carabao for money to another Lepanto Ilokano.

The Baliwang battle-ax and spear are now more generally sold for money than is any other production made or disposed of within the Bontoc area. They are said to-day to be seldom bartered for.

Medium of exchange

That a people with such incipient social and political institutions as has the Bontoc Igorot should have developed a "money" is remarkable. The North American Indian with his strong tendency and adaptability to political organization had no such money. Nothing of the kind has been presented as belonging to the Australian of ultrasocial development, and I am not aware that anything equal has been produced by other similar primitive peoples. However, it seems not improbable that allied tribes (say, of Malayan stock) which have solved the problem of subsistence in a like way have a similar currency, although I find no mention of it among four score of writers whose observations on similar tribes of Borneo have come to hand, and nothing similar has yet been found in the Philippines.

The Bontoc Igorot has a "medium of exchange" which gives a "measure of exchange value" for articles bought and sold, and which has a "standard of value." In other words he has "good money" probably the best money that could have been devised by him for his society. It is his staple product -- palay, the unthreshed rice.

Palay is at all times good money, and it is the thing commonly employed in exchange. It answers every purpose of a suitable medium of exchange. It is always in demand, since it is the staple food. It is kept eight or ten years without deterioration. Except when used to purchase clothing, it is seldom heavier or more difficult to transport than is the object for which it is exchanged. It is of very stable value, so much so that as a purchaser of Igorot labor and products its value is constant; and it can not be counterfeited.

Aside from this universal medium of exchange the characteristic production of each community, in a minor way, answers for the community the needs of a medium of exchange.

Samoki buys many things with her pots, such as tobacco and salt from Mayinit; cloth from Igorot comerciantes, breechcloth and basi from the Igorot producers; chickens, pigs, palay, and camotes from neighboring pueblos. Mayinit uses her salt in much the same way, only probably to a less extent. Salt is not consumed by all the people.

To-day, as formerly, the live pig and hog and pieces of pork and carabao meat are used a great deal in barter. As far back as the pueblo memory extends pigs have been used to purchase a particularly good breechcloth called "balakes," made in Balangao, three days east of Bontoc.

In all sales the medium of exchange is entirely in coin. Paper will not be received by the Igorot. The peso (the Spanish and Mexican silver dollar) passes in the area at the rate of two to one with American money. There is also the silver half peso, the peseta or one-fifth peso, and the half peseta. The latter two are not plentiful. The only other coin is the copper "sipen."

No centavos (cents) reach the districts of Lepanto and Bontoc from Manila, and for years the Igorot of the copper region of Suyak and Mankayan, Lepanto, have manufactured a counterfeit copper coin called "sipen." All the half-dozen copper coins current in the active commercial districts of the Islands are here counter-feited, and the "sipen" passes at the high rate of 80 per peso; it is common and indispensable. A crude die is made in clay, and has to be made anew for each "sipen" coined. The counterfeit passes throughout the area, but in Tinglayan, just beyond its eastern border, it is not known. Within two days farther east small coins are unknown, the peso being the only money value in common knowledge.

Measure of exchange value

The Igorot has as clear a conception of the relative value of two things bartered as has the civilized man when he buys or sells for money. The value of all things, from a 5-cent block of Mayinit salt to a P70 carabao, is measured in palay. To-day, as formerly, every bargain between two Igorot is made on the basis of the palay value of the articles bought or sold. This is so even though the payment is in money.

Standard of value

The standard of value of the palay currency is the sin fing-e' -- the Spanish "manojo," or handful -- a small bunch of palay tied up immediately below the fruit heads. It is about one foot long, half head and half straw. The value of such a standard is not entirely uniform, and yet there is a great uniformity in the size of the sin fing-e', and all values are satisfactorily taken from it.

<u>Palay currency</u>

An elaborate palay currency has been evolved from the standard, of which the following are the denominations:

Denomination	Number of handfuls
Sin fing-e'	1
Sin i'-ting	5
Chu'-wa i'-ting	10
To-lo' i'-ting	15
I'-pat i'-ting	20
Pu'-ak or gu'-tad	25
Sin fu tek'	50
Sin fu-tek' pu'-ak	75
Chu'-wa fu-tek'	100
To-lo' fu-tek'	150
I'-pat fu-tek'	200
Li-ma' fu-tek'	250
I-nim' fu-tek'	300
Pi-to' fu-tek'	350
Wa-lo' fu-tek'	400
Si-am' fu-tek'	450

Sim-po'-o fu-tek'	500
Sin-o'-po	1,000

Trade routes

Commerce passes quite commonly within the Bontoc culture area from one pueblo to the next, and even to the second and third pueblos if they are friends; but the general direction is along the main river (the Chico), southwest and northeast, since here the people cling. This being the case, those living to the south and north of this line have much less commerce than those along the river route. For instance, practically no people now pass through Ambawan, southeast of Bontoc. It is the last pueblo in the area along the old Spanish calzada between the culture areas of Bontoc and Quiangan to the south. No people live farther southward along the route for nearly a day, and the first pueblos met are enemies of Ambawan, fearful and feared. The only commerce between the two culture areas over this route passes when a detachment of native Constabulary soldiers makes the journey. Naturally the area traversed by a comerciante is limited by the existing feuds. The trader will not go among enemies without escort.

Besides the general trade route up and down the river, there is one between Bontoc and Barlig to the east via Kanyu and Tulubin. At Barlig the trail splits, one branch running farther eastward through Lias and Balangao and the other going southward through the Cambulo area -- a large valley of people said to be similar in culture to those of Quiangan.

Another route from Bontoc leaves the main trail at Titipan and joins the pueblos of Tunnolang, Fidelisan, and Agawa in a general southwest direction. From Agawa the trail crosses the mountains, keeping its general southwest course. It turns westward at the Rio Balasian, which it follows to Ankiling on the Rio del Abra. The route is then along the main road to Candon on the coast via Salcedo.

Mayinit, the salt-producing pueblo, has her outlet on the main trail via Bontoc, but she also passes eastward to the main trail at Sakasakan, going through Baliwang, the battle-ax pueblo. She has no outlet to the north.

Trade languages and traders

Since the commerce is to-day nearly all interpueblo, the common language of the Igorot is used almost exclusively in trade. While the Spaniards were occupying the country, Chinamen -- the "Chino" of the Islands -- passed up from the coast as far as Bontoc, and even farther; the Ilokano also came. They brought much of the iron now in the country, and also came with brass wire, cloth, cotton, gangsas, and salt. These two classes of traders took out, in the main, the money and carabaos of the Igorot, and the Spaniard's coffee, cocoa, and money. To-day no comerciante from the coast dares venture farther inland than Sagada. Of the tradesmen the Chinese did not apparently affect the trade language at all, since the Chino commonly employs the Ilokano language. The Spanish gave the words of salutation, as "Buenos dias" (good day) and "a Dios" (adieu); he also gave some of the names of coins. The peso, the silver dollar, is commonly called "peho." However, the medio peso is known as "thalepi," from the Ilokano "salepi." The peseta is called "peseta;" and the media peseta is known as "dies ay seis" (ten and six), or, simply, "seis" -- it is from the Spanish, meaning sixteen quartos.

The Ilokano language was the more readily adopted, since it is of Malayan origin, and is heard west of the Igorot with increasing frequency until its home is reached on the coast. Among the Ilokano words common in the language of commerce are the following:

Ma'-no, how much; a-sin', salt; ba'-ag, breechcloth; bu-ya'-ang, black; con-di'-man, red; fan-cha'-la, blanket, white, with end stripes; pas-li-o', Chinese bar iron from which axes, spears, and bolos are made; ba-rot', brass wire; pi-nag-pa'-gan, a woman's blanket of distinctive design.

An Americanism used commonly in commercial transactions in the area, and also widely in northern Luzon, is "no got." It is an expression here to stay, and its simplicity as a vocalization has had much to do with its adoption.

Stages of commerce

The commerce of the Igorot illustrates what seems to be the first distinctively commercial activity. Preceding it is the stage of barter between people who casually meet and who trade carried possessions on the whim of the moment. If we wish to dignify this kind of barter, it may properly be called "Fortuitous Commerce."

The next stage, one of the two illustrated by the Igorot of the Bontoc culture area, is that in which commodities are produced before a widespread or urgent demand exists for them in the minds of those who eventually become consumers through commerce. Such commodities result largely from a local demand and a local supply of raw materials. Gradually they spread over a widening area, carried by their producers whose home demand is, for the time, supplied, and who desire some commodity to be obtained among another people. Such venders never or rarely go alone to exchange their goods, which, also, are seldom produced by simply one person, but by a number of individuals or a considerable group. The motive prompting this commerce is the desire on the part of the trader to obtain the commodity for which he goes. In order to obtain it in honor, he attempts to thrust his own productions on the others by carrying his commodities among them. Commerce in this stage may be called "Irregular Intrusive Commerce." It also has its birth and development in barter.

A higher stage of commerce, an immediate outgrowth of the preceding, is that in which the producer anticipates a known demand for his commodity, and at irregular times carries his stock to the consumers. This commerce may be called "Irregular Invited Commerce." It is in this stage that a medium of exchange is likely to develop. This class of commerce is also in full operation in Bontoc to-day.

A higher form is that in which the producer keeps a supply of his commodity on hand. and periodically displays it repeatedly in a known place -- a "market." This stage also may be developed simply through barter, as is seen among certain pueblo Indians of southwestern United States, but the Bontoc man has not begun to dream of a "market" for satisfying his material wants. Such commerce may be called "Periodic Free Commerce." It is widespread in the Philippines, displaying both barter and sale. In many places in the Archipelago to-day, especially in Mindanao, periodic commerce is carried on regularly on neutral territory. Market places are selected where products are put down by one party which then retires temporarily, and are taken up by the other party which comes and leaves its own productions in exchange.

Growing out of these monthly, semimonthly, weekly, biweekly, and triweekly markets, as one sees them in the Philippines, is a still higher form of commerce carried on very largely by sale, but not entirely so. It may be called "Continual Free Commerce."

<u>Property right</u>

The idea of property right among the Igorot is clear. The recognition of property right is universal, and is seldom disputed, notwithstanding the fact that the right of ownership rests simply in the memory of the people -- the only property mark being the ear slit of the half-wild carabao.

The majority of property disputes which have come to light since the Americans have been in Bontoc probably would not have occurred nor would the occasion for them have existed in a society of Igorot control. It is claimed in Bontoc that the Spaniard there settled most disputes which came to him in favor of the party who would pay the most money. In this way, it is said, the rich became the richer at the expense of the poor. This condition is suggested by recent RECLAMOS made by poor people. Again, since the American heard the RECLAMOS of all classes of people, the poor who, according to Igorot custom, forfeited sementeras to those richer as a penalty for stealing palay, have come to dispute the ownership of certain real property.

Personal property of individual

Most articles of personal property are individual. Such property consists of clothing, ornaments, implements, and utensils of out-of-door labor, the weapons of warfare, and such chickens, dogs, hogs, carabaos, food stuffs, and money as the person may have at the time of marriage or may inherit later.

Four of the richest men of Bontoc own fifty carabaos each, and one of them owns thirty hogs. Two other men and a woman, all called equally rich, own ten head of carabaos each. Others have fewer, while two of the ten richest men in the pueblo, have no carabaos. Some of these men have eight granaries, holding from two to three hundred cargoes each, now full of palay. Carabaos are at present valued in Bontoc at about 50 pesos, and hogs average about 8 pesos. All rich people own one or more gold earrings valued at from one to two carabaos each.

The so-called richest man in Bontoc, Lak-ay'-eng, has the following visible personal property:

Articles	Value in peso
Fifty carabaos,	at 50 pesos each 2,500
Thirty hogs,	at 8 pesos each 240
Eight full granaries,	with 250 1-peso cargoes 2,000
Eight earrings,	at 75 pesos each 600
Coin from sale of palay, hogs, etc.	1,000
Total	6,340

The above figures are estimates; it is impossible to make them exact, but they were obtained with much care and are believed to be sufficiently accurate to be of value.

Personal property of group

All household implements and utensils and all money, food stuffs, chickens, dogs, hogs, and carabaos accumulated by a married couple are the joint property of the two.

Such personal property as hogs and carabaos are frequently owned by individuals of different families. It is common for three or four persons to buy a carabao, and even ten have become joint owners of one animal through purchase. Through inheritance two or more people become joint owners of single carabao, and of small herds which they prefer to own in common, pending such an increase that the herd may be divided equally without slaughtering an animal. Until recent years two, three, and even four or five men jointly owned one battle-ax.

As the Igorot acquires more money, or, as the articles desired become relatively cheaper, personal property of the group (outside the family group) is giving way to personal property of the individual. The extinction of this kind of property is logical and is approaching.

Real property of individual

The individual owns dwelling houses, granaries, camote lands about the dwellings and in the mountains, millet and maize lands. in the mountains, irrigated rice lands, and mountain lands with forests. In fact, the individual may own all forms of real property known to the people.

It is largely by the possession or nonpossession of real property that a man is considered rich or poor. This fact is due to the more apparent and tangible form of real than personal property. The ten richest people in Bontoc, nine men and a woman, own, it is said, in round numbers one hundred sementeras each. The average value of a sementera is 10 pesos for every cargo of palay it produces annually. A sementera producing 10 cargoes is rated a very good one, and yet there are those yielding 20, 25, 30, and even 40 cargoes.

It is practically impossible to get the truth concerning the value of the personal or real property of the Igorot in Bontoc, because they are not yet sure the American will not presently tax them unjustly, as they say the Spaniard did. But the following figures are believed to be true in every particular. Mang-i-lot', an old man whose ten children are all dead, and who says his property is no longer of value because he has no children with whom to leave it, is believed to have spoken truthfully when he said he has the following sementeras in the five following geographic areas surrounding the pueblo:

Geographic area	Number of sementeras	Number of cargoes produced
Magkang	6	15
Kogchog	3	5
Felas	1	8
Toyub	1	5
Samuiyu	2	10
Total	13	43

These sementeras produce the low average of 3 1/3 cargoes. The average value of Mang-i-lot's' sementeras, then, is 33 1/3 pesos -- which is thought to be a conservative estimate of the value of the Bontoc sementera. Mang-i-lot' is rated among the lesser rich men. He is relatively, as the American says, "well-to-do." However, when a man possesses twenty sementeras he is considered rich.

The richest man in Bontoc, with one hundred sementeras, has in them, say, 3,330 pesos worth of real property in addition to his 6,340 pesos of personal property.

It is claimed that each household owns its dwelling and at least two sementeras and one granary, though a man with no more property than this is a poor man and some one in his family must work much of the time for wages, because two average sementeras will not furnish all the rice needed by a family for food.

A dwelling house is valued at about 60 pesos, which is less than it usually costs to build, and a granary is valued at about 10 or 15 pesos. It is constructed with great care, is valueless unless rodent proof, and costs much more than its avowed valuation.

Title to all buildings, building lands in the pueblo, and irrigated rice lands is recognized for at least two generations, though unoccupied during that time. They say the right to such unoccupied property would be recognized perpetually if there were heirs. At least it is true that there are now acres of unused lands, once palay sementeras, which have not been cultivated for two generations because water can not be run to them, and the property right of the grandsons of the men who last cultivated them is recognized. However, if one leaves vacant any unirrigated agricultural mountain lands -- used for millet, maize, or beans -- another person may claim and plant them in one year's time, and no one disputes his title.

Real property of group

All real property accumulated by a man and woman in marriage is their joint property as long as both live and remain in union.

No form of real property, except forests, can be the joint property of other individuals than man and wife. Forests are most commonly the property of a considerable group of people -- the descendants of a single ancestral owner. The lands as well as the trees are owned, and the sale of trees carries no right to the land on which they grow. It is impossible even to estimate the value of any one's forest property, but it is true that persons are recognized as rich or poor in forests.

Public property

Public lands and forests extend in an irregular strip around most pueblos. There is no public forest, or even public lands, between Bontoc and Samoki, but Bontoc has access to the forests lying beyond her sister pueblo. Neither is there public forest, or any forest, between Bontoc and Tukukan, and Bontoc and Titipan, though there are public lands. In all other directions from Bontoc public forests surround the outlying private forests. They are usually from three to six hours distant. From them any man gathers what he pleases, but until the American came to Bontoc the Igorot seldom went that far for wood or lumber, as it was unsafe. Now, however, the individual will doubtless claim these lands, unless hindered by the Government. In this manner real property was first accumulated -- a man claimed public lands and forests which he cared for and dared to appropriate and use. There have been few irrigated sementeras built on new water supplies in two generations by people of Bontoc pueblo. The "era of public lands" for Bontoc has practically passed; there is no more undiscovered water. However, three new sementeras were built this year on an island in the river near the pueblo, and are now (May, 1903) full of splendid palay, but they can not be considered permanent property, as an excessively rainy season will make them unfit for cultivation.

Sale of property

Personal property commonly passes by transfer for value received from one party to another. Such a thing as transfer of real property from one Igorot to another for legal currency is unknown; the transfer is by barter. The transfer of personal property was considered in the preceding section on commerce.

Real property is seldom transferred for value received except at the death of the owner or a member of the family; at such times it is common, and occurs from the necessity of quantities of food for the burial feasts and the urgent need of blankets and other clothing for the interment.

Again, camote lands about the dwellings are disposed of to those who may want to build a dwelling. Dwellings are also disposed of if the original occupant is to vacate and some other person desires to possess the buildings.

Death may destroy one's personal property, such as hogs and carabaos, but almost never does an Igorot "lose his property," if it is real. Only a protracted family sickness or a series of deaths requiring the killing of great numbers of chickens, hogs, and carabaos, and the purchase of many things necessary for interment can lose to a person real property of any considerable value.

There is no formality to a "sale" of property, nor are witnesses employed. It is common knowledge within the ato when a sale is on, and the old men shortly know of and talk about the transaction -- thenceforth it is on record and will stand.

Rent, loan, and lease of property

Until recent years, long after the Spaniards came, it was customary to loan money and other forms of personal property without interest or other charge. This generous custom still prevails among most of the people, but some rich men now charge an interest on money loaned for one or more years. Actual cases show the rate to be about 6 or 7 per cent. The custom of loaning for interest was gained from contact with the Lepanto Igorot, who received it from the Ilokano.

It is claimed that dwellings and granaries are never rented.

Irrigated rice lands are commonly leased. Such method of cultivation is resorted to by the rich who have more sementeras than they can superintend. The lessee receives one-half of the palay harvested, and his share is delivered to him. The lessor furnishes all seed, fertilizers, and labor. He delivers the lessee's share of the harvest and retains the other half himself, together with the entire camote crop -- which is invariably grown immediately after the palay harvest.

Unirrigated mountain camote lands are rented outright; the rent is usually paid in pigs. A sementera that produces a yield of 10 cargoes of camotes, valued at about six pesos, is worth a 2-peso pig as annual rental. In larger sementeras a proportional rental is charged -- a rental of about 33 1/3 per cent. All rents are paid after the crops are harvested.

Inheritance and bequest

As regards property the statement that all men are born equal is as false in Igorot land as in the United States. The economic status of the present generation and the preceding one was practically determined for each man before he was born. It is fair to make the statement that the rich of the present generation had rich grandparents and the poor had poor grandparents, although it is true that a large property is now and then lost sight of in its division among numerous children.

Children before their marriage receive little permanent property during the lives of their parents, and they retain none which they may accumulate themselves. A mother sometimes gives her daughter the hair dress of white and agate beads, called "apong;" also she may give a mature daughter her peculiar and rare girdle, called "akosan." Either parent may give a child a gold earring; I know of but one such case. This custom of not allowing an unmarried child to possess permanent property is so rigid that, I am told, an unmarried son or daughter seldom receives carabaos or sementeras until the death of the parents, no matter how old the child may be.

At the time of marriage parents give their children considerable property, if they have it, giving even one-half the sementeras they possess. If parents are no longer able to cultivate their lands when their children marry, they usually give them all they have, and their wants are faithfully met by the children.

The conditions presented above are practically the only ones in which the property owner controls the disposition of his possessions which pass in gift to kin.

The laws of inheritance and bequest are as firmly fixed as are the customs of giving and not giving during life.

Since all the property of a husband and wife is individual, except that accumulated by the joint efforts of the two during union, the property of each is divided on death. The survivor of a matrimonial union receives no share of the individual property of the deceased if there are kin. It goes first to the children or grandchildren. If there are none and a parent survives, it goes to the parent. If there are neither children, grandchildren, nor parents it goes to brothers and sisters or their children. If there are none of these relatives the property goes to the uncles and aunts or cousins. This seems to be the extent of the kinship recognized by the Igorot. If there are no relatives the property passes to the survivor of the union. If there is no survivor the property passes to that friend who takes up the responsibilities of the funeral and accompanying ceremonies. The law of inheritance, then, is as follows: First, lineal descendants; second, ascendants; third, lateral descendants; fourth, surviving spouse; fifth, self-appointed executor who was a personal friend of the deceased.

Primogeniture is recognized, and the oldest living child, whether male or female, inherits slightly more than any of the others. For instance, if there were three or four or five sementeras per child, the eldest would receive one more than the others.

This law of primogeniture holds at all times, but if there are three boys and one girl the girl is given about the same advantage over the others, it is said, as though she were the eldest. If there are three girls and only one boy, no consideration is taken of sex. When there are only two children the eldest receives the largest or best sementera, but he must also take the smallest or poorest one.

It is said that division of the property of the deceased occurs during the days of the funeral ceremonies. This was done on the third day of the ceremonies at the funeral of old Som-kad', mentioned in the section on "Death and Burial?" The laws are rigid, and all that is necessary to be done is for the lawful inheritors to decide which particular property becomes the possession of each. This is neither so difficult nor so conducive of friction as might seem, since the property is very undiversified.

Tribute, tax, and "rake off"

There is no true systematic tribute, tax, or "rake off" among the Bontoc Igorot, nor am I aware that such occurs at all commonly sporadically. However, tribute, tax, and "rake off" are all found in pure Malayan culture in the Archipelago, as among the Moros of the southern islands.

Tribute may be paid more or less regularly by one group of people to a stronger, or to one in a position to harass and annoy -- for the protection of the stronger, or in acknowledgment of submission, or to avoid harassment or annoyance. Nothing of the sort exists in Bontoc. The nearest approach to it is the exchange of property, as carabaos or hogs, between two pueblos at the time a peace is made between them -- at which time the one sueing for peace makes by far the larger payment, the other payment being mere form. This transaction, as it occurs in Bontoc, is a recognition of submission and of inferiority, and is, as well, a guarantee of a certain amount of protection. However, such payments are not made at all regularly and do not stand as true tributes, though in time they might grow to be such.

Nothing in the nature of a tax for the purpose of supporting a government exists in Bontoc. The nearest approach to it is in a practice which grew up in Spanish time but is of Igorot origin. When to-day cargadors are required by Americans, as when Government supplies must be brought in, the members of each cargador's ato furnish him food for the journey, though the cargador personally receives and keeps the wage for the trip. The furnishing of food seems to spring from the feeling that the man who goes on the journey is the public servant of those who remain -- he is doing an unpleasant duty for his ato fellows. If this were carried one step further, if the rice were raised and paid for carrying on some regular function of the Igorot pueblo, it would be a true tax. It may be true, and probably is, in pure Igorot society that if men were sent by an ato on some mission for that ato they would receive support while gone. This would readily develop into a true tax if those public duties were to be performed continually, or even frequently with regularity.

"Rake off," or, as it is known in the Orient, "squeeze," is so common that every one -- Malay, Chino, Japanese, European, and American -- expects his money to be "squeezed" if it passes through another's hands or another is instrumental in making a bargain for him. In much of the Igorot territory surrounding the Bontoc area "rake off" occurs -- it follows the advent of the "headman." It is one of the direct causes why, in Igorot society, the headman is almost always a rich man. During the hunting stage of human development no "rich man" can come up, as is illustrated by the primitive hunter folk of North America. As soon, however, as there are productions which may be traded in, there is a chance for one man to take advantage of his fellows and accumulate a part of their productions -- this opportunity occurs among primitive agricultural people. The Bontoc area, however, has no "headman," no "rich man," and, consequently, no "rake off."

PART 5

Political Life and Control

It is impossible to put one's hand on any one man or any one group of men in Bontoc pueblo of whom it may be said, "Here is the control element of the pueblo."

Nowhere has the Malayan attained national organization. He is known in the Philippines as a "provincial," but in most districts he is not even that. The Bontoc Igorot has not even a clan organization, to say nothing of a tribal organization. I fail to find a trace of matriarchy or patriarchy, or any mark of a kinship group which traces relationship farther than first cousins.

The Spaniard created a "presidente" and a "vice-presidente" for the various pueblos he sought to control, but these men, as often Ilokano as Igorot, were the avenue of Spanish approach to the natives -- they were almost never the natives' mouthpiece. The influence of such officials was not at all of the nature to create or foster the feeling of political unity.

Aside from these two pueblo officers the government and control of the pueblo is purely aboriginal. Each ato, of which, as has been noted, there are seventeen, has its group of old men called "in-tug-tu'-kan." This in-tug-tu'-kan is not an organization, except that it is intended to be perpetual, and, in a measure, self-perpetuating. It is a thoroughly democratic group of men, since it is composed of all the old men in the ato, no matter how wise or foolish, rich or poor -- no matter what the man's social standing may be. Again, it is democratic -- the simplest democ-

racy -- in that is has no elective organization, no headmen, no superiors or infe-
riors whose status in the in-tug-tu'-kan is determined by the members of the
group. The feature of self-perpetuation displays itself in that it decides when the
various men of the ato become am-a'-ma, "old men," and therefore members of
the in-tug-tu'-kan. A person is told some day to come and counsel with the in-
tug-tu'-kan, and thenceforth he is a member of the group.

In all matters with which the in-tug-tu'-kan deals it is supreme in its ato, but in
the ato only; hence the opening statement of the chapter that no man or group
of men holds the control of the pueblo. The life of the several ato has been so similar for such a number of generations that, in matters of general interest, the
thoughts of one in-tug-tu'-kan will be practically those of all others. For instance,
there are eight ceremonial occasions on which the entire pueblo rests from agricultural labors, simply because each ato observes the same ceremonials on identical days. In one of these ceremonials, all the men of the entire pueblo have a rock
contest with all the men of Samoki. Again, when a person of the pueblo has been
killed by another pueblo treacherously or in ambush, or in any way except by fair
fight, the pueblo as a unit hastens to avenge the death on the pueblo of the slayer.

In such matters as these -- matters of common defense and offense, matters of religion wherein food supply is concerned -- custom has long since crystallized into
an act of democratic unity what may once have been the result of the councils of
all the in-tug-tu'-kan of the pueblo. It is customary for an ato to rest from agricultural labor on the funeral day of any adult man, but the entire pueblo thus
seeks to honor at his death the man who was old and influential.

There is little differentiation of the functions of the in-tug-tu'-kan. It hears,
reviews, and judges the individual disagreements of the members of the ato and
makes laws by determining custom. It also executes its judgments or sees that they
are executed. It makes treaties of peace, sends and accepts or rejects challenges of
war for its ato. In case of interato disagreements of individuals the two in-tug-tu'-
kan meet and counsel together, representing the interests of the persons of their
ato. In other words, the pueblo is a federation made up of seventeen geographi-
cal and political units, in each of which the members recognize that their sanest,
ripest wisdom dwells with the men who have had the longest experience in life;
and the group of old men -- sometimes only one man and sometimes a dozen --
is known as in-tug-tu'-kan, and its wisdom is respected to the degree that it is regularly sought and is accepted as final judgment, being seldom ignored or dishon-
ored. In matters of a common interest the pueblo customarily acts as a unit.
Probably could it not so act, factions would result causing separation from the

federation. This state of things is hinted as one of the causes why the ancestors of present Samoki separated from the pueblo of Bontoc. The fact that they did separate is common knowledge, and a cause frequently assigned is lack of space to develop. However, there may have been disagreement.

Crimes, detection and punishment

Theft, lying to shield oneself in some criminal act, assault and battery, adultery, and murder are the chief crimes against Igorot society.

There are tests to determine which of several suspects is guilty of a crime. One of these is the rice-chewing test. The old men of the ato interested assemble, in whose presence each suspect is made to chew a mouthful of raw rice, which, when it is thoroughly masticated, is ejected on to a dish. Each mouthful is examined, and the person whose rice is the driest is considered guilty. It is believed that the guilty one will be most nervous during the trial, thus checking a normal flow of saliva.

Another is a hot-water test. An egg is placed in an olla of boiling water, and each suspect is obliged to pick it out with his hand. When the guilty man draws out the egg the hot water leaps up and burns the forearm.

There is an egg test said to be the surest one of all. A battle-ax blade is held at an angle of about 60 degrees, and an egg is placed at the top in a position to slide down. Just before the egg is freed from the hand the question is asked "Is Liod (the name of the man under trial) guilty?" If the egg slides down the blade to the bottom the man named is innocent but if it sticks on the ax he is guilty.

There is also a blood test employed in Bontoc pueblo, and also to the west, extending, it is said, into Lepanto Province. An instrument consisting of a sharp spike of iron projecting about one-sixteenth of an inch from a handle with broad shoulders is placed against the scalp of the suspects and the handle struck a sharp blow. The projecting shoulder is supposed to prevent the spike from entering the scalp of one farther than that of another. The person who bleeds most is considered guilty -- he is "hot headed."

I was once present at an Igorot trial when the question to be decided was whether a certain man or a certain woman had lied. The old men examined and cross-questioned both parties for fully a quarter of an hour, at which time they announced that the woman was the liar. Then they brought a test to bear evidence in binding their decision. They killed a chicken and cut it open. The gall was found to be almost entirely exposed on the liver -- clearly the woman had lied. She looked at the all-knowing gall and nodded her acceptance of the verdict. If the gall had been hidden by the upper lobe of the liver, the verdict would not have been sustained.

If a person steals palay, the injured party may take a sementera from the offender.

If a man is found stealing pine wood from the forest lands of another, he forfeits not only all the wood he has cut but also his working ax.

The penalty for the above two crimes is common knowledge, and if the crime is proved there is no longer need for the old men to make a decision -- the offended party takes the customary retributive action against the offender.

Cases of assault and battery frequently occur. The chief causes are lovers' jealousies, theft of irrigating water during a period of drought, and dissatisfaction between the heirs of a property at or shortly following the time of inheritance.

It is customary for the old men of the interested ato to consider all except common offenses unless the parties settle their differences without appeal.

A fine of chickens, pigs, sementeras, sometimes even of carabaos, is the usual penalty for assault and battery.

Adultery is not a common crime. I was unable to learn that the punishment for adultery was ever the subject for a council of the old men. It seems rather that the punishment -- death of the offenders -- is always administered naturally, being prompted by shocked and turbulent emotions rather than by a council of the wise men. In Igorot society the spouse of either criminal may take the lives of both the guilty if they are apprehended in the crime. To-day the group consciousness of the penalty for adultery is so firmly fixed that adulterers are slain, not necessarily on the spur of the moment of a suspected crime but sometimes after carefully laid plans for detection. A case in question occurred in Suyak of Lepanto Province. A man knew that his faithless wife went habitually at dusk with another man to a secluded spot under a fallen tree. One evening the husband preceded them, and lay down with his spear on the tree trunk. When the guilty people arrived he killed them both in their crime, thrusting his spear through them and pinning them to the earth.

Among a primitive people whose warfare consists much in ambushing and murdering a lone person it is not always possible to predict whether the taking of human life will be considered a criminal act or an act of legitimate warfare.

It is considered warfare by the group of the murdered person, and as such to be met by return warfare unless the group of the murderer is a friendly one and at once comes to the offended people to sue for continued peace. This applies to political groups within a pueblo as well as to the people of distinct pueblos.

When murder is considered simply as a crime, its punishment may be one of two classes: First, the murderer may lose his life at the hands of his own group; second, the crime may be compounded for the equivalent of the guilty man's property. In this case the settlement is between the guilty person and the political group of the victim, and the value of the compound is consumed by feastings of the group. No part of the price is paid the family of the deceased as a compensation for the loss of his labor and other assistance.

The three following specific cases of misdemeanors will illustrate somewhat, more fully the nature of differences which arise between individuals in pure Igorot society:

In Samoki early in November, 1902, Bisbay pawned an iron pot -- a sugar boiler -- to Yagao for 4 pesos. In about two months, when sugar season was on, Bisbay went to redeem his property, but Yagao would neither receive the money nor give up the boiler. The old men of the ato counseled together over the matter, and, as a result, Yagao received the 4 pesos and returned the pot, and the matter was thus amicably settled between the two.

Early in January, 1903, Mowigas, of the pueblo of Ganang, cut and destroyed the grasshopper basket of Dadaag, of the pueblo of Mayinit, and also slightly cut Dadaag with his ax, but did not attempt to kill him. The cause of the assault was this: Mowigas had killed a chicken and was having a ceremonial in his house at the time Dadaag passed with his basket of grasshoppers. According to Igorot custom he should not have taken grasshoppers past a house in which such a ceremony was being performed. The breach made it necessary to hold another ceremony, killing another chicken. Old men from Mayinit, the pueblo of Dadaag, came to Ganang and told Mowigas he would have to pay 3 pesos for his conduct, or Mayinit would come over and destroy the town. He paid the money, whereas the basket was worth only one-sixth the price. Trouble was thus averted, and the individuals reconciled. In this case the two pueblos are friends, but Mayinit is much stronger than Ganang, and evidently took advantage of the fact.

In January, 1903, a woman and her son, of Titipan, stole camotes of another Titipan family. The old men of the two ato of the interested families fined the thieves a hog. The fine was paid, and the hog eaten by the old men of the two ato.

Very often the fine paid by the offender passes promptly down the throats of the jury. However, it is the only compensation for their services in keeping the peace of the pueblo, so they look upon it as their rightful share -- it is the "lawyer's share" with a vengeance.

PART 6

War and Head-Hunting

En-fa-lok'-net is the Bontoc word for war, but the expression "na-ma'-ka" -- take heads -- is used interchangeably with it.

For unknown generations these people have been fierce head-hunters. Nine-tenths of the men in the pueblos of Bontoc and Samoki wear on the breast the indelible tattoo emblem which proclaims them takers of human heads. The fawi of each ato in Bontoc has its basket containing skulls of human heads taken by members of the ato.

There are several different classes of head-hunters among primitive Malayan peoples, but the continuation of the entire practice is believed to be due to the so-called "debt of life" -- that is, each group of people losing a head is in duty and honor bound to cancel the score by securing a head from the offenders. In this way the score is never ended or canceled, since one or the other group is always in debt.

It seems not improbable that the heads may have been cut off first as the best way of making sure that a fallen enemy was certainly slain. The head was at all events the best proof to a man's tribesmen of the discharge of the debt of life; it was the trophy of success in defeating the foe. Whatever the cause of taking the head may have been with the first people, it would surely spread to others of a similar culture who warred with a head-taking tribe, as they would wish to appear as cruel, fierce, and courageous as the enemy.

Henry Ling Roth[33] quotes Sir Spencer St. John as follows concerning the
Seribas Dyaks of Borneo (p. 142):

A certain influential man denied that head-hunting is a religious ceremony
among them. It is merely to show their bravery and manliness, that it may be said
that so-and-so has obtained heads. When they quarrel it is a constant phrase,
"How many heads did your father or grandfather get?" If less than his own number, "Well, then, you have no occasion to be proud!" Thus the possession of heads
gives them great considerations as warriors and men of wealth, the skulls being
prized as the most valuable of goods.

Again he quotes St. John (p. 143):

Feasts in general are: To make their rice grow well, to cause the forest to abound
with wild animals, to enable their dogs and snares to be successful in securing
game, to have the streams swarm with fish, to give health and activity to the people themselves, and to insure fertility to their women. All these blessings the pos-
sessing and feasting of a fresh head are supposed to be the most efficient means of
securing.

He quotes Axel. Dalrymple as follows (p. 141)

The Uru Ais believe that the persons whose heads they take will become their
slaves in the next world.

On the same page he quotes others to the same point regarding other tribes of
Borneo.

Roth states (p. 163):

From all accounts there can be little doubt that one of the chief incentives to getting heads is the desire to please the women. It may not always have been so and
there may be and probably is the natural blood-thirstiness of the animal in man
to account for a great deal of the head-taking.

He quotes Mrs. F. F. McDougall in her statement of a Sakaran legend of the origin of head-taking to the effect that the daughter of their great ancestor residing
near the Evening Star "refused to marry until her betrothed brought her a present
worth her acceptance." First the young man killed a deer which the girl turned
from with disdain; then he killed and brought her one of the great monkeys of

the forest, but it did not please her. "Then, in a fit of despair, the lover went abroad and killed the first man he met, and, throwing his victim's head at the maiden's feet, he exclaimed at the cruelty she had made him guilty of; but, to his surprise, she smiled and said that now he had discovered the only gift worthy of herself" (p. 163). In the three following pages of his book the author quotes three or four other writers who cite in detail instances wherein heads were taken simply to advance the slayer's interests with women.

As showing the passion for head-hunting among these people, St. John tells of a young man who, starting alone to get a head from a neighboring tribe, took the head of "an old woman of their own tribe, not very distantly related to the young fellow himself." When the fact was discovered "he was only fined by the chief of the tribe and the head taken from him and buried" (p. 161).

Again (p. 159):

The maxim of the ruffians (Kayans) is that out of their own country all are fair game. "Were we to meet our father, we would slay him." The head of a child or of a woman is as highly prized as that of a man.

Mr. Roth writes that Mr. F. Witti "found that the latter (Limberan) would not count as against themselves heads obtained on head-hunting excursions, but only those of people who had been making peaceful visits, etc. In fact, the sporting head-hunter bags what he can get, his declared friends alone excepted" (p. 160).

The Ibilao of Luzon, near Dupax, of the Province of Nueva Vizcaya, give the name "debt of life" to their head-hunting practice; but they have, in addition, other reasons for head taking. No man may marry who has not first taken a head; and every year after they harvest their palay the men go away for heads, often going journeys requiring a month of time in order to strike a particular group of enemies. The Christians of Dupax claim that in 1899 the Ibilao took the heads of three Dupax women who were working in the rice sementeras close to the pueblo. These same Christians also claim that they have seen a human head above the stacks of harvested Ibilao palay; and they claim the custom is practiced annually, though the Ibilao deny it.

Some dozen causes for head-hunting among primitive Malayan peoples have been here cited. These include the debt of life, requirements for marriage, desire for abundant fruitage and harvest of cultivated products, the desire to be considered brave and manly, desire for exaltation in the minds of descendants, to increase wealth, to secure abundance of wild game and fish, to secure general health and activity of the people, general favor at the hands of the women, fecundity of women, and slaves in the future life.

From long continuance in the practice of head-hunting, many beliefs and super-stitions arise to foster it, until in the minds of the people these beliefs are greater factors in its perpetuation than the original one of the debt of life. The possession of a head, with the accompanying honor, feasts, and good omens, seems in many cases to be of first importance rather than the avenging of a life.

The custom of head taking came with the Igorot to Luzon, a custom of their ancestors in some earlier home. The people of Bontoc, however, say that their god, Lumawig, taught them to go to war. When, a very long time ago, he lived in Bontoc, he asked them to accompany him on a war expedition to Lagod, the north country. They said they did not wish to go, but finally yielded to his urg-ings and followed him. On the return trip the men missed one of their compan-ions, Gu-ma'-nub. Lumawig told them that Gu-ma'-nub had been killed by the people of the north. And thus their wars began -- Gu-ma'-nub must be avenged. They have also a legend in regard to head taking: The Moon, a woman called "Kabigat," was sitting one day making a copper pot, and one of the children of the man Chalchal, the Sun, came to watch her. She struck him with her molding paddle, cutting off his head. The Sun immediately appeared and placed the boy's head back on his shoulders. Then the Sun said to the Moon: "Because you cut off my son's head, the people of the Earth are cutting off each other's heads, and will do so hereafter."

With the Bontoc men the taking of heads is not the passion it seems to be with some of the people of Borneo. It, is, however, the almost invariable accompani-ment of their interpueblo warfare. They invariably, too, take the heads of all killed on a head-hunting expedition. They have skulls of Spaniards, and also skulls of Igorot, secured when on expeditions of punishment or annihilation with the Spanish soldiers.

But the possession of a head is in no way a requisite to marriage. A head has no part in the ceremonies for palay fruitage and harvest, or in any of the numerous agricultural or health ceremonies of the year. It in no way affects a man's wealth, and, so far as I have been able to learn, it in no way affects in their minds a man's future existence. A beheaded man, far from being a slave, has special honor in the future state, but there seems to be none for the head taker. As shown by the Lumawig legend the debt of life is the primary cause of warfare in the minds of the people of Bontoc, and it is to-day a persistent cause. Moreover, since inter-pueblo warfare exists and head taking is its form, head-hunting is a necessity with an individual group of people in a state of nature. Without it a people could have no peace, and would be annihilated by some group which believed it a coward and an easy prey.

There is no doubt that the desire to be considered brave and manly has come to be a factor in Bontoc head taking. In my presence an Igorot once told a member of ato Ungkan that the men of his ato were like girls, because they had not taken heads. The statement was false, but the pronounced judgment sincere. In this connection, also, it may be said that although the taking of a head is not a requisite to marriage, and they say that it does not win the men special favor from the women, yet, since it makes them manly and brave in the eyes of their fellows, it must also have its influence on the women.

The desire for exaltation in the minds of descendants also has a certain influence -- young men in quarrels sometimes brag of the number of heads taken by their ancestors, and the prowess or success of an ancestor seems to redound to the courage of the descendants; and it is an affront to purposely and seriously belittle the head-hunting results of a man's father.

There can be no doubt that head-hunting expeditions are often made in response to a desire for activity and excitement, with all the feasting, dancing, and rest days that follow a successful foray. The explosive nature of a man's emotional energy demands this bursting of the tension of everyday activities. In other words, the people get to itching for a head, because a head brings them emotional satisfaction.

It is believed that now the people of the two sister pueblos, Bontoc and Samoki, look on war and head-hunting somewhat as a game, as a dangerous, great sport, though not a pastime. It is a test of agility and skill, in which superior courage and brute force are minor factors.

Primarily a pueblo is an enemy of every other pueblo, but it is customary for pueblos to make terms of peace. Neighboring pueblos are usually, but not always, friendly. The second pueblo away is usually an enemy. On most of our trips through northern Luzon cargadors and guides could readily be secured to go to the nearest pueblo, but in most cases they absolutely refused to go on to the second pueblo, and could seldom be driven on by any argument or force. The actual negotiations for peace are generally between some two ato of the two interested pueblos, since the debt of life is most often between two ato.

Bontoc and Samoki claim never to have sued for peace -- a statement probably true, as they are by far the largest body of warriors in the culture area, and their war reputation is the worst. When one ato agrees on peace with another the entire pueblo honors the treaty.

The following peace agreements have been sought by outside pueblos in recent years of the following ato of Bontoc: Sakasakan sued for peace from Somowan, and Barlig from Pudpudchog; Tulubin, from Buyayyeng; Bitwagan, from Sipaat; Tukukan sought peace from both Amkawa and Polupo, and Sabangan also from Polupo; Sadanga, from Choko; and Baliwang, from Longfoy.

The relations with two of these pueblos, Barlig and Sadanga, however, are now not peaceful. Bontoc has many kin in Lias, some two days to the east, the trail to which passes Barlig; but communication between these pueblos of kin has ceased, because of the attitude of Barlig. Communication between Bontoc and Tinglayan, northeast of the Bontoc area on the river, has also ceased, because of the enmity of Sadanga, which lies close to the trail between the two pueblos.

The peace ceremonial, to which a hog or carabao is brought by the entreating people and eaten by the two parties to the agreement, is called "pwi-din." The peace is sealed by some exchange, as of a battle-ax for a blanket, the people sued having the better part of the trade.

It now and then happens that of two pueblos at peace one loses a head to the other. If the one taking the head desires continued peace, some of its most influential men hasten to the other pueblo to talk the matter over. Very likely the other pueblo will say, "If you wish war, all right; if not, you bring us two carabaos, and we will still be friends." If no effort for peace is made by the offenders, each from that day considers the other an enemy.

There is a formal way of breaking the peace between two pueblos: Should ato Somowan of Bontoc, for instance, wish to break her peace with Sakasakan she holds a ceremonial meeting, called "men-pa-kel'." In this meeting the old men freely speak their minds; and when all matters are settled a messenger departs for Sakasakan bearing a battle-ax or spear -- the customary token of war with all these Bontoc peoples. The life of the war messenger is secure, but, if possible, he is a close relative of the challenged people. There is no record that such a person was ever killed while on his mission. The messenger presents himself to some old man of the ato or pueblo, and says, "In-ya'-lak nan sud-sud in-fu-sul'-ta-ko," which means, roughly, "I bring the challenge of war."

If the challenge is accepted, as it usually is, an ax or spear is given the messenger, and he hastens home to exclaim to his people, "In-tang-i'-cha men-fu-sul'-ta-ko" -- that is, "They care to contest in war."

A peace thus canceled is followed by a battle between practically all the men of both sides. It is customary for the challenging people, within a few days, to appear before the pueblo of their late friends, and the men at once come out in answer to the challenging cries of the visitors -- "Come out if you dare to fight us?" Or it may be that those challenged appear near the other pueblo before it has time to back its challenge.

If the challenged pueblo does not wish to fight, the spokesman tells the messenger that they do not wish war; they desire continued friendship; and the messenger returns to his people, not with a weapon of war, but with a chicken or a pig; and he repeats to his people the message he received from the old man.

After a peace has been canceled the two pueblos keep up a predatory warfare, with a head lost here and there, and with now and then a more serious battle, until one or the other again sues for peace, and has its prayer granted. In this predatory warfare the entire body of enemies, one or more ato, at times lays in hiding to take a few heads from lone people at their daily toil. Or when the country about a trail is covered with close tropical growth an enemy may hide close above the path and practically pick his man as he passes beneath him. He hurls or thrusts his spear, and almost always escapes with his own life, frequently bursting through a line of people on the trail, and instantly disappearing in the cover below. Should the injured pueblo immediately retaliate, it finds its enemies alert and on guard.

At two places near the mountain trail between Samoki and Tulubin is a trellis-like structure called "ko'-mis." It consists of several posts set vertically in the ground, to which horizontal poles are tied, The posts are the stem and root sections of the beautiful tree fern. They are set root end up, and the fine, matted rootlets present a compact surface which the Igorot has carved in the traditional shape of the "anito." Some of these heads have inlaid eyes and teeth of stone. Hung on the ko'-mis are baskets and frames in which chickens and pigs have been carried to the place for ceremonial feasting.

These two ko'-mis were built four years ago when Bontoc and Samoki had their last important head-hunting forays with Tulubin. When Bontoc or Samoki (and usually they fight together) sought Tulubin heads they spent a night at one of the ko'-mis, remaining at the first one, if the signs were propitious -- but, if not, they passed on to the second, hoping for better success. They killed and ate their fowls and pigs in a ceremony called "fi-kat'," and, if all was well, approached the mountains near Tulubin and watched to waylay a few of her people when they came to the sementeras in the early morning. If a crow flew cawing over the trail, or a snake or rat crossed before the warriors, or a rock rolled down the mountain side, or a clod of earth caved away under their feet, or if the little omen bird, "i'-chu," called, the expedition was abandoned, as these were bad omens.

The ceremony of the ko'-mis is held before all head-hunting expeditions, except in the unpremeditated outburst of a people to immediately punish the successful foray or ambush of some other. The ko'-mis is built along all Bontoc war trails, though no others are known having the "anito" heads. So persistent are the warriors if they have decided to go to a particular pueblo for heads that they often go day after day to the ko'-mis for eight or ten days before they are satisfied that no good omens will come to them. If the omens are persistently bad, it is customary for the warriors to return to their ato and hold the mo-ging ceremony, during which they bury under the stone pavement of the fawi court one of the skulls then preserved in the ato.

In this way they explode their extra emotions and partially work off their disappointment.

Occasionally a town has a bad strain of blood, and two or three men break away without common knowledge and take heads. The entire body of warriors in the pueblo where those murdered lived promptly rises and pours itself unheralded on the pueblo of the murderers. If these people are not warned the slaughter is terrible -- men, women, and children alike being slain. None is spared, except mere babes, unless they belong to the offended pueblo, marriage having taken them away from home. Preceding a known attack on a pueblo it is customary for the women and children to flee to the mountains, taking with them the dogs, pigs, chickens, and valuable household effects. However, Bontoc pueblo, because of her strength, is not so evacuated -- she expects no enemy strong enough to burst through and reach the defenseless.

In the Banawi area, where the dwellings are built on prominences frequently a hundred or more feet above the surrounding territory, they say the women often remain and assist in the defense by hurling rocks. They are safer there than they would be elsewhere.

Men go to war armed with a wooden shield, a steel battle-ax, and one to three steel or wooden spears. It is a man's agility and skill in keeping his shield between himself and the enemy that preserves his life. Their battles are full of quick, incessant springing motion. There are sudden rushes and retreats, sneaking flank movements to cut an enemy off. The body is always in hand, always in motion, that it may respond instantly to every necessity. Spears are thrown with greatest accuracy and fatality up to 30 feet, and after the spears are discharged the contest, if continued, is at arms' length with the battle-axes. In such warfare no attitude or position can safely be maintained except for the shortest possible time.

Challenges and bluffs are sung out from either side, and these bluffs are usually "called." In the last Bontoc-Tulubin foray a fine, strapping Tulubin warrior sung out that he wanted to fight ten men -- he was taken at his word so suddenly that his head was a Bontoc prize before his friends could rally to assist him.

In March we were returning from a trip to Banawi of the Quiangan area, and were warned we might be attacked near a certain river. As we approached it coming down a forested mountain side three or four men were seen among the trees on the farther side of the stream. Presently they called their dogs, which began to bark; then our Bontoc Igorot Constabulary escort "joshed" the supposed enemy by loudly caning dogs and hogs. Presently the calls worked themselves into a rhythmic chorus for all like a strong college yell, "A'-su, a'-su, a'-su, a'-su, fu'-tug, fu'-tug, fu'-tug, fu'-tug." It is probable the men across the river were hunting wild hogs, but at the time the Constabulary considered the dog calls simply a bluff, which they "called" in the only way they could as they continued down the mountain trail.

Rocks are often thrown in battle, and not infrequently a man's leg is broken or he is knocked senseless by a rock, whereupon he loses his head to the enemy, unless immediately assisted by his friends.

There is little formality about the head taking. Most heads are cut off with the battle-ax before the wounded man is dead. Not infrequently two or more men have thrown their spears into a man who is disabled. If among the number there is one who has never taken a head, he will generally be allowed to cut this one from the body, and thus be entitled to a head taker's distinct tattoo. However, the head belongs to the man who threw the first disabling spear, and it finds its resting place in his ato. If there is time, men of other ato may cut off the man's hands and feet to be displayed in their ato. Sometimes succeeding sections of the arms and legs are cut and taken away, so only the trunk is left on the field.

Frequently a battle ends when a single head is taken by either side -- the victors calling out, "Now you go home, and we will go home; and if you want to fight some other day, all right!" In this way battles are ended in an hour or so, and often in half an hour. However, they have battles lasting half a day, and ten or a dozen heads are taken. Seven pueblos of the lower Quiangan region went against the scattered groups of dwellings in the Banawi area of the upper Quiangan region in May, 1902. The invaders had seven guns, but the people of Banawi had more than sixty -- a fact the invaders did not know until too late. However, they did not retire until they had lost a hundred and fifty heads. They annihilated one of the groups of the enemy, getting about fifty heads, and burned down the dwellings. This is by far the fiercest Igorot battle of which there is any memory, and its ferocity is largely due to firearms.

When a head has been taken the victor usually starts at once for his pueblo, without waiting for the further issue of the battle. He brings the head to his ato and it is put in a small funnel-shaped receptacle, called "sak-o'-long," which is tied on a post in the stone court of the fawi. The entire ato joins in a ceremony for the day and night; it is called "se'-dak." A dog or hog is killed, the greater part of which is eaten by the old men of the ato, while the younger men dance to the rhythmic beats of the gangsa. On the next day, "chao'-is," a month's ceremony, begins. About 7 o'clock in the morning the old men take the head to the river. There they build a fire and place the head beside it, while the other men of the ato dance about it for an hour. All then sit down on their haunches facing the river, and, as each throws a small pebble into the water he says, "Man-i'-su, hu! hu! hu! Tukukan!" -- or the name of the pueblo from which the head was taken. This is to divert the battle-ax of their enemy from their own necks. The head is washed in the river by sousing it up and down by the hair; and the party returns to the fawi where the lower jaw is cut from the head, boiled to remove the flesh, and becomes a handle for the victor's gangsa. In the evening the head is buried under the stones of the fawi.

In a head ceremony which began in Samoki May 21, 1903, there was a hand, a jaw, and an ear suspended from posts in the courts of ato Nag-pi', Ka'-wa, and Nak-a-wang', respectively. In each of the eight ato of the pueblo the head ceremony was performed. In their dances the men wore about their necks rich strings of native agate beads which at other dances the women usually wear on their heads. Many had boar-tusk armlets, some of which were gay with tassels of human hair. Their breechcloths were bright and long. All wore their battle-axes, two of which were freshly stained halfway up the blade with human blood -- they were the axes used in severing the trophies from the body of the slain.

On the second day the dance began about 4 o'clock in the morning, at which time a bright, waning moon flooded the pueblo with light. At every ato the dance circle was started in its swing, and barely ceased for a month. A group of eight or ten men formed, as is shown in Pl. CXXXI, and danced contraclockwise around and around the small circle. Each dancer beat his blood and emotions into sympathetic rhythm on his gangsa, and each entered intently yet joyfully into the spirit of the occasion -- they had defeated an enemy in the way they had been taught for generations.

It was a month of feasting and holidays. Carabaos, hogs, dogs, and chickens were killed and eaten. No work except that absolutely necessary was performed, but all people -- men, women, and children -- gathered at the ato dance grounds and were joyous together.

Each ato brought a score of loads of palay, and for two days women threshed it out in a long wooden trough for all to eat in a great feast. This ceremonial thresh-ing is shown in Pl. CXXXII. Twenty-four persons, usually all women, lined up along each side of the trough, and, accompanying their own songs by rhythmic beating of their pestles on the planks strung along the sides of the trough, each row of happy toilers alternately swung in and out, toward and from the trough, its long heavy pestles rising and falling with the regular "click, click, thush; click, click, thush!" as they fell rebounding on the plank, and were then raised and thrust into the palay-filled trough.

After heads have been taken by an ato any person of that ato -- man, woman, or child -- may be tattooed; and in Bontoc pueblo they maintain that tattooing may not occur at any other time, and that no person, unless a member of the success-ful ato, may be tattooed.

After the captured head has been in the earth under the fawi court of Bontoc about three years it is dug up, washed in the river, and placed in the large basket, the so-lo'-nang, in the fawi, where doubtless it is one of several which have a sim-ilar history. At such time there is a three-day's ceremony, called "min-pa-fa'-kal is nan mo'-king." It is a rest period for the entire pueblo, with feasting and dancing, and three or four hogs are killed. The women may then enter the fawi; it is said to be the only occasion they are granted the privilege.

In the fawi of ato Sigichan there are at present three skulls of men from Sagada, one of a man from Balugan, and one of a man and two of women from Baliwang. Probably not more than a dozen skulls are kept in a fawi at one time. The final resting place of the skull is again under the stones of the fawi. Samoki does not keep the skull at all; it remains where buried under the ato court. As was stated before, a skull is generally buried under the stones of the fawi court whenever the omens are such that a proposed head-hunting expedition is given up. They are doubtless, also, buried at other times when the basket in the fawi becomes too full. Sigichan has buried twenty-eight skulls in the memory of her oldest member -- making a total of thirty-five heads taken, say, in fifty years. Three of these were men's heads from Ankiling, nine were men's heads from Tukukan, three were men's heads from Barlig, three were men's heads and four women's heads from

Sabangan, and six were men's heads from Sadanga. During this same period Sigichan claims to have lost one man's head each to Sabangan and Sadanga.

No small children's skulls can be found in Bontoc, though some other head-hunters take the heads even of infants. In fact, the men of Bontoc say that babes and children up to about 5 years of age are not killed by the head-hunter. If one should take a child's head he would shortly be called to fate by some watchful pin-teng in language as follows: "Why did you take that babe's head? It does not understand war. Pretty soon some pueblo will take your head." And the pinteng is supposed to put it into the mind of some pueblo to get the head of that par-ticularly cruel man.

The friends of a beheaded person take his body home from the scene of death. It remains one day sitting in the dwelling. Sometimes a head is bought back from the victors at the end of a day, the usual price paid being a carabao. After the body has remained one day in the dwelling it is said to be buried without ceremony near the trail leading to the pueblo which took the head. The following day the entire ato has a ceremonial fishing in the river, called "mang-o'-gao" or "tid-wil." A fish feast follows for the evening meal. The next day the mang-ay'-yu ceremo-ny occurs. At that time the men of the ato, go near the place where their com-panion lost his head and ask the beheaded man's spirit, the pinteng, to return to their pueblo.

Pl. CXXXVI shows the burial of a beheaded corpse in Banawi in April, 1903.[34] After the head-taking the body was set up two days under the dwelling of the dead man, and was then carried to the mountain side in the direction of Kambulo, the pueblo which killed the man. It was tied on a war shield and the whole tied to a pole which was borne by two men, as is shown in Pl. CXXXV. The funeral pro-cession was made up as follows: First, four warriors proceeded, one after the other, along a narrow path on the dike walls, each beating a slow rhythm with a stick on the long, black, Banawi war shield, each shield, however, being striped different-ly with white-earth paint. The corpse was borne next, after which followed about a dozen more warriors, most of whom carried the white-marked shield -- an emblem of mourning.

About half a mile from the dwelling the party left the sementeras and climbed up a short, steep ascent to a spot resembling the entrance to the earth burrow of some giant animal, and there the strange corpse was placed on the ground. A small group of people, including one old woman, was awaiting the funeral party. At the back end of the burrow two men tore away the earth and disclosed a small wall of loose stones. These they removed and revealed a vertical entrance in the earth about 2 feet high and 2 1/2 feet wide. Through this small opening one of the men crawled, and crouching in the narrow sepulcher scraped up and threw out a few handfuls of earth. We were told that the corpse before us was the fifth to be placed in that old tomb, all being victims of the pueblo of Kambulo, and four of whom were descendants of the first man buried at that place -- certainly "blood vengeance" with a vengeance.

We were without means of understanding the two or three simple oral ceremonies said over the body, but the woman played a part which it is understood she does not in the Bontoc area. She carried a slender, polished stick, greatly resembling a baton or "swagger stick," and with this stood over the gruesome body, thrusting the stick again and again toward and close to the severed neck, meanwhile repeating a short, low-voiced something. After the body was cut from its shield a blanket was wrapped about it -- otherwise it was nude, save for a flayed-bark breechcloth -- and it was set up in the cramped sepulcher facing Kambulo, and sitting supported away from the earth walls by four short wooden sticks placed upright about it. An old bamboo-headed spear was broken in the shaft and the two sections placed with the corpse.

The stones were again piled across the entrance, and when all was closed except the place for one small stone a man gave a few farewell thrusts through the opening with a stick, uttering at the same time a short low sentence or two. The final stone was placed and the earth heaped against the wall.

The pole to which the corpse was tied when borne to the burial was placed horizontally before the tomb, supported with both ends resting on the high side walls of the burrow, and on it were hung a dozen white-bark headbands which were worn, evidently, as a mark of mourning, by many of the men who attended the burial.

How long it would be, in a state of nature, before the tomb would be required for another burial is a matter of chance, but a relative, frequently a son, nephew, or brother of the dead man, would be expected to avenge the dead man on the pueblo of Kambulo, with chances in favor of success, but also with equal chances of ultimate loss of the warrior's head and burial where six kinsmen had preceded him.

PART 7

AEsthetic Life

There is relatively little "color" in the life of the Bontoc Igorot. In the preceding chapter reference was made to the belief that this lack of "color," the monotony of everyday life, has to do with the continuation of head-hunting. The life of the Igorot is somber-hued indeed as compared with that of his more advanced neighbor, the Ilokano.

Dress

The Bontoc Igorot is not much given to dress -- under which term are considered the movable adornments of persons. Little effort is made by the man toward dressing the head, though before marriage he at times wears a sprig of flowers or of some green plant tucked in the hat at either side. The young man's suklang is also generally more attractive than that of the married man. With its side ornaments of human-hair tassels, its dog teeth, or mother-of-pearl disks, and its red and yellow colors, it is often very gay.

About one hundred and fifty men in Bontoc and Samoki own and sometimes wear at the girdle a large 7-inch disk of mother-of-pearl shell. It is called "fikum'," and its use is purely ornamental. (See Pls. LXXX and XXX.) It is valued highly, and I have not known half a dozen Igorot to part with one for any price. This shell ornament is widespread through the country east and also south of the Bontoc area, but nowhere is it seen plentifully, except on ceremonial days -- probably not a dozen are worn daily in Bontoc.

Other forms of adornment, though only a means to a permanent end, are the ear stretchers and variety of ear plugs which are worn in a slit in the ear lobe preparing it for the earring -- the sing-sing, which all hope to possess. The stretcher consists of two short pieces of bamboo forced apart and so held by two short cross-pieces inserted between them. The bamboo ear stretcher is generally ornamented by straight incised lines. The plugs are not all considered decorative. Some are bunches of a vegetable pith (Pl. CXXXVIII), others are wads of sugar-cane leaves. Some, however, are wooden plugs shaped quite like an ordinary large cork stopper of a bottle (Pl. CXXXVII). The outer end is often ornamented by straight incised lines or with red seeds affixed with wax or with a small piece of a cheap glass mirror roughly inlaid. The long ear slit is not the end sought, because if the owner despairs of owning the coveted earring the stretchers and plugs are eventually removed and the slit contracts from an inch and one-half to a quarter of an inch or less in length. The long slit is desired because the people consider the effect more beautiful when the ring swings and dangles at the bottom of the pendant ear. The gold earring is the most coveted, but a few silver and many copper rings are worn in substitution for the gold.

Metal earrings. (A, gold; B, copper (both are two or three generations old and their patterns are no longer made); C, copper; D, silver.)

This is practically the extent of the everyday adornment worn by the boys and men. Small boys sometimes wear a brass-wire bracelet; but the brass wire, so commonly worn on the wrists, ankles, and necks of the people east, north, and south of the Bontoc area, is not affected by the people of Bontoc.

As has been mentioned, there is an unique display of dress by the man at the head-taking ceremony of the ato, when some of the dancers wear boar-tusk armlets, called "ab-kil'," and a boar-tusk necklace, called "fu-yay'-ya."

The necklace quite resembles the Indian bear-claw necklace, but it is worn with the tusks pointing away from the breast, not toward it, as is the case with the Indian necklace. There are about six of these necklaces in Bontoc, and it is almost impossible to buy one, but the armlets are more plentiful. They are worn above the biceps, and some are adorned with a tuft of hair cut from a captured head.

The movable adornments of the woman are very similar to those of the man.

The unmarried woman wears the flowers or green sprigs in the hair, though less often than does the man. She wears the ear stretchers, ear plugs, and earrings exactly as he does. Probably 60 per cent of men and women in some way dress one ear; probably half as many dress both ears.

The chief adornment of the woman is her hairdress. It consists of strings of various beads, called "a-pong'." The hair is never combed in its dressing, except with the fingers, but the entire hair is caught at the base of the skull and lightly twisted into a loose roll; a string of beads is put beneath this twist at the back and carried forward across the head. The roll is then brought to the front of the head around the left side; at the front it is tucked forward under the beads, being thus held tightly in place. The twist is carried around the head as far as it will extend, and the end there tucked under the beads and thus secured. One and not infrequently two additional strings of beads are laid over the hair, more completely holding it in place.

The first string of beads placed on the head usually consists of compact, glossy, black seeds. Frequently brass-wire rings are regularly dispersed along the string. These beads are shown in Pl. CXLII. The second string, with its white, lozenge-shaped stone beads (Pl. CXXXIX), is very striking and attractive against the black hair. This string reaches its perfection when it is composed solely of spherical agate beads the size of small marbles and the longer white stone beads placed at regular intervals among the reddish agates. It is practically impossible to purchase these beads, since they are heirlooms. The third string is usually of dog teeth. They are strung alternately with black seeds or with sections of dog rib. This string is worn over the hair, running from the forehead around the back of the head, the white teeth resting low on the back hair, and making a very attractive adornment as they stand, points out, against the black hair. (See Pl. CLII.)

Igorot women dress their hair richly in their important ceremonials. In an in-pug-pug' ceremony of Sipaat ato in Bontoc I saw women wearing seven strings of agate beads on their hair and about their necks. The woman loves to show her friends her accumulated wealth in heirlooms, and the ato or pueblo ceremonies are the most favorable opportunities for such display. All these various hairdress beads are of Igorot manufacture.

I have seen Tukukan women come to Bontoc wearing a solid diadem about the hair. It consisted of a rattan foundation encircling the head, covered with blackened beeswax studded with three parallel rows of encircling bright-red seeds. It made a very striking headdress.

Now and then a woman is seen wearing beads around the neck, but the Bontoc woman almost never has such adornment. They are seen frequently in pueblos to the west, however. The beads for everyday wear are seeds in black, brown, and gray. There is also a small, irregular, cylindrical, wooden bead worn by the women. It is sometimes worn in strings of three or four beads by men. I believe it is considered of talismanic value when so worn.

Many women in Mayinit and some women of Bontoc wear the heirloom girdle, called "a-ko'-san," made of shells and brass wire encircling a cloth girdle (see Pl. CXL). The cloth is made in the form of a long, narrow wallet, practically concealed at the back by the encircling wire and shells. Within this wallet the cherished agate and white stone hairdress is often hidden away. In Mayinit this girdle is frequently worn beneath the skirt, when it becomes, in every essential and in the effect produced, a bustle. I have never seen it so worn in Bontoc.

Decoration

Under this head are classed all the forms of permanent adornment of the person.

First must be cited the cutting and stretching of the ear. Whereas the long, pendant earlobe is not the end in itself, nor is the long slit always permanent, yet the mutilation of the ear is permanent and desired. In a great many cases the lobe breaks, and the two, and even three, long strips of lobe hanging down seem to give their owner certain pride. Often the lower end of one of these strips is pierced and supports a ring. The sexes share alike in the preparation for and the wearing of earrings.

The woman has a permanent decoration of the nature of the "switch" of the civilized woman. The loose hair combed from the head with the fingers is saved, and is eventually rolled with the live hair of the head into long, twisted strings, some of which are an inch in diameter and three feet long; some women have more than a dozen of these twisted strings attached to the scalp. This is a common, though not universal, method of decorating the head, and the mass of lard-soaked, twisted hair stands out prominently around the crown, held more or less in place by the various bead hairdresses. (See Pls. CXLI and CXLII.)

Tattoo

The great permanent decoration of the Igorot is the tattoo. As has been stated in Chapter VI on "War and Head-Hunting," all the members -- men, women, and children -- of an ato may be tattooed whenever a head is taken by any person of the ato. It is claimed in Bontoc that at no other time is it possible for a person to be tattooed. But Tukukan tattooed some of her women in May, 1903, and this in spite of the fact that no heads had recently been taken there. However, the regulations of one pueblo are not necessarily those of another.

In every pueblo, there are one or more men, called "bu-ma-fa'-tek," who understand the art of tattooing. There are two such in Bontoc -- Toki, of Lowingan, and Finumti, of Longfoy -- and each has practiced his art on the other. Finumti has his back and legs tattooed in an almost unique way. I have seen only one other at all tattooed on the back, and then the designs were simple. A large double scallop extends from the hip to the knee on the outside of each of Finumti's legs.

The design is drawn on the skin with ink made of soot and water. Then the tattooer pricks the skin through the design. The instrument used for tattooing is called "cha-kay'-yum." It consists of from four to ten commercial steel needles inserted in a straight line in the end of a wooden handle; "cha-kay'-yum" is also the word for needle. After the pattern is pricked in, the soot is powdered over it and pressed in the openings; the tattooer prefers the soot gathered from the bottom of ollas.

The finished tattoo is a dull, blue black in color, sometimes having a greenish cast. A man in Tulubin has a tattoo across his throat which is distinctly green, while the remainder of his tattoo is the common blue black. The newly tattooed design stands out in whitish ridges, and these frequently fester and produce a mass of itching sores lasting about one month (see Pl. CXLVII).

The Igorot distinguishes three classes of tattoos: The chak-lag', the breast tattoo of the head taker; pong'-o, the tattoo on the arms of men and women; and fa'-tek, under which name all other tattoos of both sexes are classed. Fa'-tek is the general word for tattoo, and pong'-o is the name of woman's tattoo.

It is general for boys under 10 years of age to be tattooed. Their first marks are usually a small, half-inch cross on either cheek or a line or small cross on the nose. One boy in Bontoc, just at the age of puberty, has a tattoo encircling the lower jaw and chin, a wavy line across the forehead, a straight line down the nose, and crosses on the cheeks; but he is the youngest person I have seen wearing the jaw tattoo -- a mark quite commonly made in Bontoc when the chak-lag', or head-taker's emblem, is put on.

The chak-lag' is the most important tattoo of the Igorot, since it marks its wearer as a taker of at least one human head. It therefore stands for a successful issue in the most crucial test of the fitness of a person to contribute to the strength of the group of which he is a unit. It no doubt gives its wearer a certain advantage in combat -- a confidence and conceit in his own ability, and, likely, it tends to unnerve a combatant who has not the same emblem and experience. No matter what the exact social importance or advantage may be, it seems that every man in Bontoc who has the right to the emblem shows his appreciation of the privilege, since nine-tenths of the men wear the chak-lag'. It consists of a series of geometric markings running upward from the breast near each nipple and curving out on each shoulder, where it ends on the upper arm. The accompanying plates (CXLIII to CXLIX) give an excellent idea of the nature and appearance of the Igorot tattoo -- of course, reproductions in color would add to the effect. The distinctness of the markings in the photographs is about normal.

The basis of the designs is apparently geometric. If the straight-line designs originated in animal forms, they have now become so conventional that I have not discovered their original form.

The Bontoc woman is tattooed only on the arms. This tattoo begins close back of the knuckles on the back of the hands, and, as soon as it reaches the wrist, entirely encircles the arms to above the elbows. Still above this there is frequently a separate design on the outside of the arm; it is often the figure of a man with extended arms and sprawled legs.

The chak-lag' design on the man's breast is almost invariably supplemented by two or three sets of horizontal lines on the biceps immediately beneath the outer end of the main design. If the tattoo on the arms of the woman were transferred to the arms of the man, there would seldom be an overlapping -- each would supplement the other. On the men the lines are longer and the patterns simpler than those of the women, where the lines are more cross-hatched and the design partakes of the nature of patch-work.

It was not discovered that any tattoo has a special meaning, except the head-taker's emblem; and the Igorot consistently maintains that all the others are put on simply at the whim of the wearer. The face markings, those on the arms, the stomach, and elsewhere on the body, are believed to be purely aesthetic. The people compare their tattoo with the figures of an American's shirt or coat, saying they both look pretty. Often a cross-hatched marking is put over goiter, varicose veins, and other permanent swellings or enlargements. Evidently they are believed to have some therapeutic virtue, but no statement could be obtained to substantiate this opinion.

As is shown by Pls. CXLVIII and CXLIX, the tattoo of both Banawi men and women seems to spring from a different form than does the Bontoc tattoo. It appears to be a leaf, or a fern frond, but I know nothing of its origin or meaning. There is much difference in details between the tattoos of culture areas, and even of pueblos. For instance, in Bontoc pueblo there is no tattoo on a man's hand, while in the pueblos near the south side of the area the hands are frequently marked on the backs. In Benguet there is a design popularly said to represent the sun, which is seen commonly on men's hands. Instances of such differences could be greatly multiplied here, but must be left for a more complete study of the Igorot tattoo.

Music

Instrumental music

The Bontoc Igorot has few musical instruments, and all are very simple. The most common is a gong, a flat metal drum about 1 foot in diameter and 2 inches deep. This drum is commonly said to be "brass," but analyses show it to be bronze.

Two gongs submitted to the Bureau of Government Laboratories, Manila, consisted, in one case, of approximately 80 per cent copper, 15 per cent tin, and 5 per cent zinc; in the other case of approximately 84 per cent copper, 15 per cent tin, 1 per cent zinc, and a trace of iron.

Early Chinese records read that tin was one of the Chinese imports into Manila in the thirteenth century. Copper was mined and wrought by the Igorot when the Spaniards came to the Philippines, and they wrote regarding it that it was then an old and established industry and art. It may possibly be that bronze was made in the Philippines before the arrival of the Spaniard, but there is no proof of such an hypothesis.

The gong to-day enters the Bontoc area in commerce generally from the north -- from the Igorot or Tinguian of old Abra Province -- and no one in the Provinces of Benguet or Lepanto-Bontoc seems to know its source. Throughout the Archipelago and southward in Borneo there are metal drums or "gongs" apparently of similar material but of varying styles. It is commonly claimed that those of the Moro are made on the Asiatic mainland. It is my opinion that the Bontoc gong, or gang'-sa, originates in China, though perhaps it is not now imported directly from there. It certainly does not enter the Island of Luzon at Manila, or Candon in Ilokos Sur, and, it is said, not at Vigan, also in Ilokos Sur.

In the Bontoc area there are two classes of gang'-sa; one is called ka'-los, and the other co-ong'-an. The co-ong'-an is frequently larger than the other, seems to be always of thicker metal, and has a more bell-like and usually higher-pitched tone. I measured several gang'-sa in Bontoc and Samoki, and find the co-ong'-an about 5 millimeters thick, 52 to 55 millimeters deep, and from 330 to 360 millimeters in diameter; the ka'-los is only about 2 to 3 millimeters thick. The Igorot distinguishes between the two very quickly, and prizes the co-ong'-an at about twice the value of the ka'-los. Either is worth a large price to-day in the central part of the area -- or from one to two carabaos -- but it is quite impossible to purchase them even at that price.

Gang'-sa music consists of two things -- rhythm and crude harmony. Its rhythm is perfect, but though there is an appreciation of harmony as is seen in the recognition of, we may say, the "tenor" and "bass" tones of co-ong'-an and ka'-los, respectively, yet in the actual music the harmony is lost sight of by the American.

In Bontoc the gang'-sa is held vertically in the hand by a cord passing through two holes in the rim, and the cord usually has a human lower jaw attached to facilitate the grip. As the instrument thus hangs free in front of the player (always a man or boy) it is beaten on the outer surface with a short padded stick like a miniature bass-drum stick. There is no gang'-sa music without the accompanying dance, and there is no dance unaccompanied by music. A gang'-sa or a tin can put in the hands of an Igorot boy is always at once productive of music and dance.

The rhythm of Igorot gang'-sa music is different from most primitive music I have heard either in America or Luzon. The player beats 4/4 time, with the accent on the third beat. Though there may be twenty gang'-sa in the dance circle a mile distant, yet the regular pulse and beat of the third count is always the prominent feature of the sound. The music is rapid, there being from fifty-eight to sixty full 4/4 counts per minute.

It is impossible for me to represent Igorot music, instrumental or vocal, in any adequate manner, but I may convey a somewhat clearer impression of the rhythm if I attempt to represent it mathematically. It must be kept in mind that all the gang'-sa are beaten regularly and in perfect time -- there is no such thing as half notes.

The gang'-sa is struck at each italicized count, and each unitalicized count represents a rest, the accent represents the accented beat of the gang'-sa. The ka'-los is usually beaten without accent and without rest. Its beats are 1, 2, 3, 4; 1, 2, 3, 4; 1, 2, 3, 4; 1, 2, 3, 4; etc. The co-ong'-an is usually beaten with both accent and rest. It is generally as follows: 1, 2, 3', 4; 1, 2, 3', 4; 1, 2, 3', 4; 1, 2, 3', 4; etc. Sometimes, however, only the first count and again the first and second counts are struck on the individual co-ong'-an, but there is no accent unless the third is struck. Thus it is sometimes as follows: 1, 2, 3, 4; 1, 2, 3, 4; 1, 2, 3, 4; 1, 2, 3, 4; etc.; and again 1, 2, 3, 4; 1, 2, 3, 4; 1, 2, 3, 4; 1, 2, 3, 4; 1, 2, 3, 4; etc. However, the impression the hearer receives from a group of players is always of four rapid beats, the third one being distinctly accented. A considerable volume of sound is produced by the gang'-sa of the central part of the area; it may readily be heard a mile, if beaten in the open air.

In pueblos toward the western part of the area, as in Balili, Alap, and their neighbors, the instrument is played differently and the sound carries only a few rods. Sometimes the player sits in very un-Malayan manner, with legs stretched out before him, and places the gang'-sa bottom up on his lap. He beats it with the flat of both hands, producing the rhythmic pulse by a deadening or smothering of a beat. Again the gang'-sa is held in the air, usually as high as the face, and one or two soft beats, just a tinkle, of the 4/4 time are struck on the inside of the gang'-sa by a small, light stick. Now and then the player, after having thoroughly acquired the rhythm, clutches the instrument under his arm for a half minute while he continues his dance in perfect time and rhythm.

The lover's "jews'-harp," made both of bamboo and of brass, is found throughout the Bontoc area. It is played near to and in the olag wherein the sweetheart of the young man is at the time. The instrument, called in Bontoc "ab-a'-fu," is apparently primitive Malayan, and is found widespread in the south seas and Pacific Ocean.

The brass instrument, the only kind I ever saw in use except as a semitoy in the hands of small boys, is from 2 to 3 inches in length, and has a tongue, attached at one end, cut from the middle of the narrow strip of metal. (The Igorot make the ab-a'-fu of metal cartridges.) A cord is tied to the instrument at the end at which the tongue is attached, and this the player jerks to vibrate the tongue. The instrument is held at the mouth, is lightly clasped between the lips, and, as the tongue vibrates, the player breathes a low, soft tune through the instrument. One must needs get within 2 or 3 feet of the player to catch the music, but I must say after hearing three or four men play by the half hour, that they produce tunes the theme of which seems to me to bespeak a genuine musical taste.

I have seen a few crude bamboo flutes in the hands of young men, but none were able to play them. I believe they are of Ilokano introduction.

A long wooden drum, hollow and cannon-shaped, and often 3 feet and more long and about 8 inches in diameter, is common in Benguet, and is found in Lepanto, but is not found or known in Bontoc. A skin stretched over the large end of the drum is beaten with the flat of the hands to accompany the music of the metal drums or gang'-sa, also played with the flat of the hands, as described, in pueblos near the western border of Bontoc area.

Vocal music

The Igorot has vocal music, but in no way can I describe it -- to say nothing of writing it. I tried repeatedly to write the words of the songs, but failed even in that. The chief cause of failure is that the words must be sung -- even the singers failed to repeat the songs word after word as they repeat the words of their ordinary speech. There are accents, rests, lengthened sounds, sounds suddenly cut short -- in fact, all sorts of vocal gymnastics that clearly defeated any effort to "talk" the songs. I believe many of the songs are wordless; they are mere vocalizations -- the "tra la la" of modern vocal music; they may be the first efforts to sing.

I was told repeatedly that there are four classes of songs, and only four. The mang-ay-u-weng', the laborer's song, is sung in the field and trail. The mang-ay-yeng' is said to be the class of songs rendered at all ceremonies, though I believe the doleful funeral songs are of another class. The mang-ay-lu'-kay and the ting-ao' I know nothing of except in name.

Most of the songs seem serious. I never heard a mother or other person singing to a babe. However, boys and young men, friends with locked arms or with arms over shoulders, often sing happy songs as they walk along together. They often sing in "parts," and the music produced by a tenor and a bass voice as they sing their parts in rhythm, and with very apparent appreciation of harmony, is fascinating and often very pleasing.

Dancing

The Bontoc Igorot dances in a circle, and he follows the circle contraclockwise. There is no dancing without gang'-sa music, and it is seldom that a man dances unless he plays a gang'-sa. The dance step is slower than the beats on the gang'-sa; there is one complete "step" to every full 4/4 count. At times the "step" is simply a high-stepping slow run, really a springing prance. Again it is a hitching movement with both feet close to the earth, and one foot behind the other. The line of dancers, well shown in Pls. CXXXI, CLI, and CLII, passes slowly around the circle, now and again following the leader in a spiral movement toward the center of the circle and then uncoiling backward from the center to the path. Now and again the line moves rapidly for half the distance of the circumference, and then slowly backs a short distance, and again it all but stops while the men stoop forward and crouch stealthily along as though in ambush, creeping on an enemy. In all this dancing there is perfect rhythm in music and movements. There is no singing or even talking -- the dance is a serious but pleasurable pastime for those participating.

As is shown also by the illustrations, the women dance. They throw their blankets about them and extend their arms, usually clutching tobacco leaves in either hand -- which are offerings to the old men and which some old man frequently passes among them and collects -- and they dance with less movement of the feet than do the men. Generally the toes scarcely leave the earth, though a few of the older women invariably dance with a high movement and backward pawing of one foot which throws the dust and gravel over all behind them. I have more than once seen the dance circle a cloud of dust raised by one pawing woman, and the people at the margin of the circle dodging the gravel thrown back, yet they only laughed and left the woman to pursue her peculiar and discomforting "step." The dancing women are generally immediately outside the circle, and from them the rhythm spreads to the spectators until a score of women are dancing on their toes where they stand among the onlookers, and little girls everywhere are imitating their mothers. The rhythmic music is fascinating, and one always feels out of place standing stiff legged in heavy, hobnailed shoes among the pulsating, rhythmic crowd. Now and again a woman dances between two men of the line, forcing her way to the center of the circle. She is usually more spectacular than those about the margin, and frequently holds in her hand her camote stick or a ball of bark-fiber thread which she has spun for making skirts. I once saw such a dancer carry the long, heavy wooden pestle used in pounding out rice.

A few times I have seen men dance in the center of the circle somewhat as the women do, but with more movement, with a balancing and tilting of the body and especially of the arms, and with rapid trembling and quivering of the hands. The most spectacular dance is that of the man who dances in the circle brandishing a head-ax. He is shown in Pls. CLII and CLIII. At all times his movements are in perfect sympathy and rhythm with the music. He crouches around between the dancers brandishing his ax, he deftly all but cuts off a hand here, an arm or leg there, an ear yonder. He suddenly rushes forward and grinningly feigns cutting off a man's head. He contorts himself in a ludicrous yet often fiendish manner. This dance represents the height of the dramatic as I have seen it in Igorot life. His is truly a mimetic dance. His colleague with the spear and shield, who sometimes dances on the outskirts of the circle, now charging a dancer and again retreating, also produces a true mimetic and dramatic spectacle. This is somewhat more than can be said of the dance of the women with the camote sticks, pestles, and spun thread. The women in no way "act" -- they simply purposely present the implements or products of their labors, though in it all we see the real beginning of dramatic art.

Other areas, and other pueblos also, have different dances. In the Benguet area the musicians sit on the earth and play the gang'-sa and wooden drum while the dancers, a man and woman, pass back and forth before them. Each dances independently, though the woman follows the man. He is spectacular with from one to half a dozen blankets swinging from his shoulders, arms, and hands.

Captain Chas. Nathorst, of Cervantes, has told me of a dance in Lepanto, believed by him to be a funeral dance, in which men stand abreast in a long line with arms on each other's shoulders. In this position they drone and sway and occasionally paw the air with one foot. There is little movement, and what there is is sluggish and lifeless.

Games

Cockfighting is the Philippine sport. Almost everywhere the natives of the Archipelago have cockfights and horse races on holidays and Sundays. They are also greatly addicted to the sport of gambling. The Bontoc Igorot has none of the common pastimes or games of chance. This fact is remarkable, because the modern Malayan is such a gamester.

Only in toil, war, and numerous ceremonials does the Bontoc man work off his superfluous and emotional energy. One might naturally expect to find Jack a dull boy, but he is not. His daily round of toil seems quite sufficient to keep the steady accumulation of energy at a natural poise, and his head-hunting offers him the greatest game of skill and chance which primitive man has invented.

Formalities

The Igorot has almost no formalities, the "etiquette" which one can recognize as binding "form." When the American came to the Islands he found the Christians exceedingly polite. The men always removed their hats when they met him, the women always spoke respectfully, and some tried to kiss his hand. Every house, its contents and occupants, to which he might go was his to do with as he chose. Such characteristics, however, seem not to belong to the primitive Malayan. The Igorot meets you face to face and acts as though he considers himself your equal -- both you and he are men -- and he meets his fellows the same way.

When Igorot meet they do not greet each other with words, as most modern people do. As an Igorot expressed it to me they are "all same dog" when they meet. Sometimes, however, when they part, in passing each other on the trial, one asks where the other is going.

The person with a load has the right of way in the trail, and others stand aside as best they can.

There is commonly no greeting when a person comes to one's house, nor is there a greeting between members of a family when one returns home after an absence even of a week or more.

Children address their mothers as "I'-na," their word for mother, and address their father as "A'-ma," their word for father. They do this throughout life.

Igorot do not kiss or have other formal physical expression to show affection between friends or relatives. Mothers do not kiss their babes even.

The Igorot has no formal or common expression of thankfulness. Whatever gratitude he feels must be taken for granted, as he never expresses it in words.

When an Igorot desires to beckon a person to him he, in common with the other Malayans of the Archipelago, extends his arm toward the person with the hand held prone, not supine as is the custom in America, and closes the hand, also giving a slight inward movement of the hand at the wrist. This manner of beckoning is universal in Luzon.

The hand is almost never used to point a direction. Instead, the head is extended in the direction indicated -- not with a nod, but with a thrusting forward of the face and a protruding of the open lips; it is a true lip gesture. I have seen it practically everywhere in the Islands, among pagans, Mohammedans, and Christians.

PART 8

Religion

Spirit belief

The basis of Igorot religion is every man's belief in the spirit world -- the animism found widespread among primitive peoples. It is the belief in the ever-present, ever-watchful a-ni'-to, or spirit of the dead, who has all power for good or evil, even for life or death. In this world of spirits the Igorot is born and lives; there he constantly entreats, seeks to appease, and to cajole; in a mild way he threatens, and he always tries to avert; and there at last he surrenders to the more than matchful spirits, whose numbers he joins, and whose powers he acquires.

All things have an invisible existence as well as a visible, material one. The Igorot does not explain the existence of earth, water, fire, vegetation, and animals in invisible form, but man's invisible form, man's spirit, is his speech. During the life of a person his spirit is called "ta'-ko." After death the spirit receives a new name, though its nature is unchanged, and it goes about in a body invisible to the eye of man yet unchanged in appearance from that of the living person. There seems to be no idea of future rewards or punishments, though they say a bad a-ni'-to is sometimes driven away from the others.

The spirit of all dead persons is called "a-ni'-to" -- this is the general name for the soul of the dead. However, the spirits of certain dead have a specific name. Pin-teng' is the name of the a-ni'-to of a beheaded person; wul-wul is the name of the a-ni'-to of deaf and dumb persons -- it is evidently an onomatopoetic word. And wong-ong is the name of the a-ni'-to of an insane person. Fu-ta-tu is a bad a-ni'-to, or the name applied to the a-ni'-to which is supposed to be ostracized from respectable a-ni'-to society.

Besides these various forms of a-ni'-to or spirits, the body itself is also sometimes supposed to have an existence after death. Li-mum' is the name of the spiritual form of the human body. Li-mum' is seen at times in the pueblo and frequently enters habitations, but it is said never to cause death or accident. Li-mum' may best be translated by the English term "ghost," although he has a definite function ascribed to the rather fiendish "nightmare" -- that of sitting heavily on the breast and stomach of a sleeper.

The ta'-ko, the soul of the living man, is a faithful servant of man, and, though accustomed to leave the body at times, it brings to the person the knowledge of the unseen spirit life in which the Igorot constantly lives. In other words, the people, especially the old men, dream dreams and see visions, and these form the meshes of the net which has caught here and there stray or apparently related facts from which the Igorot constructs much of his belief in spirit life.

The immediate surroundings of every Igorot group is the home of the a-ni'-to of departed members of the group, though they do not usually live in the pueblo itself. Their dwellings, sementeras, pigs, chickens, and carabaos -- in fact, all the possessions the living had -- are scattered about in spirit form, in the neighboring mountains. There the great hosts of the a-ni'-to live, and there they reproduce, in spirit form, the life of the living. They construct and live in dwellings, build and cultivate sementeras, marry, and even bear children; and eventually, some of them, at least, die or change their forms again. The Igorot do not say how long an a-ni'-to lives, and they have not tried to answer the question of the final disposition of a-ni'-to, but in various ceremonials a-ni'-to of several generations of ancestors are invited to the family feast, so the Igorot does not believe that the a-ni'-to ceases, as an a-ni'-to, in what would be the lifetime of a person.

When an a-ni'-to dies or changes its form it may become a snake -- and the Igorot never kills a snake, except if it bothers about his dwelling; or it may become a rock -- there is one such a-ni'-to rock on the mountain horizon north of Bontoc; but the most common form for a dead a-ni'-to to take is li'-fa, the phosphorescent glow in the dead wood of the mountains. Why or how these various changes occur the Igorot does not understand.

In many respects the dreamer has seen the a-ni'-to world in great detail. He has seen that a-ni'-to are rich or poor, old or young, as were the persons at death, and yet there is progression, such as birth, marriage, old age, and death. Each man seems to know in what part of the mountains his a-ni'-to will dwell, because some one of his ancestors is known to inhabit a particular place, and where one ancestor is there the children go to be with him. This does not refer to desirability of location, but simply to physical location -- as in the mountain north of Bontoc, or in one to the east or south.

As was stated in a previous chapter, with the one exception of toothache, all injuries, diseases, and deaths are caused directly by a-ni'-to. In certain ceremonies the ancestral a-ni'-to, are urged to care for living descendants, to protect them from a-ni'-to that seek to harm -- and children are named after their dead ancestors, so they may be known and receive protection. In the pueblo, the sementeras, and the mountains one knows he is always surrounded by a-ni'-to. They are ever ready to trip one up, to push him off the high stone sementera dikes or to visit him with disease. When one walks alone in the mountain trail he is often aware that an a-ni'-to walks close beside him; he feels his hair creeping on his scalp, he says, and thus he knows of the a-ni'-to's presence. The Igorot has a particular kind of spear, the sinalawitan, having two or more pairs of barbs, of which the a-ni'-to is afraid; so when a man goes alone in the mountains with the sinalawitan he is safer from a-ni'-to than he is with any other spear.

The Igorot does not say that the entire spirit world, except his relatives, is against him, and he does not blame the spirits for the evils they inflict on him -- it is the way things are -- but he acts as though all are his enemies, and he often entreats them to visit their destruction on other pueblos. It is safe to say that one feast is held daily in Bontoc by some family to appease or win the good will of some a-ni'-to.

At death the spirit of a beheaded person, the pin-teng', goes above to chayya, the sky. The old men are very emphatic in this belief. They always point to the surrounding mountains as the home of the a-ni'-to, but straight above to chayya, the sky, as the home of the spirit of the beheaded. The old men say the pin-teng' has a head of flames. There in the sky the pin-teng' repeat the life of those living in the pueblo. They till the soil and they marry, but the society is exclusive -- there are none there except those who lost their heads to the enemy.

The pin-teng' is responsible for the death of every person who loses his head. He puts murder in the minds of all men who are to be successful in taking heads. He also sees the outrages of warfare, and visits vengeance on those who kill babes and small children.

In his relations with the unseen spirit world the Igorot has certain visible, material friends that assist him by warnings of good and evil. When a chicken is killed its gall is examined, and, if found to be dark colored, all is well; if it is light, he is warned of some pending evil in spirit form. Snakes, rats, crows, falling stones, crumbling earth, and the small reddish-brown omen bird, i'-chu, all warn the Igorot of pending evil.

<u>Exorcist</u>

Since the anito is the cause of all bodily afflictions the chief function of the person who battles for the health of the afflicted is that of the exorcist, rather than that of the therapeutist.

Many old men and women, known as "in-sup-ak'," are considered more or less successful in urging the offending anito to leave the sick. Their formula is simple. They place themselves near the afflicted part, usually with the hand stroking it, or at least touching it, and say, "Anito, who makes this person sick, go away." This they repeat over and over again, mumbling low, and frequently exhaling the breath to assist the departure of the anito -- just as, they say, one blows away the dust; but the exhalation is an open-mouthed outbreathing, and not a forceful blowing. One of our house boys came home from a trip to a neighboring pueblo with a bad stone bruise for which an anito was responsible. For four days he faithfully submitted to flaxseed poultices, but on the fifth day we found a woman in-sup-ak' at her professional task in the kitchen. She held the sore foot in her lap, and stroked it; she murmured to the anito to go away; she bent low over the foot, and about a dozen times she well feigned vomiting, and each time she spat out a large amount of saliva. At no time could purposeful exhalations be detected, and no explanation of her feigned vomiting could be gained. It is not improbable that when she bent over the foot she was supposed to be inhaling or swallowing the anito which she later sought to cast from her. In half an hour she succeeded in "removing" the offender, but the foot was "sick" for four days longer, or until the deep-seated bruise discharged through a scalpel opening. The woman unquestionably succeeded in relieving the boy's mind.

When a person is ill at his home he sends for an in-sup-ak', who receives for a professional visit two manojos of palay, or two-fifths of a laborer's daily wage. In-sup-ak' are not appointed or otherwise created by the people, as are most of the public servants. They are notified in a dream that they are to be in-sup-ak'.

As compared with the medicine man of some primitive peoples the in-sup-ak' is a beneficial force to the sick. The methods are all quiet and gentle; there is none of the hubbub or noise found in the Indian lodge -- the body is not exhausted, the mind distracted, or the nerves racked. In a positive way the sufferer's mind receives comfort and relief when the anito is "removed," and in most cases probably temporary, often permanent, physical relief results from the stroking and rubbing.

The man or woman of each household acts as mediator between any sick member of the family and the offending anito. There are several of these household ceremonials performed to benefit the afflicted.

If one was taken ill or was injured at any particular place in the mountains near the pueblo, the one in charge of the ceremony goes to that place with a live chicken in a basket, a small amount of basi (a native fermented drink), and usually a little rice, and, pointing with a stick in various directions, says the Wa-chao'-wad or Ay'-ug si a-fi'-ik ceremony -- the ceremony of calling the soul. It is as follows:

"A-li-ka' ab a-fi'-ik Ba-long'-long en-ta-ko' is a'-fong sang'-fu." The translation is: "Come, soul of Ba-long'-long; come with us to the house to feast." The belief is that the person's spirit is being enticed and drawn away by an anito. If it is not called back shortly, it will depart permanently.

The following ceremony, called "ka-taol'," is said near the river, as the other is in the mountains:

"A-li-ka' ta-en-ta-ko is a'-fong ta-ko' tay la-ting' is'-na." Freely translated this is: "Come, come with us into the house, because it is cold here."

A common sight in the Igorot pueblo or in the trails leading out is a man or woman, more frequently the latter, carrying the small chicken basket, the tube of basi, and the short stick, going to the river or the mountains to perform this ceremony for the sick.

After either of these ceremonies the person returns to the dwelling, kills, cooks, and, with other members of the family, eats the chicken.

For those very ill and apparently about to die there is another ceremony, called "a'-fat," and it never fails in its object, they affirm -- the afflicted always recovers. Property equal to a full year's wages is taken outside the pueblo to the spot where the affliction was received, if it is known, and the departing soul is invited to return in exchange for the articles displayed. They take a large hog which is killed where the ceremony is performed; they take also a large blue-figured blanket --

the finest blanket that comes to the pueblo -- a battle-ax and spear, a large pot of "preserved" meat, the much-prized woman's bustle-like girdle, and, last, a live chicken. When the hog is killed the person in charge of the ceremony says: "Come back, soul of the afflicted, in trade for these things."

All then return to the sick person's dwelling, taking with them the possessions just offered to the soul. At the house they cook the hog, and all eat of it; as those who assisted in the ceremony go to their own dwellings they carry each a dish of the cooked pork.

The next day, since the afflicted person does not die, they have another ceremony, called "mang-mang," in the house of the sick. A chicken is killed, and the following ceremonial is spoken from the center of the house:

"The sick person is now well. May the food become abundant; may the chickens, pigs, and rice fruit heads be large. Bring the battle-ax to guard the door. Bring the winnowing tray to serve the food; and bring the wisp of palay straw to sweep away the many words spoken near us."

For certain sick persons no ceremony is given for recovery. They are those who are stricken with death, and the Igorot claims to know a fatal affliction when it comes.

Lumawig, the Supreme Being

The Igorot has personified the forces of nature. The personification has become a single person, and to-day this person is one god, Lu-ma'-wig. Over all, and eternal, so far as the Igorot understands, is Lu-ma'-wig -- Lu-ma'-wig, who had a part in the beginning of all things; who came as a man to help the survivors and perpetuators of Bontoc; who later came as a man to teach the people whom he had befriended, and who still lives to care for them. Lu-ma'-wig is the greatest of spirits, dwelling above in chayya, the sky. All prayers for fruitage and increase -- of men, of animals, and of crops -- all prayers for deliverance from the fierce forces of the physical world are made to him; and once each month the pa'-tay ceremony, entreating Lu-ma'-wig for fruitage and health, is performed for the pueblo group by an hereditary class of men called "pa'-tay -- a priesthood in process of development. Throughout the Bontoc culture area Lu-ma'-wig, otherwise known but less frequently spoken of as Fu'-ni and Kam-bun'-yan, is the supreme being. Scheerer says the Benguet Igorot call their "god" Ka-bu-ni'-an -- the same road as Kam-bun'-yan.

In the beginning of all things Lu-ma'-wig had a part. The Igorot does not know how or why it is so, but he says that Lu-ma'-wig gave the earth with all its characteristics, the water in its various manifestations, the people, all animals, and all vegetation. To-day he is the force in all these things, as he always has been.

Once, in the early days, the lower lands about Bontoc were covered with water. Lu-ma'-wig saw two young people on top of Mount Po'-kis, north of Bontoc. They were Fa-tang'-a and his sister Fu'-kan. They were without fire, as all the fires of Bontoc were put out by the water. Lu-ma'-wig told them to wait while he went quickly to Mount Ka-lo-wi'-tan, south of Bontoc, for fire. When he returned Fu'-kan was heavy with child. Lu-ma'-wig left them, going above as a bird flies. Soon the child was born, the water subsided in Bontoc pueblo, and Fa-tang'-a with his sister and her babe returned to the pueblo. Children came to the household rapidly and in great numbers. Generation followed generation, and the people increased wonderfully.

After a time Lu-ma'-wig decided to come to help and teach the Igorot. He first stopped on Ka-lo-wi'-tan Mountain, and from there looked over the young women of Sabangan, searching for a desirable wife, but he was not pleased with the girls of Sabangan because they had short hair. He next visited Alap, but the young women of that pueblo were sickly; so he came on to Tulubin. There the marriageable girls were afflicted with goiter. He next stopped at Bontoc, where he saw two young women, sisters, in a garden. Lu-ma'-wig came to them and sat down. Presently he asked why they did not go to the house. They answered that they must work; they were gathering beans. Lu-ma'-wig was pleased with this, so he picked one bean of each variety, tossed them into the baskets -- when presently the baskets were filled to the rim. He married Fu'-kan, the younger of the two industrious sisters, and namesake of the mother of the people of Bontoc.

After marriage he lived at Chao'-wi, in the present ato of Sigichan, near the center of Bontoc pueblo. The large, flat stones which were once part of Lu-ma'-wig's dwelling are still lying in position, and are shown in Pl. CLIII.

Lu-ma'-wig at times exhibited his marvelous powers. They say he could take a small chicken, feed it a few grains of rice, and in an hour it would be full grown. He could fill a basket with rice in a very few moments, simply by putting in a handful of kernels. He could cut a stick of wood in the mountains, and with one hand toss it to his dwelling in the pueblo. Once when out in I-shil' Mountains northeast of Bontoc, Fa-tang'-a, the brother-in-law of Lu-ma'-wig, said to him, "Oh, you of no value! Here we are without water to drink. Why do you not give us water?" Lu-ma'-wig said nothing, but he turned and thrust his spear in the side of the mountain. As he withdrew the weapon a small stream of water issued from the opening. Fa-tang'-a started to drink, but Lu-ma'-wig said, "Wait; the others first; you last." When it came Fa-tang'-a's turn to drink, Lu-ma'-wig put his hand on him as he drank and pushed him solidly into the mountain. He became a rock, and the water passed through him. Several of the old men of Bontoc have seen this rock, now broken by others fallen on it from above, but the stream of water still flows on the thirsty mountain.

In an isolated garden, called "fil-lang'," now in ato Chakong, Lu-ma'-wig taught Bontoc how best to plant, cultivate, and garner her various agricultural products. Fil-lang' to-day is a unique little sementera. It is the only garden spot within the pueblo containing water. The pueblo is so situated that irrigating water can not be run into it, but throughout the dry season of 1903 -- the dryest for years in Bontoc -- there was water in at least a fourth of this little garden. There is evidently a very small. but perpetual spring within the plat. Taro now occupies the garden and is weeded and gathered by Na-wit', an old man chosen by the old men of the pueblo for this office. Na-wit' maintains and the Igorot believe that the vegetable springs up without planting. As the watering of fil-lang' is through the special dispensation of Lu-ma'-wig, so the taro left by him in his garden school received from him a peculiar lease of life -- it is perpetual. The people claim that all other taro beds must be planted annually.

Lu-ma'-wig showed the people how to build the fawi and pabafunan, and with his help those of Lowingan and Sipaat were constructed. He also told them their purposes and uses. He gave the people names for many of the things about them; he also gave the pueblo its name.

He gave them advice regarding conduct -- a crude code of ethics. He told them not to lie, because good men do not care to associate with liars. He said they should not steal, but all people should take care to live good and honest lives. A man should have only one wife; if he had more, his life would soon be required of him. The home should be kept pure; the adulterer should not violate it; all should be as brothers.

As has been previously said, the people of Bontoc claim that they did not go to war or kill before Lu-ma'-wig came.

They say no Igorot ever divorced a wife who bore him a child, yet they accuse Lu-ma'-wig of such conduct, but apparently seek to excuse the act by saying that at the time he was partially insane. Fu'-kan, Lu-ma'-wig's wife, bore him several children. One day she spoke very disrespectfully to him. This change of attitude on her part somewhat unbalanced him, and he put her with two of her little boys in a large coffin, and set them afloat on the river. He securely fastened the cover of the coffin, and on either end tied a dog and a cock. The coffin floated downstream unobserved as far as Tinglayan. There the barking of the dog and the crowing of the cock attracted the attention of a man who rushed out into the river with his ax to secure such a fine lot of pitch-pine wood. When he struck his ax in the wood a voice called from within, "Don't do that; I am here." Then the man opened the coffin and saw the woman and children. The man said his wife was dead, and the woman asked whether he wanted her for a wife. He said he did, so she became his wife.

After a time the children wanted to return to Bontoc to see their father. Before they started their mother instructed them to follow the main river, but when they arrived at the mouth of a tributary stream they became confused, and followed the river leading them to Kanyu. There they asked for their father, but the people killed them and cut them up. Presently they were alive again, and larger than before. They killed them again and again. After they had come to life seven times they were full-grown men; but the eighth time Kanyu killed them they remained dead. Bontoc went for their bodies, and told Kanyu that, because they killed the children of Lu-ma'-wig, their children would always be dying -- and to-day Bontoc points to the fewness of the houses which make up Kanyu. The bodies were buried close to Bontoc on the west and northwest; scarcely were they interred when trees began to grow upon and about the graves -- they were the transformed bodies of Lu-ma'-wig's children. The Igorot never cut trees in the two small groves nearby the pueblo, but once a year they gather the fallen branches. They say that a Spaniard once started to cut one of the trees, but he had struck only a few blows when he was suddenly taken sick. His bowels bloated and swelled and he died in a few minutes.

These two groves are called "Pa-pa-tay'" and "Pa-pa-tay' ad So-kok'," the latter one shown in Pl. CLIV. Each is said to be a man, but among some of the old men the one farthest to the north is now said to be a woman. The reason they assign for now calling one a woman is because it is situated lower down on the mountain than the other. They are held sacred, and the monthly religious ceremonial of patay is observed beneath their trees.

It seems that Lu-ma'-wig soon became irritated and jealous, because Fu'-kan was the wife of another man, and he sent word forbidding her to leave her house. About this time the warriors of Tinglayan returned from a head-hunting expedition. When Fu'-kan heard their gongs and knew all the pueblo was dancing, she danced alone in the house. Soon those outside felt the ground trembling. They looked and saw that the house where Fu'-kan lived was trembling and swaying. The women hastened to unfortunate Fu'-kan and brought her out of the house. However, in coming out she had disobeyed Lu-ma'-wig, and shortly she died.

Lu-ma'-wig's work was ended. He took three of his children with him to Mount Po'-kis, on the northern horizon of Bontoc, and from there the four passed above into the sky as birds fly. His two other children wished to accompany him, but he denied them the request; and so they left Bontoc and journeyed westward to Loko (Ilokos Provinces) because, they said, if they remained, they would die. What became of these two children is not known; neither is it known whether those who went above are alive now; but Lu-ma'-wig is still alive in the sky and is still the friendly god of the Igorot, and is the force in all the things with which he originally had to do.

Throughout the Bontoc culture area Lu-ma'-wig is the one and only god of the people. Many said that he lived in Bontoc, and, so far as known, they hold the main facts of the belief in him substantially as do the people of his own pueblo.

"Changers" in religion

In the western pueblos of Alap, Balili, Genugan, Takong, and Sagada there has been spreading for the past two years a changing faith. The people allying themselves with the new faith call themselves "Su-pa-la'-do," and those who speak Spanish say they are "guardia de honor."

The Su-pa-la'-do continue to eat meat, but wash and cleanse it thoroughly before cooking. They are said also not to hold any of the ceremonials associated with the old faith. They keep a white flag flying from a pole near their dwelling, or at least one such flag in the section of the pueblo in which they reside. They also believe that Lu-ma'-wig will return to them in the near future.

A Tinguian man of the pueblo of Pay-yao', Lepanto, a short journey from Agawa, in Bontoc, is said to be the leading spirit in this faith of the "guardia de honor." It is believed to be a movement taking its rise from the restless Roman Catholic Ilokano of the coast.

In Bontoc pueblo the thought of the return of Lu-ma'-wig is laughed at. The people say that if Lu-ma'-wig was to return they would know of it. However, two families in Bontoc, one that of Finumti, the tattooer, and the other that of Kayyad, a neighbor of Finumti, have a touch of a changing faith. They are known in Bontoc as O-lot'.

I was not able to trace any connection between the O-lot' and the Su-pa-la'-do, though I presume there is some connection; but I learned of the O-lot' only during the last few days of my stay in Bontoc. The O-lot' are said not to eat meat, not to kill chickens, not to smoke, and not to perform any of the old ceremonies. However, I do not believe they or in fact the Su-pa-la'-do neglect all ceremonials, because such a turning from a direct, positive, and very active religious life to one of total neglect of the old religious ceremonials would seem to be impossible for an otherwise normal Igorot.

Priesthood

That the belief in spirits is the basis of Igorot religion is shown in the fact that each person or each household has the necessary power and knowledge to intercede with the anito. No class of persons has been differentiated for this function, excepting the limited one of the dream-appointed insupak or anito exorcists.

That belief in a supreme being is a later development than the belief in spirits is clear when the fact is known that a differentiated class of persons has arisen whose duty it is to intercede with Lumawig for the people as a whole.

This religious intercessor has few of the earmarks of a priest. He teaches no morals or ethics, no idea of future rewards or punishments, and he is not an idle, non-productive member of the group. He usually receives for the consumption of his family the food employed in the ceremonies to Lumawig, but this would not sustain the family one week in the fifty-two. The term "priesthood" is applied to these people for lack of a better one, and because its use is sufficiently accurate to serve the present purpose.

There are three classes of persons who stand between the people and Lumawig, and to-day all hold an hereditary office. The first class is called "Wa-ku'," of which there are three men, namely, Fug-ku-so', of ato Somowan, Fang-u-wa', of ato Lowingan, and Cho-Iug', of ato Sigichan. The function of these men is to decide and announce the time of all rest days and ceremonials for the pueblo. These Wa-ku' inform the old men of each ato, and they in turn announce the days to the ato. The small boys, however, are the true "criers." They make more noise in the evening before the rest day, crying "Teng-ao'! whi! teng-ao'!" ("Rest day! hurrah! rest day!"), than I have heard from the pueblo at any other time.

The title of the second class of intercessors is "Pa'-tay," of whom there are two in Bontoc -- Kad-lo'-san, of ato Somowan, and Fi'-Iug, of ato Longfoy.

The Pa'-tay illustrate the nature of the titles borne by all the intercessors. The title is the same as the name of the ceremony or one of the ceremonies which the person performs.

Once every new moon each Pa'-tay performs the pa'-tay ceremony in the sacred grove near the pueblo. This ceremony is for the general well-being of the pueblo.

The third class of intercessors has duties of a two-fold nature. One is to allay the rain and wind storms, called "baguios," and to drive away the cold; and the other is to petition for conditions favorable to crops. There are seven of these men, and each has a distinct title. All are apparently of equal importance to the group.

Le-yod', of ato Lowingan, whose title is "Ka-lob'," has charge of the ka-lob' ceremony held once or twice each year to allay the baguios. Ang'-way, of ato Somowan, whose title is "Chi-nam'-wi," presides over the chi-nam'-wi ceremony to drive away the cold and fog. This ceremony usually occurs once or twice each year in January, February, or March. He also serves once each year in the fa-kil' ceremony for rain. Cham-lang'-an, of ato Filig, has the title "Po-chang'," and he has one annual ceremony for large palay. A fifth intercessor is Som-kad', of ato Sipaat; his title is "Su'-wat." He performs two ceremonies annually -- one, the su'-wat, for palay fruitage, and the other a fa-kil' for rains. Ong-i-yud', of ato Fatayyan, is known by the title of "Ke'-eng." He has two ceremonies annually, one ke'-eng and the other tot-o-lod'; both are to drive the birds and rats from the fruiting palay. Som-kad', of ato Sigichan, with the title "O-ki-ad'," has charge of three ceremonies annually. One is o-ki-ad', for the growth of beans; another is los-kod', for abundant camotes, and the third is fa-kil', the ceremony for rain. There are four annual fa-kil' ceremonies, and each is performed by a different person.

Sacred days

Teng-ao' is the sacred day, the rest day, of Bontoc. It occurs on an average of about every ten days throughout the year, though there appears to be no definite regularity in its occurrence. The old men of the two ato of Lowingan and Sipaat determine when teng-ao' shall occur, and it is a day observed by the entire pueblo.

The day is publicly announced in the pueblo the preceding evening. If a person goes to labor in the fields on a sacred day -- not having heard the announcement, or in disregard of it -- he is fined for "breaking the Sabbath." The old men of each ato discover those who have disobeyed the pueblo law by working in the field, and they announce the names to the old men of Lowingan and Sipaat, who promptly take from the lawbreaker firewood or rice or a small chicken to the value of about 10 cents, or the wage of two days. March 3, 1903, was teng-ao' in Bontoc, and I saw ten persons fined for working. The fines are expended in buying chickens and pigs for the pa'-tay ceremonies of the pueblo.

Ceremonials

A residence of five months among a primitive people about whom no scientific knowledge existed previously is evidently so scant for a study of ceremonial life that no explanation should be necessary here. However, I wish to say that no claim is made that the following short presentation is complete -- in fact, I know of several ceremonies by name about which I can not speak at all with certainty. Time was also insufficient to get accurate translations of all ceremonial utterances which are here presented.

There is great absence of formalism in uttering ceremonies, scarcely two persons speak exactly the same words, though I believe the purport of each ceremony, as uttered by two people, to be the same. This looseness may be due in part to the absence of a developed cult having the ceremonies in charge from generation to generation.

Ceremonies connected with agriculture

Pochang

This ceremony is performed at the close of the period Pa-chog', the period when rice seed is put in the germinating beds.

It is claimed there is no special oral ceremony for Po-chang'. The proceeding is as follows: On the first day after the completion of the period Pa-chog' the regular monthly Pa'-tay ceremony is held. On the second day the men of ato Sigichan, in which ato Lumawig resided when he lived in Bontoc, prepare a bunch of runo as large around as a man's thigh. They call this the "cha-nug'," and store it away in the ato fawi, and outside the fawi set up in the earth twenty or more runo, called "pa-chi'-pad -- the pud-pud' of the harvest field.

The bunch of runo is for a constant reminder to Lumawig to make the young rice stalks grow large. The pa-chi'-pad are to prevent Igorot from other pueblos entering the fawi and thus seeing the efficacious bundle of runo.

During the ceremony of Lis-lis, at the close of the annual harvest of palay, both the cha-nug' and the pa-chi'-pad are destroyed by burning.

Chaka

On February 10, 1903, the rice having been practically all transplanted in
Bontoc, was begun the first of a five-day general ceremony for abundant and good
fruitage of the season's palay. It was at the close of the period I-na-na'.

The ceremony of the first day is called "Su-yak'." Each group of kin -- all descendants of one man or woman who has no living ascendants -- kills a large hog and
makes a feast. This day is said to be passed without oral ceremony.

The ceremony of the second day was a double one. The first was called "Wa-lit'"
and the second "Mang'-mang." From about 9.30 until 11 in the forenoon a person from each family -- usually a woman -- passed slowly up the steep mountain
side immediately west of Bontoc. These people went singly and in groups of two
to four, following trails to points on the mountain's crest. Each woman carried a
small earthen pot in which was a piece of pork covered with basi. Each also carried a chicken in an open-work basket, while tucked into the basket was a round
stick about 14 inches long and half an inch in diameter. This stick, "lo'-lo," is
kept in the family from generation to generation.

When the crest of the mountain was reached, each person in turn voiced an invitation to her departed ancestors to come to the Mang'-mang feast. She placed her
olla of basi and pork over a tiny fire, kindled by the first pilgrim to the mountain
in the morning and fed by each arrival. Then she took the chicken from her basket and faced the west, pointing before her with the chicken in one hand and the
lo'-lo in the other. There she stood, a solitary figure, performing her sacred mission alone. Those preceding her were slowly descending the hot mountain side in
groups as they came; those to follow her were awaiting their turn at a distance
beneath a shady tree. The fire beside her sent up its thin line of smoke, bearing
through the quiet air the fragrance of the basi.

The woman invited the ancestral anito to the feast, saying:

"A-ni'-to ad Lo'-ko, su-ma-a-kay'-yo ta-in-mang-mang'-ta-ko ta-ka-ka'-nen si
mu'-teg." Then she faced the north and addressed the spirit of her ancestors there:
"A-ni'-to ad La'-god, su-ma-a-kay'-yo ta-in-mang-mang'-ta-ko ta-ka-ka'-nen si
mu'-teg." She faced the east, gazing over the forested mountain ranges, and called
to the spirits of the past generation there: "A-ni'-to ad Bar'-lig su-ma-a-kay'-yo ta-
in-mang-mang'-ta-ko ta-ka-ka-nen si mu'-teg."

As she brought her sacred objects back down the mountain another woman stood alone by the little fire on the crest.

The returning pilgrim now puts her fowl and her basi olla inside her dwelling, and likely sits in the open air awaiting her husband as he prepares the feast. Outside, directly in front of his door, he builds a fire and sets a cooking olla over it. Then he takes the chicken from its basket, and at his hands it meets a slow and cruel death. It is held by the feet and the hackle feathers, and the wings unfold and droop spreading. While sitting in his doorway holding the fowl in this position the man beats the thin-fleshed bones of the wings with a short, heavy stick as large around as a spear handle. The fowl cries with each of the first dozen blows laid on, but the blows continue until each wing has received fully half a hundred. The injured bird is then laid on its back on a stone, while its head and neck stretch out on the hard surface. Again the stick falls, cruelly, regularly, this time on the neck. Up and down its length it is pummeled, and as many as a hundred blows fall -- fall after the cries cease, after the eyes close and open and close again a dozen times, and after the bird is dead. The head receives a few sharp blows, a jet of blood spurts out, and the ceremonial killing is past. The man, still sitting on his haunches, still clasping the feet of the pendent bird, moves over beside his fire, faces his dwelling, and voices the only words of this strangely cruel scene. His eyes are open, his head unbending, and he gazes before him as he earnestly asks a blessing on the people, their pigs, chickens, and crops.

The old men say it is bad to cut off a chicken's head -- it is like taking a human head, and, besides, they say that the pummeling makes the flesh on the bony wings and neck larger and more abundant -- so all fowls killed are beaten to death.

After the oral part of the ceremony the fowl is held in the flames till all its feathers are burned off. It is cut up and cooked in the olla before the door of the dwelling, and the entire family eats of it.

Each family has the Mang'-mang ceremony, and so also has each broken household if it possesses a sementera -- though a lone woman calls in a man, who alone may perform the rite connected with the ceremonial killing, and who must cook the fowl. A lone man needs no woman assistant.

Though the ancestral anito are religiously bidden to the feast, the people eat it all, no part being sacrificed for these invisible guests. Even the small olla of basi is drunk by the man at the beginning of the meal.

The rite of the third day is called "Mang-a-pu'-i." The sementeras of growing palay are visited, and an abundant fruitage asked for. Early in the morning some member of each household goes to the mountains to get small sprigs of a plant named "pa-lo'-ki." Even as early as 7.30 the pa-lo'-ki had been brought to many of the houses, and the people were scattering along the different trails leading to the most distant sementeras. If the family owned many scattered fields, the day was well spent before all were visited.

Men, women, and boys went to the bright-green fields of young palay, each carrying the basket belonging to his sex. In the basket were the sprigs of pa-lo'-ki, a small olla of water, a small wooden dish or a basket of cooked rice, and a bamboo tube of basi or tapui. Many persons had also several small pieces of pork and a chicken. As they passed out of the pueblo each carried a tightly bound club-like torch of burning palay straw; this would smolder slowly for hours.

On the stone dike of each sementera the owner paused to place three small stones to hold the olla. The bundle of smoldering straw was picked open till the breeze fanned a blaze; dry sticks or reeds quickly made a small, smoking fire under the olla, in which was put the pork or the chicken, if food was to be eaten there. Frequently, too, if the smoke was low, a piece of the pork was put on a stick punched into the soil of the sementera beside the fire and the smoke enwrapped the meat and passed on over the growing field.

As soon as all was arranged at the fire a small amount of basi was poured over a sprig of pa-lo'-ki which was stuck in the soil of the sementera, or one or two sprigs were inserted, drooping, in a split in a tall, green runo, and this was pushed into the soil. While the person stood beside the efficacious pa-lo'-ki an invocation was voiced to Lumawig to bless the crop.

The olla and piece of pork were at once put in the basket, and the journey conscientiously continued to the next sementera. Only when food was eaten at the sementera was the halt prolonged.

A-sig-ka-cho' is the name of the function of the fourth day. On that day each household owning sementeras has a fish feast.

At that season of the year (February), while the water is low in the river, only the very small, sluggish fish, called "kacho," is commonly caught at Bontoc. Between 200 and 300 pounds of those fish, only one in a hundred of which exceeded 2 1/2 inches in length, were taken from the river during the three hours in the afternoon when the ceremonial fishing was in progress.

Two large scoops, one shown in Pl. XLIX, were used to catch the fish. They were a quarter of a mile apart in the river, and were operated independently.

At the house the fish were cooked and eaten as is described in the section on "Meals and mealtime."

When this fish meal was past the last observance of the fourth day of the Cha'-ka ceremonial was ended.

The rite of the last day is called "Pa'-tay." It is observed by two old Pa'-tay priests. Exactly at high noon Kad-lo'-san left his ato carrying a chicken and a smoldering palay-straw roll in his hand, and the unique basket, tak-fa', on his shoulder. He went unaccompanied and apparently unnoticed to the small grove of trees, called "Pa-pa-tay' ad So-kok'." Under the trees is a space some 8 or 10 feet across, paved with flat rocks, and here the man squatted and put down his basket. From it he took a two-quart olla containing water, a small wooden bowl of cooked rice, a bottle of native cane sugar, and a head-ax. He next kindled a blaze under the olla in a fireplace of three stones already set up. Then followed the ceremonial killing of the chicken, as described in the Mang'-mang rite of the second day. With the scarcely dead fowl held before him the man earnestly addressed a short supplication to Lumawig.

The fowl was then turned over and around in the flame until all its feathers were burned off. Its crop was torn out with the fingers. The ax was struck blade up solid in the ground, and the legs of the chicken cut off from the body by drawing them over the sharp ax blade, and they were put at once into the pot. An incision was cut on each side of the neck, and the body torn quickly and neatly open, with the wings still attached to the breast part. A glad exclamation broke from the man when he saw that the gall of the fowl was dark green. The intestines were then removed, ripped into a long string, and laid in the basket. The back part of the fowl, with liver, heart, and gizzard attached, went into the now boiling pot, and the breast section followed it promptly. Three or four minutes after the bowl of rice was placed immediately in front of the man, and the breast part of the chicken laid in the bowl on the rice. Then followed these words: "Now the gall is good, we shall live in the pueblo invulnerable to disease."

The breast was again put in the pot, and as the basket was packed up in preparation for departure the anito of ancestors were invited to a feast of chicken and rice in order that the ceremony might be blessed.

At the completion of this supplication the Pa'-tay shouldered his basket and hastened homeward by a different route from which he came.

If a chicken is used in this rite it is cooked in the dwelling of the priest and is eaten by the family. If a pig is used the old men of the priest's ato consume it with him.

The performance of the rite of this last day is a critical half hour for the town. If the gall of the fowl is white or whitish the palay fruitage will be more or less of a failure. The crop last year was such -- a whitish gall gave the warning. If a crow flies cawing over the path of the Pa'-tay as he returns to his dwelling, or if the dogs bark at him, many people will die in Bontoc. Three years ago a man was killed by a falling bowlder shortly after noon on this last day's ceremonial -- a flying crow had foretold the disaster. If an eagle flies over the path, many houses will burn. Two years ago an eagle warned the people, and in the middle of the day fifty or more houses burned in Bontoc in the three ato of Pokisan, Luwakan, and Ungkan.

If none of these calamities are foretold, the anito enemies of Bontoc are not revengeful, and the pueblo rests in contentment.

Suwat

This ceremony, performed by Som-kad' of ato Sipaat, occurs in the first period of the year, I-na-na'. The usual pig or chicken is killed, and the priest says: "In-fi-kus'-na ay pa-ku' to-mo-no'-ka ad chay'-ya." This is: "Fruit of the palay, grow up tall, even to the sky."

Keeng

Ke'-eng ceremony is for the protection of the palay. Ong-i-yud', of ato Fatayyan, is the priest for this occasion, and the ceremony occurs when the first fruit heads appear on the growing rice. They claim two good-sized hogs are killed on this day. Then Ong-i-yud' takes a ki'-lao, the bird-shaped bird scarer, from the pueblo and stealthily ducks along to the sementera where he suddenly erects the scarer. Then he says:

U-mi-chang'-ka Sik'-a
Ti-lin' in kad La'-god yad Ap'-lay
Sik'-a o'-tot in lo-ko-lo'-ka nan fu-i'-mo.

Freely translated, this is --

Ti-lin' [the rice bird], you go away into the north country and the south country
You, rat, you go into your hole.

Totolod

This ceremony, tot-o-lod', occurs on the day following ke'-eng, and it is also for the protection of the rice crop. Ong-i-yud' is the priest for both ceremonies.

The usual hog is killed, and then the priest ties up a bundle of palay straw the size of his arm, and walks to the south side of the pueblo "as though stalking deer in the tall grass." He suddenly and boldly throws the bundle southward, suggesting that the birds and rats follow in the same direction, and that all go together quickly.

Safosab

This ceremony is recorded in the chapter on "Agriculture" in the section on "Harvesting," page 103. It is simply referred to here in the place where it would logically appear if it were not so intimately connected with the harvesting that it could not be omitted in presenting that phase of agriculture.

Lislis

At the close of the rice harvest, at the beginning of the season Li'-pas, the lis-lis ceremony is widely celebrated in the Bontoc area. It consists, in Bontoc pueblo, of two parts. Each family cooks a chicken in the fireplace on the second floor of the dwelling. This part is called "cha-peng'." After the cha-peng' the public part of the ceremony occurs. It is called "fug-fug'-to," and is said to continue three days.

Fug-fug'-to in Bontoc is a man's rock fight between the men of Bontoc and Samoki. The battle is in the broad bed of the river between the two pueblos. The men go to the conflict armed with war shields, and they pelt each other with rocks as seriously as in actual war. There is a man now in Bontoc whose leg was broken in the conflict of 1901, and three of our four Igorot servant boys had scalp wounds received in lis-lis rock conflicts.

A river cuts in two the pueblo of Alap, and that pueblo is said to celebrate the harvest by a rock fight similar to that of Bontoc and Samoki.

It is said by Igorot that the Sadanga lis-lis is a conflict with runo (or reed) spears, which are warded off with the war shields.

It is claimed that in Sagada the public part of the ceremony consists of a mud fight in the sementeras, mud being thrown by each contending party.

Loskod

This ceremony occurs once each year at the time of planting camotes, in the period of Ba-li'-ling.

Som-kad' of ato Sigichan is the pueblo "priest" who performs the los-kod' ceremony. He kills a chicken or pig, and then petitions Lumawig as follows: "Lo-mos-kod'-kay to-ki'." This means, "May there be so many camotes that the ground will crack and burst open."

Okiad

Som-kad' of ato Sigichan performs the o-ki-ad' ceremony once each year during the time of planting the black beans, or ba-la'-tong, also in the period of Ba-li'-ling.

The petition addressed to Lumawig is said after a pig or chicken has been ceremonially killed; it runs as follows: "Ma-o'-yed si ba-la'-tong, Ma-o'-yed si fu'-tug, Ma-o'-yed nan i-pu-kao'." A free translation is, "May the beans grow rapidly; may the pigs grow rapidly; and may the people [the children] grow rapidly."

Kopus

Ko'-pus is the name given the three days of rest at the close of the period of Ba-li'-ling. They say there is no special ceremony for ko'-pus, but some time during the three days the pa'-tay ceremony is performed.

Ceremonies connected with climate

Fakil

The Fa-kil' ceremony for rain occurs four times each year, on four succeeding days, and is performed by four different priests. The ceremony is simple. There is the usual ceremonial pig killing by the priest, and each night preceding the ceremony all the people cry: "I-teng'-ao ta-ko nan fa-kil'." This is only an exclamation, meaning, "Rest day! We observe the ceremony for rain!" I was informed that the priest has no separate oral petition or ceremony, though it is probable that he has.

Kalob

Once or twice each year, or maybe once in two years, in January or February, a cold, driving rain pours itself on Bontoc from the north. It often continues for two or three days, and is a miserable storm to be out in.

If this storm continues three or four days, Le-yod', of ato Lowingan, performs the following ceremony in his dwelling: "Ma-kis-kis'-kay li-fo'-o min-chi-kang'-ka ay fat-a'-wa ta-a'-yu nan fa'-ki lo-lo'-ta." A very free translation of this is as follows: "You fogs, rise up rolling. Let us have good weather in all the world! All the people are very poor."

Following this ceremony Le-yod' goes to Chao'-wi, the site of Lumawig's former dwelling in the pueblo, shown in Pl. CLIII, and there he builds a large fire. It is claimed the fierce storm always ceases shortly after the ka-lob' is performed.

Chinamwi

Ang'-way of ato Somowan performs the chi-nam'-wi ceremony once or twice each year during the cold and fog of the period Sama, when the people are standing in the water-filled sementeras turning the soil, frequently working entirely naked.

Many times I have seen the people shake -- arms, legs, jaw, and body -- during those cold days, and admit that I was touched by the ceremony when I saw it.

A hog is killed and each household gives Ang'-way a manojo of palay. He pleads to Lumawig: "Tum-ke'-ka ay li-fo'-o ta-a-ye'-o nan in sa-ma'-mi." This prayer is: "No more cold and fog! Pity those working in the sementera!"

Ceremonies connected with head taking[35]

Kafokab

Ka-fo'-kab is the name of a ceremony performed as soon as a party of successful head-hunters returns home. The old man in charge at the fawi says: "Cha-kay'-yo fo'-so-mi ma-pay-ing'-an. Cha-kay'-mi in-ked-se'-ka-mi nan ka-nin'-mi to-kom-ke'-ka." This is an exultant boast -- it is the crow of the winning cock. It runs as follows: "You, our enemies, we will always kill you! We are strong; the food we eat makes us strong!"

Changtu

There is a peculiar ceremony, called "chang'-tu," performed now and then when i'-chu, the small omen bird, visits the pueblo.

This ceremony is held before each dwelling and each pabafunan in the pueblo. A chicken is killed, and usually both pork and chicken are eaten. The man performing the Chang'-tu says:

"Sik'-a tan-ang'-a sik'-a lu'-fub ad Sa-dang'-a nan ay-yam' Sik'-a ta-lo'-lo ad La'-god nan ay-yam' Sik'-a ta-lo'-lo ye'-mod La'-god nan fa-no wat'-mo yad Ap'-lay."

This speech is a petition running as follows:

"You, the anito of a person beheaded by Bontoc, and you, the anito of a person who died in a dwelling, you all go to the pueblo of Sadanga [that is, you destructive spirits, do not visit Bontoc; but we suggest that you carry your mischief to the pueblo of Sadanga, an enemy of ours]. You, the anito of a Bontoc person beheaded by some other pueblo, you go into the north country, and you, the anito of a Bontoc person beheaded by some other pueblo, you carry the palay-straw torch into the north country and the south country [that is, friendly anito, once our fellow-citizens, burn the dwellings of our enemies both north and south of us]."

In this petition the purpose of the Chang'-tu is clearly defined. The faithful i'-chu has warned the pueblo that an anito, perhaps an enemy, perhaps a former friend, threatens the pueblo; and the people seek to avert the calamity by making feasts -- every dwelling preparing a feast. Each household then calls the names of the classes of malignant anito which destroy life and property, and suggests to them that they spend their fury elsewhere.

Ceremony connected with ato

Young men sometimes change their membership from one a'-to to another. It is said that old men never do. There is a ceremony of adoption into a new a'-to when a change is made; it is called "pu-ke'" or "pal-ug-peg'." At the time of the ceremony a feast is made. and some old man welcomes the new member as follows:

If you die first, you must look out for us, since we wish to live long [that is, your spirit must protect us against destructive spirits], do not let other pueblos take our heads. If you do not take this care, your spirit will find no food when it comes to the a'-to, because the a'-to will be empty -- we will all be dead.

PART 9

Mental Life

The Igorot does not know many things in common with enlightened men, and yet one constantly marvels at his practical knowledge. Tylor says primitive man has "rude, shrewd sense." The Igorot has more -- he has practical wisdom.

Actual knowledge

Concerning cosmology, the Igorot believes Lumawig gave the earth and all things connected with it. Lumawig makes it rain and storm, gives day and night, heat and cold. The earth is "just as you see it." It ceases somewhere a short distance beyond the most distant place an Igorot has visited. He does not know how it is supported. "Why should it fall?" he asks. "A pot on the earth does not fall." Above is chayya, the sky -- the Igorot does not know or attempt to say what it is. It is up above the earth and extends beyond and below the visible horizon and the limit of the earth. The Igorot does not know how it remains there, and a man once interrupted me to ask why it did not fall down below the earth at its limit.

"Below us," an old Igorot told me, "is just bones."

The sun is a man called "Chal-chal'." The moon is a woman named "Ka-bi-gat'." "Once the moon was also a sun, and then it was always day; but Lumawig made a moon of the woman, and since then there is day and night, which is best."

There are two kinds of stars. "Fat-ta-ka'-kan" is the name of large stars and "tuk-fi'-fi" is the name of small stars. The stars are all men, and they wear white coats.

Once they came down to Bontoc pueblo and ate sugar cane, but on being discovered they all escaped again to chayya.

Thunder is a gigantic wild boar crying for rain. A Bontoc man was once killed by Ki-cho', the thunder. The unfortunate man was ripped open from his legs to his head, just as a man is ripped and torn by the wild boar of the mountains. The lightning, called "Yup-yup," is also a hog, and always accompanies Ki-cho'.

Lumawig superintends the rains. Li-fo'-o are the rain clouds -- they are smoke. "At night Lumawig has the li-fo'-o come down to the river and get water. Before morning they have carried up a great deal of water; and then they let it come down as rain."

Earthquakes are caused by Lumawig. He places both hands on the edge of the earth and quickly pushes it back and forth. They do not know why he does it.

Regarding man himself the Igorot knows little. He says Lumawig gave man and all man's functionings. He does not know the functioning of blood, brain, stomach, or any other of the primary organs of the body. He says the bladder of men and animals is for holding the water they drink. He knows that a man begets his child and that a woman's breasts are for supplying the infant food, but these two functionings are practically all the facts he knows or even thinks he knows about his body.

<u>Mensuration</u>

Under this title are considered all forms of measurement used by the Igorot.

Numbers

The most common method of enumerating is that of the finger count. The usual method is to count the fingers, beginning with the little finger of the right hand, in succession touching each finger with the forefinger of the other hand. The count of the thumb, li'-ma, five, is one of the words for hand. The sixth count begins with the little finger of the left hand, and the tenth reaches the thumb. The eleventh count begins with the little finger of the right hand again, and so the count continues. The Igorot system is evidently decimal. One man, however, invariably recorded his eleventh count on his toes, from which he returned to the little finger of his right hand for the twenty-first count.

A common method of enumerating is one in which the record is kept with small pebbles placed together one after another on the ground.

Another method in frequent use preserves the record in the number of sections of a slender twig which is bent or broken half across for each count.

When an Igorot works for an American he records each day by a notch in a small stick. A very neat record for the month was made by one of our servants who prepared a three-sided stick less than 2 inches long. Day by day he cut notches in this stick, ten on each edge.

When a record is wanted for a long time -- as when one man loans another money for a year or more -- he ties a knot in a string for each peso loaned.

The Igorot subtracts by addition. He counts forward in the total of fingers or pebbles the number he wishes to subtract, and then he again counts the remainder forward.

Lineal measure

The distance between the tips of the thumb and middle finger extended and opposed is the shortest linear measure used by the Igorot, although he may measure by eye with more detail and exactness, as when he notes half the above distance. This span measure is called "chang'-an" or "i'-sa chang'-an," "chu'-wa chang'-an," etc.

Chi-pa' is the measure between the tips of the two middle fingers when the arms are extended full length in opposite directions. Chi-wan' si chi-pa' is half the above measure, or from the tip of the middle finger of one hand, arm extended from side of body, to the sternum.

These three measures are most used in handling timbers and boards in the construction of buildings.

Cloth for breechcloths is measured by the length of the forearm, being wound about the elbow and through the hand, quite as one coils up a rope.

Long distances in the mountains or on the trail are measured by the length of time necessary to walk them, and the length of time is told by pointing to the place of the sun in the heavens at the hour of departure and arrival.

Rice sementeras are measured by the number of cargoes of palay they produce. Besides this relatively exact measure, sementeras producing up to five cargoes are called "small," pay-yo' ay fa-nig'; and those producing more than five are said to be "large," pay-yo' chuk-chuk'-wag.

Measurement of animals

The idea of the size of a carabao, and at the same time a crude estimate of its age and value, is conveyed by representing on the arm the length of the animal's horns.

The size of a hog and, as with the carabao, an estimate of its value is shown by representing the size of the girth of the animal by clasping the hands around one's leg. For instance, a small pig is represented by the size of the speaker's ankle, as he clasps both hands around it; a larger one is the size of his calf; a still larger one is the size of a man's thigh; and one still larger is represented by the thigh and calf together, the calf being bent tightly against the upper leg. To represent a still larger hog, the two hands circle the calf and thigh, but at some distance from them.

The Bontoc Igorot has no system of liquid or dry measure, nor has he any system of weight.

The calendar

The Igorot has no mechanical record of time or events, save as he sometimes cuts notches in a stick to mark the flight of days. He is apt, however, in memorizing the names of ancestors, holding them for half a dozen generations, but he keeps no record of age, and has no adequate conception of such a period as twenty years. He has no conception of a cycle of time greater than one year, and, in fact, it is the rare man who thinks in terms of a year. When one does he speaks of the past year as tin-mo-win', or i-san' pa-na'-ma.

Prominent Igorot have insisted that a year has only eight moons, and other equally sane and respected men say it has one hundred. But among the old men, who are the wisdom of the people, there are those who know and say it has thirteen moons.

They have noted and named eight phases of the moon, namely: The one-quarter waxing moon, called "fis-ka'-na;" the two-quarters waxing moon, "ma-no'-wa," or "ma-lang'-ad;" the three-quarters waxing moon, "kat-no-wa'-na" or "nap-no';" the full moon, "fit-fi-tay'-eg;" the three-quarters waning moon, "ka-tol-pa-ka'-na" or "ma-til-pa'-kan;" the two-quarters waning moon, "ki-sul-fi-ka'-na;" the one-quarter waning moon, sig-na'-a-na" or "ka-fa-ni-ka'-na;" and the period following the last, when there is but a faint rim of light, is called "li'-meng" or "ma-a-mas'."

Recognized phases of the moon.
Fis-ka'-na.
Ma-no'-wa.
Kat-no-wa'-na.
Fit-fi-tay'-eg.
Ka-tol-pa-ka'-na.
Ki-sul-fi-ka'-na.
Sig-na'-a-na.
Li'-meng.

However, the Igorot do seldom count time by the phases of the moon, and the only solar period of time they know is that of the day. Their word for day is the same as for sun, a-qu'. They indicate the time of day by pointing to the sky, indicating the position the sun occupied when a particular event occurred.

There are two seasons in a year. One is Cha-kon', having five moons, and the other is Ka-sip', having eight moons. The seasons do not mark the wet and dry periods, as might be expected in a country having such periods. Cha-kon' is the season of rice or "palay" growth and harvest, and Ka-sip' is the remainder of the year. These two seasons, and the recognition that there are thirteen moons in one year, and that day follows night, are the only natural divisions of time in the Igorot calendar.

He has made an artificial calendar differing somewhat in all pueblos in name and number and length of periods. In all these calendars the several periods bear the names of the characteristic industrial occupations which follow one another successively each year. Eight of these periods make up the calendar of Bontoc pueblo, and seven of them have to do with the rice industry. Each period receives its name from that industry which characterizes its beginning, and it retains this name until the beginning of the next period, although the industry which characterized it may have ceased some time before.

I-na-na' is the first period of the year, and the first period of the season Cha-kon'. It is the period, as they say, of no more work in the rice sementeras -- that is, practically all fields are prepared and transplanted. It began in 1903 on February 11. It lasts about three months, continuing until the time of the first harvest of the rice or "palay" crop in May; in 1903 this was until May 2. This period is not a period of "no work" -- it has many and varied labors.

The second period is La'-tub. It is that of the first harvests, and lasts some four weeks, ending about June 1.

Cho'-ok is the third period. It is the time when the bulk of the palay is harvested. It occupies about four weeks, running over in 1903 two days in July.

Li'-pas is the fourth period. It is that of "no more palay harvest," and lasts for about ten or fifteen days, ending probably about July 15. This is the last period of the season Cha-kon'.

The fifth period is Ba-li'-ling. It is the first period of the season Ka-sip'. It takes its name from the general planting of camotes, and is the only one of the calendar periods not named from the rice industry. It continues about six weeks, or until near the 1st of September.

Sa-gan-ma' is the sixth period. It is the time when the sementeras to be used as seed beds for rice are put in condition, the earth being turned three different times. It lasts about two months. November 15, 1902, the seed rice was just peeping from the kernels in the beds of Bontoc and Sagada, and the seed is sown immediately after the third turning of the earth, which thus ended early in November.

Pa-chog' is the seventh period of the annual calendar. It is the period of seed sowing, and begins about November 10. Although the seed sowing does not last many days, the period Pa-chog' continues five or six weeks.

Sa'-ma is the last period of the calendar. It is the period in which the rice sementeras are prepared for receiving the young plants and in which these seedlings are transplanted from the seed beds. The last Sa'-ma was near seven weeks' duration. It began about December 20, 1902, and ended February 10, 1903. Sa'-ma is the last period of the season Ka-sip', and the last of the year.

The Igorot often says that a certain thing occurred in La'-tub, or will occur in Ba-li'-ling, so these periods of the calendar are held in mind as the civilized man thinks of events in time as occurring in some particular month.

The Igorot have a tradition that formerly the moon was also a sun, and at that time it was always day. Lumawig told the moon to be "moon," and then there was night. Such a change was necessary, they say, so the people would know when to work -- that is, when was the right time, the right moon, to take up a particular kind of labor.

Folk tales

The paucity of the pure mental life of the Igorot is nowhere more clearly shown than in the scarcity of folk tales.

I group here seven tales which are quite commonly known among the people of Bontoc. The second, third, fourth, and fifth are frequently related by the parents to their children, and I heard all of them the first time from boys about a dozen years old. I believe these tales are nearly all the pure fiction the Igorot has created and perpetuated from generation to generation, except the Lumawig stories.

The Igorot story-tellers, with one or two exceptions, present the bare facts in a colorless and lifeless manner. I have, therefore, taken the liberty of adding slightly to the tales by giving them some local coloring, but I have neither added to nor detracted from the facts related.

The sun man and moon woman; or, origin of head-hunting

The Moon, a woman called "Ka-bi-gat'," was one day making a large copper cooking pot. The copper was soft and plastic like potter's clay. Ka-bi-gat' held the heavy sagging pot on her knees and leaned the hardened rim against her naked breasts. As she squatted there -- turning, patting, shaping, the huge vessel -- a son of the man Chal-chal', the Sun, came to watch her. This is what he saw: The Moon dipped her paddle, called "pip-i'," in the water, and rubbed it dripping over a smooth, rounded stone, an agate with ribbons of colors wound about in it. Then she stretched one long arm inside the pot as far as she could. "Tub, tub, tub," said the ribbons of colors as Ka-bi-gat' pounded up against the molten copper with the stone in her extended hand. "Slip, slip, slip, slip," quickly answered pip-i', because the Moon was spanking back the many little rounded domes which the stone bulged forth on the outer surface of the vessel. Thus the huge bowl grew larger, more symmetrical, and smooth.

Suddenly the Moon looked up and saw the boy intently watching the swelling pot and the rapid playing of the paddle. Instantly the Moon struck him, cutting off his head.

Chal-chal' was not there. He did not see it, but he knew Ka-bi-gat' cut off his son's head by striking with her pip-i'.

He hastened to the spot, picked the lad up, and put his head where it belonged -- and the boy was alive.

Then the Sun said to the Moon:

"See, because you cut off my son's head, the people of the Earth are cutting off each other's heads, and will do so hereafter."

"And it is so," the story-tellers continue; "they do cut off each other's heads."

Origin of coling, the serpent eagle[36]

A man and woman had two boys. Every day the mother sent them into the mountains for wood to cook her food. Each morning as she sent them out she complained about the last wood they brought home.

One day they brought tree limbs; the mother complained, saying:

"This wood is bad. It smokes so much that I can not see, and soon I shall be blind." And then she added, as was her custom:

"If you do not work well, you can have only food for dogs and pigs."

That day, as usual, the boys had in their topil for dinner only boiled camote vines, such as the hogs eat, and a small allowance of rice, just as much as a dog is fed. At night the boys brought some very good wood -- wood of the pitch-pine tree. In the morning the mother complained that such wood blackened the house. She gave them pig food in their topil, saying:

"Pig food is good enough for you because you do not work well."

That night each boy brought in a large bundle of runo. The mother was angry, and scolded, saying:

"This is not good wood; it leaves too many ashes and it dirties the house."

In the morning she gave them dog food for dinner, and the boys again went away to the mountains. They were now very thin and poor because they had no meat to eat. By and by the older one said:

"You wait here while I climb up this tree and cut off some branches." So he climbed the tree, and presently called down:

"Here is some wood" -- and the bones of an arm dropped to the ground.

"Oh, oh," exclaimed the younger brother, "it is your arm!"

Again the older boy called, "Here is some more wood" -- and the bones of his other arm fell at the foot of the tree.

Again he called, and the bones of a leg dropped; then his other leg fell. The next time he called, down came the right half of his ribs; and then, next, the left half of his ribs; and immediately thereafter his spinal column. Then he called again, and down fell his hair.

The last time he called, "Here is some wood," his skull dropped on the earth under the tree.

"Here, take those things home," said he. "Tell the woman that this is her wood; she only wanted my bones."

"But there is no one to go with me down the mountains," said the younger boy.

"Yes; I will go with you, brother," quickly came the answer from the tree top.

So the boy tied up his bundle, and, putting it on his shoulder, started for the pueblo. As he did so the other -- he was now Co-ling' -- soared from the tree top, always flying directly above the boy.

When the younger brother reached home he put his bundle down, and said to the woman:

"Here is the wood you wanted."

The woman and the husband, frightened, ran out of the house; they heard something in the air above them.

"Qu-iu'-kok! qu-iu'-kok! qu-iu'-kok!" said Co-ling', as he circled around and around above the house. "Qu-iu'-kok! qu-iu'-kok!" he screamed, "now camotes and palay are your son. I do not need your food any longer."

Origin of tilin, the ricebird[37]

As the mother was pounding out rice to cook for supper, her little girl said:

"Give me some mo'-ting to eat."

"No," answered the mother, "mo'-ting is not good to eat; wait until it is cooked."

"No, I want to eat mo'-ting," said the little girl, and for a long time she kept asking her mother for raw rice.

At last her mother interrupted, "It is bad to talk so much."

The rice was then all pounded out. The mother winnowed it clean, and put it in her basket, covering it up with the winnowing tray. She placed an empty olla on her head and went to the spring for water.

The anxious little girl reached quickly for the basket to get some rice, but the tray slipped from her grasp and fell, covering her beneath it in the basket.

The mother returned with the water to cook supper. She heard a bird crying, "King! king! nik! nik! nik!" When the woman uncovered the basket, Tilin, the little brown ricebird, flew away, calling:

"Good-bye, mother; good-bye, mother; you would not give me mo'-ting!"

Origin of kaag, the monkey

The palay was in the milk and maturing rapidly. Many kinds of birds that knew how delicious juicy palay is were on hand to get their share, so the boys were sent to stay all day in the sementeras to frighten these little robbers away.

Every day a father sent out his two boys to watch his palay in a narrow gash in the mountain; and every day they carried their small basket full of cooked rice, white and delicious, but their mother put no meat in the basket.

Finally one of the boys said:

"It is bad not to have meat to eat; every day we have only rice."

"Yes, it is bad," said his brother. "We can not keep fat without meat; we are getting poor and thin, and pretty soon we shall die."

"That is true," answered the other boy; "pretty soon we shall die. I believe I shall be ka'-ag."

And during the day thick hair came on this boy's arms; and then he became hairy all over; and then it was so -- he was ka'-ag, and he vanished in the mountains.

Then soon the other boy was ka'-ag, too. At night he went home and told the father:

"Your boy is ka'-ag; he is in the mountains."

The boy ran out of the house quickly. The father went to the mountains to get his boy, but ka'-ag ran up a tall tree; at the foot of the tree was a pile of bones. The father called his son, and ka'-ag came down the tree, and, as the father went toward him, ka'-ag stood up clawing and striking at the man with his hands, and breathing a rough throat cry like this:

"Haa! haa! haa!"

Then the man ran home crying, and he never got his boys.

Pretty soon there was a-sa'-wan nan ka'-ag[38] with a babe. Then there were many little children; and then, pretty soon, the mountains were full of monkeys.

Origin of gayyang, the crow, and fanias, the large lizard

There were two young men who were the very greatest of friends.

One tattooed the other beautifully. He tattooed his arms and his legs, his breast and his belly, and also his back and face. He marked him beautifully all over, and he rubbed soot from the bottom of an olla into the marks, and he was then very beautiful.

When the tattooer finished his work he turned to his friend, and said: "Now you tattoo me beautifully, too."

So the young men scraped together a great pile of black, greasy soot from pitch-pine wood; and before the other knew what the tattooed one was doing he rubbed soot over him from finger tip to finger tip. Then the black one asked:

"Why do you tattoo me so badly?"

Without waiting for an answer they began a terrible combat. When, suddenly, the tattooed one was a large lizard, fa-ni'-as,[39] and he ran away and hid in the tall grass; and the sooty black one was gay-yang, the crow,[40] and he flew away and up over Bontoc, because he was ashamed to enter the pueblo after quarreling with his old friend.

Owug, the snake

The old men say that a man of Mayinit came to live in Bontoc, as he had married a Bontoc woman and she wished to live in her own town.

After a while the man died. His friends came to the funeral, and a snake, o-wug', also came. When the people wept, o-wug' cried also. When they put the dead man in the grave, and when they stood there looking, o-wug' came to the grave and looked upon the man, and then went away.

Later, when the friends observed the death ceremony, o-wug' also came.

"O-wug' thus showed himself to be a friend and companion of the Igorot. Sometime in the past he was an Igorot, but we have not heard," the old men say, "when or how he was o-wug'."

"We never kill o-wug'; he is our friend. If he crosses our path on a journey, we stop and talk. If he crosses our path three or four times, we return home, because, if we continue our journey then, some of us will die. O-wug' thus comes to tell us not to proceed; he knows the bad anito on every trail."

Who took my father's head?

The Bontoc people have another folk tale regarding head taking. In it Lumawig, their god, taught them how to discover which pueblo had taken the head of one of their members. They repeat this story as a ceremony in the pabafunan after every head lost, though almost always they know what pueblo took it. It is as follows:

"A very great time ago a man and woman had two sons. Far up in the mountains they owned some garden patches. One day they told the boys to go and see whether the stone wall about the garden needed repair; but the boys said they did not wish to go, so the father went alone. As he did not return at nightfall, his sons started into the mountains to find him. They bound together two small bunches of runo for torches to light up the steep, rough, twisting trail. One torch was burning when they went out, and they carried the other to light them home again. Nowhere along the trail did they find their father; he had not been injured in the path, nor could they find where he had fallen over a cliff. So they passed on to the garden; there they found their father's headless body. They searched for blood in the bushes and grass, but they found nothing -- no blood, no enemies' tracks.

"They carried the strange corpse down the mountain trail to their home in Bontoc. Then they hastened to the pabafunan, and there they told the men what had befallen their father. The old men counseled together, and at last one of them said: 'Lumawig told the old men of the past, so the old men last dead told me, that should any son find his father beheaded, he should do this: He should ask, "Who took my father's head? Did Tukukan take it? Did Sakasakan take it?" ' and Lumawig said, 'He shall know who took his father's head.'

"So the boys took a basket, the fangao, to represent Lumawig, and stuck it full of chicken feathers. Before the fangao they placed a small cup of basi. Then squatting in front with the cup at their feet they put a small piece of pork on a stick and held it over the cup. 'Who took my father's head? -- did Tukukan?' they asked. But the pork and the cup and the basket all remained still. 'Did Sakasakan?' asked the boys all was as before. They went over a list of towns at enmity with Bontoc, but there was no answer given them. At last they asked, 'Did the Moon?' -- but still there was no answer. 'Did the Sun?' the boys asked, and suddenly the piece of pork slid from the stick into the basi. And this was the way Lumawig had said a person should know who took his father's head.

"The Sun, then, was the guilty person. The two boys took some dogs and hastened to the mountains where their father was killed. There the dogs took up the scent of the enemy, and followed it in a straight line to a very large spring where the water boiled up, as at Mayinit where the salt springs are. The scent passed into this bubbling, tumbling water, but the dogs could not get down. When the dogs returned to land the elder brother tried to enter, but he failed also. Then the younger brother tried to get down; he succeeded in going beneath the water, and there he saw the head of his father, and young men in a circle were dancing around it -- they were the children of the Sun. The brother struck off the head of one of these young men, caught up his father's head, and, with the two heads, escaped. When he reached his elder brother the two hastened home to their pueblo."

PART 10

Language

Introduction

The language of the Bontoc Igorot is sufficiently distinct from all others to be classed as a separate dialect. However, it is originally from a parent stock which to-day survives more or less noticeably over probably a much larger part of the surface of the earth than the tongue of any other primitive people.

The language of every group of primitive people in the Philippine Archipelago, except the Negrito, is from that same old tongue. Mr. Homer B. Hulbert[41] has recorded vocabularies of ten groups of people in Formosa; and those vocabularies show that the people belong to the same great linguistic family as the Bontoc Igorot. Mr. Hulbert believes that the language of Korea is originally of the same stock as that of Formosa. In concluding his article he says:

We find therefore that out of a vocabulary of fifty words there are fifteen in which a distinct similarity [between Korean and Formosan] can be traced, and in not a few of the fifteen the similarity amounts to practical identity.

The Malay language of Malay Peninsula, Java, and Sumatra is from the same stock language. So are many, perhaps all, the languages of Borneo, Celebes, and New Zealand. This same primitive tongue is spread across the Pacific and shows unmistakably in Fiji, New Hebrides, Samoa, and Hawaii. It is also found in Madagascar.

Alphabet

The Bontoc man has not begun even the simplest form of permanent mechanical record in the line of a written language, and no vocabulary of the language has before been published.

The following alphabet was used in writing Bontoc words in this study:

A as in FAR; Spanish RAMO
A is in LAW; as O in French OR
AY as in AI in AISLE; Spanish HAY
AO as OU in OUT; as AU in Spanish AUTO
B as in BAD; Spanish BAJAR
CH as in CHECK; Spanish CHICO
D as in DOG; Spanish DAR
E as in THEY; Spanish HALLE
E as in THEN; Spanish COMEN
F as in FIGHT; Spanish FIRMAR
G as in GO; Spanish GOZAR
H as in HE; Tagalog BAHAY
I as in PIQUE; Spanish HIJO
I as in PICK
K as in KEEN
L as in LAMB; Spanish LENTE
M as in MAN; Spanish MENOS
N as in NOW; Spanish JABON
NG as in FINGER; Spanish LENGUA
O as in NOTE; Spanish NOSOTROS
OI as in BOIL
P as in POOR; Spanish PERO
Q as CH in German ICH
S as in SAUCE; Spanish SORDO
SH as in SHALL; as CH in French CHARMER
T as in TOUCH; Spanish TOMAR
U as in RULE; Spanish UNO
U as in BUT
U as in German KUHL
V as in VALVE; in Spanish VOLVER
W as in WILL; nearly as OU in French OUI
Y as in YOU; Spanish YA

The sounds which I have represented by the unmarked vowels A, E, I, O, and U, Swettenham and Clifford in their Malay Dictionary represent by the vowels with a circumflex accent. The sound which I have indicated by U they indicate by A. Other variations will be noted.

The sound represented by A, it must be noted, has not always the same force or quantity, depending on an open or closed syllable and the position of the vowel in the word.

So far as I know there is no R sound in the Bontoc Igorot language. The word "Igorot" when used by the Bontoc man is pronounced Igolot. In an article on "The Chamorro language of Guam"[42] it is noted that in that language there was originally no R sound but that in modern times many words formerly pronounced by an L sound now have that letter replaced by R.

Linguistic inconsistencies

The language of the Bontoc area is not stable, but is greatly shifting. In pueblos only a few hours apart there are not only variations in pronunciation but in some cases entirely different words are used, and in a single pueblo there is great inconsistency in pronunciation.

It is often impossible to determine the exact sound of vowels, even in going over common words a score of times with as many people. The accent seems very shifting and it is often difficult to tell where it belongs.

Several initial consonants of words and syllables are commonly interchanged, even by the same speaker if he uses a word more than once during a conversation. That this fickleness is a permanency in the language rather than the result of the present building of new words is proved by ato names, words in use for many years -- probably many hundred years.

One of the most frequent interchanges is that of B and F. This is shown in the following ato names: Bu-yay'-yeng or Fu-yay'-yeng; Ba-tay'-yan or Fa-tay'-yan; Bi'-lig or Fi'-lig; and Long-boi' or Long-foi'. It is also shown in two other words where one would naturally expect to find permanency -- the names of the men's public buildings in the ato, namely, ba'-wi or fa'-wi, and pa-ba-bu'-nan or pa-ba-fu'-nan. Other common illustrations are found in the words ba-to or fa-to (stone) and ba-bay'-i or fa-fay'-i (woman).

Another constant interchange is that of CH and D. This also is shown well in names of ato, as follows: Cha-kong' or Da-kong'; Pud-pud-chog' or Pud-pud-dog'; and Si-gi-chan' or Si-gi-dan'. It is shown also in chi'-la or di'-la (tongue).

The interchange of initial K and G is constant. These letters are interchanged in the following names of ato: Am-ka'-wa or Am-ga'-wa; Lu-wa'-kan or Lu-wa'-gan; and Ung-kan' or Ung-gan'. Other illustrations are ku'-lid or gu'-lid (itch) and ye'-ka or ye'-ga (earthquake).

The following three words illustrate both the last two interchanges: Cho'-ko or Do'-go (name of an ato); pag-pa-ga'-da or pag-pa-ka'-cha (heel); and ka-cho' or ga-de'-o (fish).

<u>Nouns</u>

The nouns appear to undergo slight change to indicate gender, number, or case. To indicate sex the noun is followed by the word for woman or man -- as, a'-su fa-fay'-i (female dog), or a'-su la-la'-ki (male dog). The same method is employed to indicate sex in the case of the third personal pronoun Si'-a or Si-to-di'. Si'-a la-le'-ki or Si-to-di' la-la'-ki is used to indicate the masculine gender, and Si'-a fa-fay'-i or Si-to-di' fa-fay'-i the feminine.

The plural form of the noun is sometimes the same as the singular. Plural number may also be expressed by use of the word ang-san (many) or am-in' (all) in addition to the noun. It is sometimes expressed by repetition of syllables, as la-la'-ki (man), la-la-la'-ki (men); sometimes, also, by the prefix ka together with repetition of syllables, as li-fo'-o (cloud), ka-li'-fo-li-fo'-o (clouds). There seems to be no definite law in accordance with which these several plural forms are made. When in need of plurals in this study the singular form has always been used largely for simplicity.

<u>Pronouns</u>

The personal pronouns are:

I Sak-in'

You Sik-a'

He, she Si'-a and Si-to-di'

We Cha-ta'-ko and Cha-ka'-mi

You Cha-kay'-yo

They Cha-i-cha and Cha-to-di'

Examples of the possessive as indicated in the first person are given below:

My father A-mak'

My dog A-suk'

My hand Li-mak'

Our father A-ma'-ta

Our dog A-su'-ta

Our house A-fong'-ta

Other examples of the possessive are not at hand, but these given indicate that, as in most Malay dialects, a noun with a possessive suffix is one form of the possessive.

Scheerer[43] gives the possessive suffixes of the Benguet Igorot as follows:

My K, after A, I, O, and U, otherwise 'KO

Thy } M, after A, I, O, and U, otherwise 'MO

Your

His } IO

Her

Our (inc.) 'TAYO

Our (exc.) 'ME

Your 'DIO

Their 'CHA or 'RA

These possessive suffixes in the Benguet Igorot language are the same, according to Scheerer, as the suffixes used in verbal formation.

The verbal suffixes of the Bontoc Igorot are very similar to those of the Benguet. It is therefore probable that the possessive suffixes are also very similar.

It is interesting to note that in the Chamorro language of Guam the possessive suffixes for the first person correspond to those of the Igorot -- MY is KO and OUR is TA.

Verbs

Mention has been made of the verbal suffixes. Their use is shown in the following paradigms:

I eat Sak-in' mang-an-ak'

You eat Sik-a' mang-an-ka'

He eats Si-to-di' mang-an'

We eat Cha-ka'-mi mang-an-ka-mi'

You eat Cha-kay'-yo mang-an-kay'-o

They eat Cha-to-di' mang-an-cha'

I go Sak-in' u-mi-ak'

You go Sik-a' u-mi-ka'

He goes Si-to-di' u-mi'

We go Cha-ka-mi' u-mi-ka-mi'

You go Cha-kay'-yo u-mi-kay'-yo

They go Cha-to-di' u-mi-cha'

The suffixes are given below, and the relation they bear to the personal pronouns is also shown by heavy-faced type:

I 'ak Sak-in'

You (sing) 'ka Sik-a'

He ... Si'-a or Si-to-di'

We kami or tako Cha-ka'-mi or Cha-ta'-ko

You kayo Cha-kay'-yo

They cha Cha-to-di' or cha-i'-cha

The Benguet suffixes as given by Scheerer are:

I 'ko or 'ak

You 'mo or 'ka

He 'to

We { me

tayo

You 'kayo or 'dio

They 'ra or 'cha

The verbal suffixes seem to be commonly used by the Bontoc Igorot in verbal formations. The tense of a verb standing alone seems always indefinite; the context alone tells whether the present, past, or future is indicated.

Comparative vocabularies

About eighty-five words have been selected expressing simple ideas. These are given in the Bontoc Igorot language and as far as possible in the Benguet Igorot; they are also given in the Malay and the Sulu languages.

Of eighty-six words in both Malay and Bontoc 32 per cent are clearly derived from the same root words, and of eighty-four words in the Sulu and Bontoc 45 per cent are from the same root words. Of sixty-eight words in both Malay and Benguet 34 per cent are from the same root words, and 47 per cent of sixty-seven Benguet and Sulu words are from the same root words. Of sixty-four words in Bontoc and Benguet 58 per cent are the same or nearly the same.

These facts suggest the movement of the Philippine people from the birthplace of the parent tongue, and also the great family of existing allied languages originating in the primitive Malayan language. They also suggest that the Bontoc and the Benguet peoples came away quite closely allied from the original nest, and that they had association with the Sulu later than with the Malay.

[In the following compilation works have been consulted respectively as follows: Malay -- Hugh Clifford and Frank Athelstane Swettenham, A Dictionary of The Malay Language (Taiping, Perak; in parts, Part I appearing 1894, Part III appearing 1904); Sulu -- Andson Cowie, English-Sulu-Malay Vocabulary, with Useful Sentences, Tables, etc. (London, 1893); Benguet Igorot -- Otto Scheerer, The Ibaloi Igorot, MS. in MS. Coll., The Ethnological Survey for the Philippine Islands.]

English
Malay
Sulu
Benguet Igorot
Bontoc Igorot

Ashes
Abu
Abu
De-pok
Cha-pu'

Bad
Jahat (wicked)
Mang-i, ngi
...
Ngag

Black

Hitam
Itam
An-to'-leng
In-ni'-tit

Blind
Buta
Buta
Sa-gei a ku'-rab[44]
Na-ki'-mit

Blood
Darah
Duguh
Cha'-la
Cha'-la

Bone
Tulang
Bukog
Pu'-gil
Ung-et'

Burn, to
Bakar
Sunog
...
Fin-mi'-chan

Chicken
Anak ayam
Anak-manok
...
Mo-nok'

Child
Anak
Batah, anak
A-a'-nak
Ong-ong'-a

Come
Mari
Mari
...
A-li-ka'

Cut, to
Potong
Hoyah
Kom-pol'
Ku-ke'-chun

Day
Hari
Adlau
A-kou
A-qu'

Die, to
Mati
Matai
...
Ma-ti'

Dog
Anjing
Erok
A-su'
A'-su

Drink, to
Minum
Hinom, minom
...
U-mi-num'

Ear
Telinga
Tainga
Tang-i'-da
Ko-weng'

Earthquake
Gempa tanah
Linog
Yek-yek
Ye'-ga

Eat, to
Makan
Ka-aun
Kanin
Mang-an', Ka-kan'

Eight
Dilapan
Walu
Gua'-lo
Wa-lo'

Eye
Mata
Mata
Ma-ta
Ma-ta'

Father
Baba
Amah
A-ma
A'-ma

Finger nail
Kuku
Kuku
Ko-go
Ko-ko'

Fire
Api
Kayu
A-pui
A-pu'-i

Five
Lima
Lima
Di'-ma
Li-ma'

Foot
Kaki
Siki
Cha-pan
Cha-pan'

Four
Ampat
Opat
Ap'-pat
I-pat'

Fruit
Buah
Bunga-kahol
Damos
Fi-kus'-na

Get up, to
Bangun
Bangun
...
Fo-ma-ong'

Good
Baik
Maraiau
...
Cug-a-wis'

Grasshopper
Bi-lalang
Ampan
Chu'-ron
Cho'-chon

Ground (earth)
Tanah
Lopah
Bu'-dai
Lu'-ta

Hair of head
Rambut
Buhok
Bu-og
Fo-ok'

Hand
Tangan
Lima
Di-ma
Li-ma', Ad-pa'

Head
Kepala
O
Tok-tok
O'-lo

Hear, to
Dengar
Dungag
...
Chung-nen'

Here
Sini
Di, di-ha-inni
Chiai
Is'-na

Hog
Babi
Baboi
Ke-chil
Fu-tug'

I
Shaya
Aku
Sikak; Sidiak
Sak-in'

Kill, to
Bunoh
Bunoh
Bunu'-in
Na-fa'-kug

Knife
Pisau
Lading
Ta'-ad
Ki-pan'

Large
Besar
Dakolah
Abatek
Chuk-chuk'-i

Lightning
Kilat
Kilat
Ba-gi'-dat
Yup-Yup

Louse
Kutu
Kutu
Ku-to
Ko'-to

Man
Orang
Tau
Da'-gi
La-la'-ki

Monkey
Munyit, Kra
Amok
Ba-ges
Ka-ag'

Moon
Bulan
Bulan
Bu'-lan
Fu-an'

Mortar (for rice)
Lesong
Lusong
...
Lu-song'

Mother
Mak, ibu
Inah
I-na
I'-na

Night
Malam
Dum
Kal-leian, A-da'-wi
Mas-chim, la-fi'

Nine
S'ambilan
Siam
Dsi'-am
Si-am'

No
Tidak
Waim di
...
A-di'

Nose
Hidong
Ilong
A-deng
I-ling'

One
Satu, suatu, sa
Isa
Sa-gei'
I-sa'

Rain
Hujan
Ulan
U'-ran
O-chan'

Red
Merah
Pula, lag
Am-ba'-alang-a
Lang-at'

Rice (threshed)
Padi
Pai
...
Pa-ku'

Rice (boiled)
Nasi
K'aun-an
I-na-pui
Mak-an'

River
Sungei
Sobah
Pa'-dok
Wang'-a

Run, to
Lari
Dag-an
...
In-tug'-tug

Salt
Garam
Asin
A-sin
Si'-mut

Seven
Tujoh
Peto
Pit'-to
Pi-to'

Sit, to
Dudok
Lingkud
...
Tu-muck'-chu

Six
Anam
Unom
An-nim
I-nim'

Sky
Langit
Langit
Dang-it
Chay'-ya

Sleep, to
Tidor
Ma-tog
...
Ma-si-yip'

Small
Kechil
Asivi
O-o'-tik
Fan-ig'

Smoke
Asap
Aso
A-sok
A-sok'

Steal, to
Men-churi
Takau
Magibat
Mang-a-qu'

Stone
Batu
Batu
Ba-to
Ba-to

Sun
Mata-Hari
Mata suga
A-kau, Si-kit
A-qu'

Talk, to
Ber-chakap
Nug-pamong
...
En-ka-li'

Ten
Sa'puloh
Hangpoh
Sam-pu'-lo
Sim-po'-o

There
Di-situ, Di-sana
Ha ietu, dun
Chitan, Chiman
Is'-chi

Three
Tiga
To
Tad'-do
To-lo'

To-morrow
Esok, Besok
Kin-shum
Ka-bua-san
A-swa'-kus

Tree
Poko'kayu
Kahoi
Po-on
Cha-pon', Kay'-o

Two
Dua
Rua, Dua
Chu'-a
Chu'-wa

Walk, to
Ber-jalan
Panau
...
Ma-na'-lun

Water
Ayer
Tubig
Cha-num
Che-num'

White
Puteh
Ma-putih
Am-pu-ti'
Im-po'-kan

Wind
Angin
Hangin
Cha-num
Che-num'

Woman
Prempuan
Babai
Bi-i, a-ko'-dau
Fa-fay'-i

Wood
Kayu
Kahol
Ki'-u
Kay'-o

Yellow
Kuning
...
Chu-yao[45]
Fa-king'-i

Yes
Ya
...
...
Ay

You (singular)
Ankau
Ekau
Sikam
Sik'-a

Bontoc vocabulary

The following vocabulary is presented in groups with the purpose of throwing additional light on the grade of culture the Igorot has attained.

No words follow which represent ideas borrowed of a modern culture; for instance, I do not record what the Igorot calls shoes, pantaloons, umbrellas, chairs, or books, no one of which objects he naturally possesses.

Whereas it is not claimed that all the words spoken by the Igorot follow under the various headings, yet it is believed that the man's vocabulary is nearly exhausted under such headings as "Cosmology," "Clothing, dress, and adornment," and "Weapons, utensils, etc.:"

English, with Bontoc equivalent

Cosmology

Afternoon Mug-a-qu'

Afternoon, middle of Mak-sip'

Air Si'-yak

Ashes Cha-pu'

Blaze Lang-lang

Cloud, rain Li-fo'-o

Creek Ki-nan'-wan

Dawn Wi-wi-it'

Day A-qu'

Day after to-morrow Ka-sin' wa'-kus

Day before yesterday Ka-sin' ug'-ka

Dust Cha'-pog

Earthquake Ye'-ga

East Fa-la'-an si a-qu'

Evening Ni-su'-yao

Fire A-pu'-i

Ground (earth) Lu'-ta

Hill Chun'-tug

Horizon Nang'-ab si chay'-ya

Island Pa'-na

Lightning Yup-yup

Midnight Teng-ang si la-fi'

Milky way Ang'-san nan tuk-fi'-fi[46]

Moon Fu-an'

Moon, eclipse of Ping-mang'-et nan fu-an'

Moon, full Fit-fi-tay'-eg

Moon, waxing, one-quarter Fis-ka'-na

Moon, waxing, two-quarters Ma-no'-wa

Moon, waxing, three-quarters Kat-no-wa'-na

Moon, waning, three-quarters Ka-tol-pa-ka'-na

Moon, waning, two-quarters Ki-sul-fi-ka'-na

Moon, waning, one-quarter Sig-na'-a-na

Moon, period following Li'-meng

Morning Fib-i-kut'

Morning, mid Ma-a-qu'

Mountain Fi'-lig

Mud Pi'-tek

Nadir Ad-cha'-im

Night La-fi' or mas-chim

Noon Nen-ting'-a or teng-ang si a-qu'

Periods of time in a year I-na-na', La'-tub, Cho'-ok, Li'-pas, Ba-li'-ling, Sa-gan-ma', Pa-chog', Sa'-ma

Plain Cha'-ta

Pond Tab-lak'

Precipice Ki-chay'

Rain O-chan'

Rainbow Fung-a'-kan

River Wang'-a

River, down the river[47] La'-god

River, mouth of Sa-fang-ni'-na

River, up the river[48] Ap'-lay

Sand O-fod'

Sea Po'-sang

Season, rice culture Cha-kon'

Season, remainder of year Ka-sip'

Sky Chay'-ya

Smoke A-sok'

Spring Ib-ib

Spring, hot Lu-ag'

Stars, large Fat-ta-ka'-kan

Stars, small Tuk-fi'-fi

Stone Ba-to

Storm, heavy (rain and winds) O-chan' ya cha-kim

Storm, heavy prolonged (baguio) Lim-lim

Sun A-qu'

Sun, eclipse of Ping-mang'-et

Sunrise Lap-lap-on'-a

Sunset Le-nun-nek' nan a-qu'

Thunder Ki-cho'

To-day Ad-wa'-ni

To-morrow A-swa'-kus

Valley, or canon Cha-lu'-lug

Water Che-num'

Waterfall Pa-lup-o'

West Lum-na-kan' si a-qu'

Whirlwind Al-li-pos'-pos or fa-no'-on

Wind Cha-kim

Year Ta'-win

Year, past Tin-mo-win

Yesterday A-dug-ka'

Zenith Ad-tong'-cho

Human Body

Ankle Ung-et'

Ankle bone King-king-i'

Arm Li'-ma

Arm, left I-kid'

Arm, right A-wan'

Arm, upper Pong'-o

Arm, upper, near shoulder Tak-lay'

Armpit Yek-yek'

Back I-chug'

Beard, side of face Sap-ki'

Belly Fo'-to

Bladder Fi-chung'

Blood Cha'-la

Body A'-wak

Bone Ung-et' or tung-al'

Brain U'-tek

Breast So'-so

Breath Ing-ga'-es

Cheek Ta-mong' or i-ping'

Chest Ta'-kib

Chin Pang'-a

Ear Ko-weng'

Elbow Si'-ko

Excreta Tay-i

Eye Ma-ta'

Eyebrow Ki-chi'

Eyelash Ki-chi'

Eyelid Ta-nib si ma'-ya

Finger Li-cheng'

Finger, index or first Mes-ned' si am-am'-a

Finger, little Ik-ik-king'

Finger, second Ka-wa'-an

Finger, third Mes-ned si nan ka-wa'-an

Finger nail Ko-ko'

Foot Cha-pan'

Foot, instep of O'-son si cha-pan'

Forehead Ki'-tong

Gall A-ku'

Groin Lip-yak'

Hair in armpit Ki-lem' si yek-yek'

Hair on crown of head Tug-tug'-o

Hair on head Fo-ok'

Hair, pubic, man's Ki-lem' si o'-ti

Hand Ad-pa' or li'-ma

Hand, inside of Ta'-lad

Head O'-lo

Heart Po'-so

Heel Pag-pa-ga'-da

Hip Tip-ay

Intestine Fu-ang'

Jaw Pang'-a

Kidney Fa-tin'

Knee Gung-gung'-o

Leg Si-ki'

Leg, calf of Fit'-kin

Lip, lower So'-fil ay nin-gub'

Lip, upper So'-fil

Liver A-tu'-i

Lung Fa'-la

Mouth To-puk'

Navel Pu'-sig

Neck Fuk-kang'

Neck, back of Tung-ed'

Nipple So'-so

Nose I-ling'

Nostril Pa-nang'-e-tan

Palate A-lang-a-ang'

Penis O'-ti

Rib Tag-lang'

Rump U-fit

Saliva Tuv'-fa

Shoulder Po-ke'

Shoulder blade Gang-gang'-sa

Skin Ko-chil'

Spinal cord U'-tuk si ung-et'

Spine Ka-ung-e-ung-et'

Spirit of living person Leng-ag'

Spirit of dead person A-ni'-to

Spirit of beheaded dead Pin-teng'

Sternum Los-los-it'

Stomach Fa'-sag

Sweat (perspiration) Ling-et

Testicle Lug-lug'-ong

Thigh U'-po

Throat A-lo-go'-og

Thumb Am-am'-a

Toe Go-mot'

Toe, first Mes-ned si am-am'-a si cha-pan'

Toe, fourth Ik-ik-king' si cha-pan'

Toe, third Mes-ned si nan ka-wa'-an si cha-pan'

Toe, great Am-am'-a si cha-pan'

Toe nail Ko-ko' si go-mot'

Toe, second Ka-wa'-an si cha-pan'

Tongue Chi'-la

Tooth Fob-a'

Urine Is-fo

Vagina Ti'-li

Vein Wath

Vertebrae Ung-et' si i-chug'

Wrist Pang-at si'-nang

Wrist joint Ung-et'

Bodily Conditions

Ague Wug-wug

Beri-beri Fu-tut

Blindness, eyelids closed Na-ki'-mit

Blindness, eyelids open Fu-lug

Blood, passage of In-is-fo cha'-la, or in-tay'-es cha'-la

Boil, a Fu-yu-i'

Burn, a Ma-la-fub-chong'

Childbirth In-sa'-cha

Cholera Pish-ti'

Circumcision Sig-i-at'

Cold, a Mo-tug'

Consumption O'-kat

Corpse A'-wak

Cut, a Na-fa'-kag

Deafness Tu'-wing

Diarrhea O-gi'-ak

Dumbness Gna-nak

Eyes, crossed Li'-i

Eyes, sore In-o'-ki

Feet, cracked from wading in rice paddies Fung-as'

Fever Im-po'-os nan a'-wak

Goiter Fin-to'-kel or fi-kek'

Headache Sa-kit' si o'-lo or pa-tug' si o'-lo

Health Ka-wis' nan a'-wak

Itch or mange Ku'-lid

Itch, first stage of small sores Ka'-ti

Pain In-sa-ki'

Pitted-face Ga-la'-ga

Rheumatism Fig-fig

Scar Sap-luk

Sickness Nay-yu' nan a'-wak

Smallpox Ful-tang'

Swelling Nay-am-an' or kin-may-yon'

Syphilis Na-na

Toe, inturning Fa'-wing

Toothache Pa-tug' nan fob-a'

Ulcers and sores, disease of Lang-ing'-i

Varicose vein O'-pat

Consanguineal and Social Relationships

Aunt A-ki-na

Babe, boy Kil-lang'

Babe, girl Gna-an'

Brother U'-na

Child Ong-ong'-a

Consanguineal group or family Sim-pang' a-nak', Sim-pang' a-po', Sim-pang' a'-fong

Father A'-ma

Man La-la'-ki

Man, old Am-a'-ma

Man, poor Pu'-chi

Man, rich Ka-chan-a-yan'

Mother I'-na

Orphan Nang-o'-so

Orphan, father dead Nan-a-ma'-na

Orphan, mother dead Nan-i-na'-na

People I-pu-kao'

People, of another pueblo Mang-i'-li

People, of one's own pueblo Kay-il-yan'

Person, one Ta'-ku

Relative I-ba'

Sister A-no'-chi

Twins Na-a-pik'

Wife A-sa'-wa

Woman Fa-fay'-i

Woman, old In-i'-na

Clothing, Dress, and Adornment

Armlet, bejuco Sung-ub'

Armlet, boar tusk Ab-kil'

Bag, flint and steel Pal-ma-ting'-un

Bag, tobacco, cloth Cho'-kao

Bag, tobacco, bladder carabao or hog Fi-chong'

Bag, tobacco, bladder deer Ka'-tat

Beads, string of A-pong'

Beads, dog tooth Sa-ong

Beads, seed, black Gu-sao'

Beads, seed, blue gray At-lok-ku'-i

Beads, red agate Si'-lung

Beads, white, large Fo'-kus

Blanket E-wis' or pi'-tay

Blanket, girl's Kud-pas'

Blanket, black, white stripes Fa-yi-ong'

Blanket, blue Pi-nag-pa'-gan

Blanket, used to carry baby on back I-fan'

Blanket, white, blue stripes Fan-cha'-la

Blanket, white, wide blue stripes Ti-na'-pi

Breechcloth Wa'-nis

Breechcloth, bark, red Ti-nan'-agt

Breechcloth, bark, white So'-put

Breechcloth, bark, white, burial Chi-nang-ta'

Breechcloth, blue Fa'-a

Breechcloth, blue, small stripes Bi-no-slun'

Breechcloth, woman's menstruation Fa'-la

Ear plug or ear stretcher Su-wip'

Earring, three varieties Sing-sing, i-pit, sing-ut'

Girdle, man's, chain Ka'-ching

Girdle, man's, bejuco rope Ka'-kot

Girdle, man's, bejuco string I-kit'

Girdle, man's, fiber Song-kit-an'

Girdle, woman's Wa'-kis

Girdle, woman's, bustle-like A-ko'-san

Hair, false Fo-bo-ok'

Hat, man's Suk'-lang

Hat, man's fez-shaped, of Bontoc pueblo Ti-no-od'

Hat, man's rain Seg-fi'

Hat, sleeping Kut'-lao

Headcloth, burial To-chong'

Jacket, woman's La-ma

Necklace, boar tusk Fu-yay'-ya

Neck ring, brass Bang-gu

Pipe Fo-bang'-a

Pipe, clay Ki-na-lo'-sab

Pipe, brass "anito" Tin-ak-ta'-go

Pipe, smooth cast metal Pin-e-po-yong'

Rain protector, woman's Tug-wi'

Rain protector, camote leaf Ang-el'

Shell, mother-of-pearl, worn at waist by men Fi-kum'

Shirt, man's blue burial Los-a'-dan

Shirt, man's blue burial, red and yellow threads A-ni'-wis

Skirt, woman's burial Kay-in'

Skirt, cotton Lu-fid' i kad-pas

Skirt, cotton, Bognen Qa'-bou

Skirt, fiber Pi-tay'

Skirt, made of falatong Lu-fid'

Skirt, twine of Mi-no'-kan

Tattoo Fa'-tek

Tattoo, arm Pong'-o

Tattoo, breast Chak-lag'

Foods and Beverages

Beverage, fermented rice Ta-pu'-i

Beverage, fermented rice, ferment of Fu-fud

Beverage, fermented sugar cane Ba'-si

Beverage, fermented sugar cane, ferment of Tub-fig'

Beverage, fermented vegetables and meats Sa-fu-eng'

Food, beans and rice Sib-fan'

Food, camotes and rice Ke-le'-ke

Food, locusts and rice Pi-na-lat'

Food, preserved meat It-tag'

Salt Si-mut

Salt, cake of Luk'-sa

Weapons, Utensils, Etc.

Ax, battle Pi'-tong

Ax, cutting edge of To-pek'

Ax, handle of Pa-lik'

Ax, handle, bejuco ferrule of Tok'-no

Ax, handle, iron ferrule of Ka-lo'-lot

Ax, handle, top point of blade of Pow-wit'

Ax, working tool Wa'-say

Ax, working tool, blade turned as adz Sa'-ka

Ax, working tool, handle of Pa-ka'-cha

Basket, baby's food bottle Tuk-to'-pil

Basket, ceremonial, chicken Fi-ki'

Basket, dinner To'-pil

Basket, fish Kot-ten'

Basket, fish, small Fak-king'

Basket, gangsa Fa'-i si gang'-sa

Basket, grasshopper I-wus'

Basket, house, holding about a peck Fa-lo'-ko

Basket, man's carrying Ka-lu'-pit

Basket, man's dirt Ko-chuk-kod'

Basket, man's dirt scoop Tak-o-chug'

Basket, man's transportation Ki-ma'-ta

Basket, man's transportation, handle of Pa'-tang

Basket, man's traveling Sang'-i

Basket, man's traveling, with rain-proof covering (so-called "head basket") Fang'-ao

Basket, salt Fa-ni'-ta

Basket, side, small, for tobacco A-ku'-pan

Basket, spoon So'-long

Basket, threshed rice Ko'-lug

Basket, tobacco, small Ka-lu'-pit

Basket, woman's rum Ag-ka-win'

Basket, woman's transportation Lu'-wa

Basket, woman's transportation, large Tay-ya-an'

Basket, woman's vegetable A-fo-fang

Basket, woman's vegetable scoop Sug-fi'

Bellows Op-op'

Bellows, piston of Dot-dot'

Bellows, tube of, to fire To-bong'

Bird scarer, carabao horn Kong-ok'

Box, small wooden, for hair grease Tug-tug'-no

Chair, for corpse Sung-a'-chil

Coffin A-lo'-ang

Deadfall, for wild hogs Il-tib'

Dish, small wooden Chu'-yu

Dish, small wooden, bowl-shaped Suk-ong'

Drumstick Pat-tong'

Fire machine, bamboo Co-li'-li

Fire machine, flint and steel Pal-ting'

Fire machine, flint and steel, cotton used with as tinder A-mek'

Gong, bronze Gang'-sa

Gong, bronze (two varieties) Ka'-los, Co-ong'-an

Gourd, large bejuco-bound, for meat Fa'-lay

Head pad, woman's, for supporting load on head Ki'-kan

Jews-harp, wooden Ab-a'-fu

Jug, gourd, for basi Tak-ing'

Knife, man's small Ki-pan'

Ladle, common wooden, for rice Fa'-nu

Ladle, gourd Ki-ud

Ladle, narrow wooden Fak-ong'

Loom In-a-fu'-i

Mortar, double, for threshing rice Lu-song'

Needle Cha-kay'-yum

Net, grasshopper Se-chok'

Olla, roughly spherical jar Fang'-a

Olla, more paralleled-side jar Fu-o-foy'

Olla, preserved meat Tu-u'-nan

Paddle, olla-molding Pip-i

Pail, wooden, for feeding pigs Kak-wan'

Pestle, rice Al'-o

Pit-fall, for hogs Fi'-to

Plate, eating, of braided bamboo Ki'-ug

Scarecrows Pa-chek', ki'-lao

Scarecrows, water power, line of Pi-chug'

Scarecrows, water power, wood in rapids Pit-ug'

Sieve, rice A-ka'-ug

Snare, wild chicken Shi'-ay

Snare, spring, bird Si-sim' and Ling-an'

Snare, spring, wild chicken and cat Kok-o'-lang

Spear Fal-feg'

Spear, blade of Tu'-fay

Spear, blade, barbless Fang'-kao

Spear, blade, many-barbed Si-na-la-wi'-tan

Spear, blade, single-barbed Fal-feg'

Spear, blade Kay-yan'

Spoon, large wooden, for drinking Tug-on'

Spoon, large wooden, for pig's feed Ka-od'

Spoon, small wooden, for eating I-chus'

Stick, soil-turning Kay-kay

Stick, woman's camote Su-wan'

Sweep runo, for catching birds Ka-lib'

Tattooing instrument Cha-kay'-yum

Torch Si-lu'

Trap, fish, funnel, large O-kat'

Trap, fish, funnel, small Ob-o'-fu

Trap, fish, scoop Ko-yug'

Trap, wild-cat Fa-wang'

Tray, winnowing Lig-o'

Trough, for salt at Mayinit Ko-long'-ko

Tube, for basi Fu-us

Whetstone A-san'

Home and Field

Canal, irrigating A'-lak

Council house for men Fa'-wi

Council house, open court of Chi-la'

Council house, open court of, posts in Po-si'

Council house, roofed portion of Tung-fub'

Council house, closed room of A'-fo

Council house, closed room, doorway of Pan-tu

Council house, closed room, fireplace of A-ni-chu'-an

Council house, closed room, floor of Chap-ay'

Council house, wall of To-ping

Dam, in river Lung-ud'

Dormitory, boys' Pa-ba-fu'-nan

Dormitory, girls' O'-lag

Dwelling A'-fong

Dwelling, better class of Fay'-u

Dwelling, better class, aisle in Cha-la'-nan

Dwelling, better class, door of Tang-ib

Dwelling, better class, first room on left of aisle Chap-an'

Dwelling, better class, second room on left of aisle Cha-le-ka-nan' si mo-o'-to

Dwelling, better class, sleeping room of Ang-an'

Dwelling, better class, small recesses at ends of sleeping room Kub-kub

Dwelling, better class, stationary shelf in Chuk'-so

Dwelling, poorer class Kat-yu'-fong

Fence, garden A'-lad

Granary A-lang'

Lands, public Pag-pag'

Sementera, rice Pay-yo'

Sementera, abandoned Nud-yun a pay-yo'

Sementera, large, producing more than five cargoes Pay-yo' chuk-chuk'-wag

Sementera, small, producing less than five cargoes Pay-yo' ay fa-nig

Sementera, irrigated by hand Pay-yo' a kao-u'-chan

Sementera, unirrigated mountain Fo-ag'

Sementera, used as seed bed Pad-cho-kan'

Stones, groups of in pueblo, said to be places to rest and talk O-bub-fu'-nan

Troughs, irrigation Ta-la'-kan

Troughs, irrigation, scaffolding of To-kod'

Walls, sementera Fa-ning'

Animals

Ant, large black Ku'-sim

Ant, large red A-lala-sang'

Ant, large red, pincers of Ken'-ang

Ant, small red Fu'-wis

Bedbug Ki'-teb

Bee Yu'-kan

Bee, wax of A-tid'

Bird Ay-ay'-am

Butterfly, large Fi-no-lo-fo'-lo

Butterfly, small Ak-a'-kop

Carabao No-ang'

Carabao, backbone of Tig-tig-i'

Carabao, body of Po'-to

Carabao bull Tot'-o

Carabao calf I-na-nak' ay no-ang'

Carabao cow Kam-bat'-yan

Carabao cow, udder of So'-so

Carabao, dew claw of Pa-king-i'

Carabao, foot of Ko'-kod

Carabao, fore leg of Kong-kong'-o ay pang-u-lo

Carabao, forequarters of Pang-u-lo

Carabao, hair of Tot-chut'

Carabao, hind leg of Kong-kong'-o ay o-chi-chi'

Carabao, horn of Sa-kod'

Carabao, white mark on neck of La-fang'

Carabao, point of shoulder of Mok-mok-ling pang-u-lo

Carabao, rear quarters of O-chi-chi'

Carabao, rump of Ba-long'-a

Carabao, tail of I'-pus

Carabao, wild Ay-ya-wan'

Caterpillar Ge'-cheng

Chicken Mo-nok'

Chicken, cock Kao-wi'-tan

Chicken, cock, spur of Pa-ging-i'

Chicken, cock, wild Sa'-fug

Chicken, comb of Ba-long-a-bing'

Chicken, crop of Fi-chong'

Chicken, ear lobe of, white Ko-weng'

Chicken, egg Et-log'

Chicken, foot of Go-mot'

Chicken, gall of Ak-ko'

Chicken, gizzard of Fit-li'

Chicken, heart of Leng-ag'

Chicken, hen Mang-a'-lak

Chicken, leg of Pu-yong' or o-po'

Chicken, liver of A'-ti

Chicken, mandible of To-kay'

Chicken, pullet Chi'-sak

Chicken, stomach of Fu-ang'

Chicken, tail of Ga-tod'

Chicken, toe of Ga'-wa

Chicken, toe nail of Ko-ko'

Chicken, wattles of Ba-long-a-bing'

Chicken, wing of Pay-yok'

Chicken, young Im'-pas

Crab Ag-ka'-ma

Crab (found in sementeras) Song'-an

Cricket Fil-fil'-ting

Crow Gay-yang

Deer Og'-sa

Dog A'-su

Dog, male La-la'-ki ay a'-su

Dog, female Fa-fay'-i ay a'-su

Dog, puppy O-ken'

Dragon fly Lang-fay'-an

Fish, large, 3 to 5 feet long Cha-lit'

Fish, 6 to 10 inches long Li'-ling

Fish, small Ka-cho'

Flea Ti'-lang

Fly (house fly) La'-lug

Hawk La-fa'-an

Hog Fu-tug'

Hog, barrow Na-fit-li'-an

Hog, boar Bu'-a

Hog, boar, tusk of Tang-o'-fu

Hog, sow O-go'

Hog, wild La'-man or fang'-o

Hog, young A-mug'

Horse Ka-fay'-o

Horse, colt I-na-nak' ay ka-fay'-o

Horse, mare Fa-fay'-i ay ka-fay'-o

Horse, stallion La-la'-ki ay ka-fay'-o

Lizard Fa-ni'-as

Locust Cho'-chon

Locust, young, without wings O-non

Louse Ko'-to

Louse, nit I'-lit

Maggot Fi'-kis

Monkey Ka-ag'

Mosquito Tip'-kan

Mouse Cho-cho'

Owl Ko-op'

Rat O-tot'

Snail, in river Ko'-ti

Snail, in sementera (three mollusks) Kit-an', Fing'-a, Lis'-chug

Snake O-wug'

Spider Ka-wa'

Wasp A-tin-fa-u'-kan

Wild-cat In'-yao

Wild-cat (so called) Si'-le, co'-lang

Worm Ka-lang'

Vegetal Life

Bamboo Ka-way'-gan

Bamboo, used for baskets A'-nis

Bamboo, used to tie bunches of palay Fi'-ka

Bamboo, used to tie bunches of palay, fiber of Ping-el

Banana Fa'-lat

Banana, green variety Sa-ging

Banana, yellow variety Mi-nay'-ang

Bark Sip-sip

Bark, from which brown fiber is made Lay-i'

Bark, inner, for spinning Ko-pa'-nit

Bean, black and gray I'-tab

Bean, black, small Ba-la'-tong

Bean, pale green, small Ka'-lap

Bejuco (rattan) Wu-e

Bud Fo'-a

Camote To-ki'

Camote, blossom of Tup-kao'

Camote, red, two varieties Si'-sig, Pit-ti'-kan

Camote vine Fi-na-li'-ling

Camote, white, six varieties Li-no'-ko, Pa-to'-ki, Ki'-nub fa-fay'-i, Pi-i-nit', Ki-weng', Tang-tang-lab'

Flower Feng'-a

Forest Pag-pag

Fruit Fi-kus'-na

Leaf To-fo'-na

Limb, tree Pang'-a

Maize Pi'-ki

Millet Sa'-fug

Millet, dark grain, "black" Pi-ting'-an

Millet, white, three varieties Mo-di', Poy-ned', Si-nang'-a

Plant, cultivated for spinning fiber Pu-ug'

Plant, wild, fiber gathered for spinning A-pas

Plant, wild, fiber of above Las-las'

Rice Pa-ku'

Rice, beard of Fo-ok'

Rice, boiled Mak-an'

Rice, head of Sin-lu'-wi

Rice, kernel of I-ta'

Rice, red varieties, smooth Chay-yet'-it, Gu-mik'-i

Rice, red variety, bearded Fo-o'-kan

Rice, roots of Tad-lang'

Rice, shelled grain Fi-na-u'

Rice, stalk of Pang-ti-i'

Rice, white, four varieties Ti'-pa, Ga'-sang, Pu-i-a-pu'-i, Tu'-peng

Root, of plant La-mot'

Runo Lu'-lo

Squash Ka-lib-as'

Tree Kay'-o, cha-pon'

Tree, dead Na-lu'-yao

Tree, knot on Ping-i'

Tree, stump of Tung-ed'

Vine, wild, from which fiber for spinning is gathered Fa-ay'-i

Wood, from which pipes are made, three varieties Ga-sa'-tan, La-no'-ti, Gi-gat'

Wood, fire May-i-su'-wo

Wood, fire, pitch pine Kay'-o

Wood, fire, from all other trees Cha'-pung

Verbs

Burn, to Fin-mi'-chan

Come (imperative) A-li-ka'

Cut, to Ku-ke'-chun

Die, to Ma-ti'

Drink, to U-mi-num'

Eat, to Mang-an'; ka-kan'

Get heads, to Na-ma'-kil

Get up, to Fo-ma-ong'

Go, I Um-i-ak'

Hear, to Chung-nen'

Kill, to Na-fa'-kug

Run, to In-tug'-tug

Sit down, to Tu-muck'-chu

Sleep, to Ma-si-yip'

Steal, to Mang-a-qu'

Talk, to En-ka-li'

Wake, to Ma-na'-lun

Adjectives

All Am-in'

Bad An-an-a-lut' or ngag

Black In-ni'-tit

Good Cug-a-wis'

Large Chuk-chuk'-i

Lazy Sang-a-an'

Long An-cho'

Many Ang-san

Red Lang-at'

Small Fan-ig'

White Im-po'-kan

Yellow Fa-king-i

Adverbs

Here Is'-na

No A-di'

There Is'-chi

Yes Ay

Cardinal Numerals

1 I-sa'

2 Chu'-wa

3 To-lo'

4 I-pat'

5 Li-ma'

6 I-nim'

7 Pi-to'

8 Wa-lo'

9 Si-am'

10 Sim po'-o

11 Sim po'-o ya i-sa'

12 Sim po'-o ya chu'-wa

13 Sim po'-o ya to-lo'

14 Sim po'-o ya i-pat'

15 Sim po'-o ya li-ma'

16 Sim po'-o ya i-nim

17 Sim po'-o ya pi-to'

18 Sim po'-o ya wa-lo'

19 Sim po'-o ya si-am'

20 Chu-wan po'-o

21 Chu-wan po'-o ya i-sa'

30 To-lon' po'-o

31 To-lon' po'-o ya i-sa'

40 I-pat' po'-o

41 I-pat' po'-o ya i-sa'

50 Li-man' po'-o

51 Li-man' po'-o ya i-sa'

60 I-nim' po'-o

61 I-nim' po'-o ya i-sa'

70 Pi-ton' po'-o

71 Pi-ton' po'-o ya i-sa'

80 Wa-lon' po'-o

81 Wa-lon' po'-o ya i-sa'

90 Si-am' ay po'-o

91 Si-am' ay po'-o ya i-sa'

100 La-sot' or Sin la-sot'

101 Sin la-sot' ya i-sa'

102 Sin la-sot' ya chu'-wa

200 Chu'-wan la-sot'

201 Chu'-wan la-sot' ya i-sa'

300 To-lon' la-sot'

301 To-lon' la-sot' ya i-sa'

400 I-pat' la-sot'

401 I-pat' la-sot' ya i-sa'

500 Li-man' la-sot'

501 Li-man' la-sot' ya i-sa'

600 I-nim' la-sot'

601 I-nim' la-sot' ya i-sa'

700 Pi-ton' la-sot'

701 Pi-ton' la-sot' ya i-sa'

800 Wa-lon' la-sot'

801 Wa-lon' la-sot' ya i-sa'

900 Si-am' ay la-sot'

901 Si-am' ay la-sot' ya i-sa'

1,000 Sin li'-fo

1,001 Sin li'-fo ya i-sa'

1,100 Sin li'-fo ya sin la-sot'

1,200 Sin li'-fo ya chu'-wan la-sot'

1,300 Sin li'-fo ya to-lon' la-sot'

1,400 Sin li'-fo ya i-pat' la-sot'

1,500 Sin li'-fo ya li-man' la-sot'

1,600 Sin li'-fo ya i-nim' la-sot'

1,700 Sin li'-fo ya pi-ton' la-sot'

1,800 Sin li'-fo ya wa-lon' la-sot'

1,900 Sin li'-fo ya si-am' la-sot'

2,000 Chu'-wa ay li'-fo

3,000 To-loy' li'-fo

4,000 I-pat' li'-fo

5,000 Li-may' li'-fo

6,000 I-nim' li'-fo

7,000 Pi-ton' li'-fo

8,000 Wa-lon' li'-fo

9,000 Si-am' ay li'-fo

10,000 Sin po'-oy li'-fo

11,000 Sin po'-o ya i-sang ay li'-fo

12,000 Sin po'-o ya nan chu'-wa li'-fo

[49]13,000 Sin po'-o ya nan to'-lo li'fo

Ordinal Numerals[50]

First Ma-ming'-san

Second Ma-mid-du'-a

Third Ma-mit-lo'

Fourth Mang-i-pat'

Fifth Mang-a-li-ma'

Sixth Mang-a-nim'

Seventh Mang-a-pi-to'

Eighth Mang-a-wa-lo'

Ninth Mang-nin-si-am'

Tenth Mang-a-po'-o

Eleventh Mang-a-po'-o ya i-sa'

Twelfth Mang-a-po'-o ya chu'-wa

Thirteenth Mang-a-po'-o ya to'-lo

Twentieth Ma-mid-du'-a' po'-o

Twenty-first Ma-mid-du'-a' po'-o ya i-sa'

Thirtieth Ma-mit-lo'-i po'-o

Thirty-first Ma-mit-lo'-i po'-o ya i-sa'

Fortieth Mang-i-pat' ay po'-o

Forty-first Mang-i-pat' ay po'-o ya i-sa'

Fiftieth Mang-a-li-ma' ay po'-o

Fifty-first Mang-a-li-ma' ay po'-o ya i-sa'

Sixtieth Mang-a-nim ay po'-o

Sixty-first Mang-a-nim ay po'-o ya i-sa'

Seventieth Mang-a-pi-to' ay po'-o

Seventy-first Mang-a-pi-to' ay po'-o ya i-sa'

Eightieth Mang-a-wa-lo' ay po'-o

Eighty-first Mang-a-wa-lo' ay po'-o ya i-sa'

Ninetieth Mang-a-si-am ay po'-o

Ninety-first Mang-a-si-am ay po'-o ya i-sa'

One hundredth Mang-a-po'-o ya po'-o

One hundred and first Mang-a-po'-o ya po'-o ya i-sa'

Two hundredth Ma-mid-dua' la-sot'

Two hundred and first Ma-mid-dua' la-sot' ya i-sa'

Three hundredth Ma-mit-lo'-i la-sot'

Three hundred and first Ma-mit-lo'-i la-sot' ya i-sa'

Four hundredth Mang-i-pat' ay la-sot'

Four hundred and first Mang-a-pat' ay la-sot' ya i-sa'

Thousandth Ka-la-so la-sot' or ka-li-fo-li'-fo

Last A-nong-os'-na

Distributive Numerals

One to each I-sas' nan i-sa'

Two to each Chu-was' nan i-sa'

Three to each To-los' nan i-sa'

Ten to each Po-os' nan i-sa'

Eleven to each Sim po'-o ya i-sas' nan i-sa'

Twelve to each Sim po'-o ya chu'-wa is nan i-sa'

Twenty to each Chu-wan' po-o' is nan i-sa'

NOTES

[1] -- The proof sheets of this paper came to me at the Philippine Exposition, St. Louis, Mo., July, 1904. At that time Miss Maria del Pilar Zamora, a Filipino teacher in charge of the model school at the Exposition, told me the Igorot children are the brightest and most intelligent of all the Filipino children in the model school. In that school are children from several tribes or groups, including Christians, Mohammedans, and pagans.

[2] -- There are many instances on record showing that people have been planted on Pacific shores many hundred miles from their native land. It seems that the primitive Pacific Islanders have sent people adrift from their shores, thus adding a rational cause to those many fortuitous causes for the interisland migration of small groups of individuals.

"In 1696, two canoes were driven from Ancarso to one of the Philippine Islands, a distance of eight hundred miles. They had run before the wind for seventy days together, sailing from east to west. Thirty-five had embarked, but five had died from the effects of privation and fatigue during the voyage, and one shortly after their arrival. In 1720, two canoes were drifted from a remote distance to one of the Marian Islands. Captain Cook found, in the island of Wateo Atiu, inhabitants of Tahiti, who had been drifted by contrary wind in a canoe, from some islands to the eastward, unknown to the natives. Several parties have, within the last few years, (prior to 1834), reached the Tahitian shores from islands to the eastward, of which the Society Islands had never before heard. In 1820, a canoe arrived at Maurua, about thirty miles west of Borabora, which had come from Rurutu, one of the Austral Islands. This vessel had been at sea between a fortnight and three weeks; and, considering its route, must have sailed seven or eight hundred miles. A more recent instance occurred in 1824: a boat belonging to Mr. Williams of Raiatea left that island with a westerly wind for Tahiti. The wind changed after the boat was out of sight of land. They were driven to the island of Atiu, a distance of nearly eight hundred miles in a south-westerly direction, where they were discovered several months afterwards. Another boat, belonging to Mr. Barff of Huahine, was passing between that island and Tahiti about the same time, and has never since been heard of; and subsequent instances of equally distant and perilous voyages in canoes or open boats might be cited." -- (Ellis) Polynesian Researches, vol. I, p. 125.

"In the year 1799, when Finow, a Friendly Island chief, acquired the supreme power in that most interesting group of islands, after a bloody and calamitous civil war, in which his enemies were completely overpowered, the barbarian forced a number of the vanquished to embark in their canoes and put to sea; and during the revolution that issued in the subversion of paganism in Otaheite, the rebel chiefs threatened to treat the English missionaries and their families in a similar way. In short, the atrocious practice is, agreeably to the Scotch law phrase, "use and wont," in the South Sea Islands." -- John Dunmore Lang, View of the Origin and Migrations of the Polynesian Nation, London, 1834, pp. 62, 63.

[3] -- The Christianized dialect groups are: Bikol, of southern Luzon and adjacent islands; Cagayan, of the Cagayan Valley of Luzon; Ilokano, of the west coast of northern Luzon; Pampango and Pangasinan, of the central plain of Luzon; Tagalog, of the central area South of the two preceding; and the Visayan, of the central islands and northern Mindanao.

[4] -- No pretense is now made for permanency either in the classification of the many groups of primitive people in the Philippines or for the nomenclature of these various groups; but the groups of non-Christian people in the Archipelago, as they are to-day styled in a more or less permanent way by The Ethnological Survey, are as follows: Ata, north and west of Gulf of Davao in southeastern Mindanao; Batak, of Paragua; Bilan, in the southern highlands west of Gulf of Davao, Mindanao; Bagobo, of west coast of Gulf of Davao, Mindanao; Bukidnon, of Negros; Ibilao or Ilongot, of eastern central Luzon; Igorot, of northern Luzon; the Lanao Moro, occupying the central territory of Mindanao between the Bays of Iligan and Illana, including Lake Lanao; Maguindanao Moro, extending in a band southeast from Cotabato, Mindanao, toward Sarangani Bay, including Lakes Liguasan and Buluan; Mandaya, of southeastern Mindanao east of Gulf of Davao; Mangiyan, of Mindoro: Manobo, probably the most numerous tribe in Mindanao, occupying the valley of the Agusan River draining northward into Butuan Bay and the extensive table-land west of that river, besides in isolated territories extending to both the east and west coasts of the large body of land between Gulf of Davao and Illana Bay; Negrito, of several

areas of wild mountains in Luzon, Negros, Mindanao, and other smaller islands; the Sama, of the islands in Gulf of Davao, Mindanao; Samal Moro, of scattered coastal areas in southern Mindanao, besides the eastern and southern islands of the Sulu or Jolo Archipelago; the Subano, probably the second largest tribal group in Mindanao, occupying all the mountain territory west of the narrow neck of land between Illana Bay and Pangul Bay; the Sulu Moro, of Jolo Island; the Tagabili, on the southern coast of Mindanao northwest of Sarangani Bay; the Tagakola, along the central part of the west coast of Gulf of Davao, Mindanao; Tagbanua, of Paragua; Tinguian, of western northern Luzon; Tiruray, south of Cotabato, Mindanao; Yakan Moro, in the mountainous interior of Basilan Island, off the Mindanao coast at Zamboanga. Under the names of these large groups must be included many more smaller dialect groups whose precise relationship may not now be confidently stated. For instance, the large Igorot group is composed of many smaller groups of different dialects besides that of the Bontoc Igorot of which this paper treats.

[5] -- IMPERATA ARUNDICEA.

[6] -- BUBALUS KERABAU FERUS (Nehring).

[7] -- Pages 72 -- 74 of the Report of the Director of the Philippine Weather Bureau, 1901 -- 1902; Part First, The Climate of Baguio (Benguet), by Rev. Fr. Jose Algue, S. J. (Manila, Observatory Printing Office, 1902.)

[8] -- Map No. 7 in the Atlas of the Philippine Islands. (Washington, Government Printing Office, 1900.)

[9] -- R. P. Fr. Angel Perez, Igorrotes, Estudio Geografico y Etnografico, etc. (Manila, 1902), p. 7.

[10] -- Op. cit., p. 29.

[11] -- Major Godwin-Austen says of the Garo hill tribes, Bengal, India:

"In every village is the 'bolbang,' or young men's house. ... In this house all the unmarried males live, as soon as they attain the age of puberty, and in this any travelers are put up." -- The Journal of the Anthropological Institute of Great Britain and Ireland, vol. II, p. 393. See also op. cit., vol. XI, p. 199.

S. E. Peal says:

"Barracks for the unmarried young men are common in and around Assam among non-Aryan races. The institution is here seen in various stages of decline or transition. In the case of 'head-hunters' the young men's barracks are invariably guardhouses, at the entrance to the village, and those on guard at night keep tally of the men who leave and return." -- Op. cit., vol. XXII, p. 248.

Gertrude M. Godden writes at length of the young men's house of the Naga and other frontier tribes of northeast India: "Before leaving the Naga social customs one prominent feature of their village society must be noticed. This is the DEKHA CHANG, an institution in some respects similar to the bachelors' hall of the Melanesians, which again is compared with the BALAI and other public halls of the Malay Archipelago. This building, also called a MORANG, was used for the double purpose of a sleeping place for the young men and as a guard or watch house for the village. The custom of the young men sleeping together is one that is constantly noticed in accounts of the Naga tribes, and a like custom prevailed in some, if not all, cases for the girls. ... "The young men's hall is variously described and named. An article in the Journal of the Indian Archipelago, 1848, says that among the Nagas the bachelors' hall of the Dayak village is found under the name of 'Mooring.' In this all the boys of the age of 9 or 10 upward reside apart. In a report of 1854 the 'morungs' are described as large buildings generally situated at the principal entrances and varying in number according to the size of the village; they are in fact the main guardhouse, and here all the young unmarried men sleep. In front of the morung is a raised platform as a lookout, commanding an extensive view of all approaches, where a Naga is always kept on duty as a sentry. ... In the Morungs are kept skulls carried off in battle; these are suspended by a string along the wall in one or more rows over each other. In one of the Morungs of the Changuae village, Captain Brodie counted one hundred and thirty skulls. ... Besides these there was a large basket full of broken pieces of skulls. Captain Holroyd, from whose memorandum the above is quoted, speaks later of the Morung as the 'hall of justice' in which the consultations of the clan council are held.

"The 'MORANGS' of another tribe, the 'Naked' Naga, have recently been described as situated close to the village gate, and consist of a central hall, and back and front verandahs. In the large front verandah are collected all the trophies of war and the chase, from a man's skull down to a monkey's. Along both sides of the central hall are the sleeping berths of the young men. ...

"Speaking of the Mao and Muran tribes [continues Miss Godden], Dr. Brown says, 'the young men never sleep at home, but at their clubs, where they keep their arms always in a state of readiness.' ...

"With the Aos at the present day the custom seems to be becoming obsolete; sleeping houses are provided for bachelors, but are seldom used except by small boys. Unmarried girls sleep by twos and threes in houses otherwise empty, or else tenanted by one old woman.

"The analogy between the DAKHA CHANG, or MORANG, of the Nagas and the men's hall of the Melanesians is too close to be overlooked, and in view of the significance of all evidence concerning the corporate life of early communities a description of the latter is here quoted. I am aware of no recorded instance of the women's house, other than these Naga examples. 'In all the Melanesian groups it is the rule that there is in every village a building of public character where the men eat and spend their time, the young men sleep, strangers are entertained; where as in the Solomon Islands the canoes are kept; where images are seen, and from which women are generally excluded; ... and all these no doubt correspond to the balai and other public halls of the Malay Archipelago.' " -- Op. cit., vol. XXVI, pp. 179 -- 182.

Similar institutions appear to exist also in Sumatra.

In Borneo among the Land Dyaks "head houses," called "pangah," are found in each village. Low says of them: "The Pangah is built by the united efforts of the boys and unmarried men of the tribe, who, after having attained the age of puberty, are obliged to leave the houses of the village; and do not generally frequent them after they have attained the age of 8 or 9 years." -- Sir Hugh Low, Sarawak, its Inhabitants and Productions (London, 1848), p. 280.

Lieutenant F. Elton writes of the natives of Solomon Islands: "In every village they have at least one so-called tamboo house of TOHE, generally the largest building in the settlement. This is only for the men, it being death for a female to enter there. It is used as a public place and belongs to the community. Any stranger coming to the village goes to the tamboo house and remains there until the person he is in quest of meets him there." -- The Journal of the Anthropological Institute of Great Britain and Ireland, vol. XVII, p. 97.

Mr. H. O. Forbes writes of the tribes of Timor (islands between New Guinea and Australia) that they have a building called "Uma-lulik." He says: "The LULIK can be at once recognized, were it by nothing else than by the buffalo crania with which it is decorated on the outside." An officer who holds one of the highest and certainly the most influential positions in the kingdom has charge of the building, and presides over the sacred rites which are conducted in them. ... The building is cared for by some old person, sometimes by a man and his wife, but they must not both -- being of opposite sex -- stay all night." -- Op. cit., XIII, pp. 411, 412.

[12] -- The o'-lag of Buyayyeng is known as La-ma'-kan; that of Amkawa, in Buyayyeng, is Ma-fa'-lat; that of Polupo is Ma-lu-fan'. The two of Fatayyan are Ka-lang'-kang and A-la'-ti. Ta-ting' is the o'-lag in the Tang-e-ao' section of Fatayyan. Chung-ma' is the one in Filig. Lang-i-a' and Ab-lo' are the two of Mageo, both in Pudpudchog. The o'-lag of Chakong is called Kat'-sa, and that of Lowingan is Si-mang'-an. The one of Pudpudchog is Yud-ka'. Sung-ub' is the o'-lag of Sipaat, situated in Lowingan. Kay-pa', Tek-a-ling, and Sak-a-ya' are, respectively, the o'-lag of Sigichan, Somowan, and Pokisan. Ag-lay'-in is the o'-lag of Luwakan, and Tal-pug and Say-ki'-pit are o'-lag of Choko and Longfoy, respectively.

[13] -- The Journal of The Anthropological Institute of Great Britain and Ireland, vol. XXVI, pp. 179, 180.

[14] -- Op. cit., vol. XXII, p. 248.

[15] -- Sweet potato, IPOMOEA BATATAS. -- J.H.

[16] -- An anito, as is developed in a later chapter, is the name given the spirit of a dead person. The anito dwell in and about the pueblo, and, among other of their functions, they cause almost all diseases and ailments of the people and practically all deaths.

[17] -- Earthenware pot. -- J.H.

[18] -- Gong. -- J.H.

[19] -- David J. Doherty, M.D., translator of The Philippines, A Summary Account of their Ethnological, Historical, and Political Conditions, by Ferdinand Blumentritt, etc. (Chicago, 1900), p. 16.

[20] -- A fermented drink.

[21] -- A fermented drink.

[22] -- The accompanying photo was an instantaneous exposure, taken in the twilight. The people could not be induced to wait for a time exposure.

[23] -- No true cats are known to be indigenous to the Philippines, but the one shown in the plate was a wild mountain animal and was a true cat, not a civet. Its ancestors may have been domestic.

[24] -- This estimate was obtained by a primitive surveying outfit as follows:

A rifle, with a bottle attached used for a liquid level, was sighted from a camera tripod. A measuring tape attached to the tripod showed the distance of the rifle above the surface of the water. A surveyor's tape measured the distance between the tripod and the leveling rod, which also had an attached tape to show the distance of the point sighted above the surface of the water.

I am indebted to Mr. W. F. Smith, American teacher in Bontoc, for assisting me in obtaining these measurements.

The strength of the scaffolding supporting the troughs is suggested by the statement that the troughs were brimming full of swift-running water, while our "surveying" party of four adults, accompanied by half a dozen juvenile Igorot sightseers, weighed about 900 pounds, and was often distributed along in the troughs, which we waded, within a space of 30 feet.

[25] -- MUNIA JAGORI (Martens).

[26] -- Mr. Elmer D. Merrill.

[27] -- Mr. F. A. Thanisch.

[28] -- Igorrotes, Estudio Geografico y Etnografico sobre algunos Distritos del Norte de Luzon, by R. P. Fr. Angel Perez (Manila), 1902.

[29] -- This typical Malayan bellows is also found in Siam, and is shown in a half tone from a photograph facing page 186 of Maxwell Somerville's Siam on the Meinam from the Gulf to Aynthia (London, Sampson Low, Marston & Co., 1897).

There is also a crude woodcut of this bellows printed as fig. 2, Pl. XIV, in The Journal of the Anthropological Institute of Great Britain and Ireland, vol. XXII. With the illustration is the information that the bellows is found in Assam, Salwin, Sumatra, Java, Philippines, and Madagascar.

[30] -- It is believed to be either a PORCELAIN (PORCELANA) or a SPIDER (MAIOIDEA) crab.

[31] -- Analysis made for this study by Bureau of Government Laboratories, Manila, P.I., February 21, 1903.

[32] -- Charles A. Goessmann in Universal Cyclopaedia, vol. X (1900), p. 274.

[33] -- The Natives of Sarawak and British North Borneo (2 vols., London, 1896); pp. 140 -- 174, vol. II.

[34] -- A party, consisting of the Secretary of the Interior for the Philippine Islands, Hon. Dean C. Worcester; the governor and lieutenant-governor of Lepanto-Bontoc, William Dinwiddie and Truman K. Hunt, respectively; Captain Chas. Nathorst of the Constabulary, and the writer, was in Banawi in time to witness the procession and burial but not the previous ceremonies at the dwelling.

[35] -- See also the story, "Who took my father's head?" Chapter IX, p 225.

[36] -- The bird called "co-ling'" by the Bontoc Igorot is the serpent eagle (SPILOMIS HOLOSPLILUS Vigors). It seems to be found in no section of Bontoc Province except near Bontoc pueblo.

There were four of these large, tireless creatures near the pueblo, but an American shot one in 1900. The other three may be seen day in and day out, high above the mountain range west of the pueblo, sailing like aimless pleasure boats. Now and then they utter their penetrating cry of "qu-iu'-kok."

[37] -- MUNIA JAGORI (Martens).

[38] -- "A wife monkey."

[39] -- An iguana some two feet long.

[40] -- CORONE PHILIPPA (Bonap.).

[41] -- The Korean Review, July, 1903, pp. 289 -- 294.

[42] -- William Edwin Safford, American Anthropologist, April -- June, 1903, p. 293.

[43] -- Otto Scheerer (MS.), The Ibaloi Igorot, MS. Coll., Ethnological Survey for the Philippine Islands.

[44] -- One blind.

[45] -- From Ilokano.

[46] -- Many small stars

[47] -- The country northward

[48] -- The country southward

[49] -- It is probable they seldom count as high as 13,000

[50] -- These people say they have no separate adverbs denoting repetition of action -- as, once, twice, thrice, four times, ten times, etc. They use the ordinal numerals for this purpose also.

Printed in Great Britain
by Amazon